God in Chinatown

God in Chinatown

Religion and Survival in New York's Evolving Immigrant Community

Kenneth J. Guest

New York University Press

NEW YORK AND LONDON

NEW YORK UNIVERSITY PRESS
New York and London
www.nyupress.org

Library of Congress Cataloging-in-Publication Data
Guest, Kenneth J.
God in Chinatown : religion and survival in New York's
evolving immigrant community / Kenneth J. Guest.
p. cm. — (Religion, race, and ethnicity)
Includes bibliographical references (p. 209) and index.
ISBN 0-8147-3153-8 (cloth) — ISBN 0-8147-3154-6 (paper)
1. Immigrants—Religious life——New York (State)—New York.
2. Chinese Americans—New York (State)—New York—Religious life.
3. Chinatown (New York, N.Y.) I. Title. II. Series.
BL2527.N7G84 2003
200'.89'95107471—dc21   2003000761

New York University Press books are printed on acid-free paper,
and their binding materials are chosen for strength and durability.

Manufactured in the United States of America
10 9 8 7 6 5 4 3 2 1

For Thomas Luke

Contents

Acknowledgments

My interest in New York's Chinatown and in the people of Fuzhou, China—
the most recent wave of Chinese immigrants to the United States—began in
a seminar taught by Peter Kwong and Ida Susser entitled "New New Yorkers
in Global Perspective" at the City University of New York Graduate Center.
I am indebted to these two scholars and my advisor, Jane Schneider, for seeing me through the Ph.D. process and shaping much of the analytical
framework and intellectual voice that run through this book. Many others
at CUNY inspired me, read chapters, allowed me to test ideas, and offered
timely direction and encouragement. Louise Lennihan, executive officer of
the Anthropology Program, has been a generous mentor and advocate. June
Nash and Ida Susser supervised a National Science Foundation–funded
fieldwork training program that first took me to Fuzhou in 1997. Ongoing
research was supported by a Graduate Teaching Fellowship at Hunter College, where members of the Anthropology Department provided a collegial
and encouraging environment. A CUNY Graduate Center Alumni Dissertation Year Fellowship enabled me to dedicate the time needed to write up
my fieldwork.

   Along the academic journey, Irene Liu, Peter Awn, Celia Weisman, and
Scott Matheney served as my mentors and teachers when I was an under-
graduate at Columbia University, as did Chung Hyun-kyung, Will Kennedy,
Tom Driver, Beverly Harrison, and Aloysius Pieris at Union Theological
Seminary. Saskia Sassen at Columbia advanced my understanding of glob-
alization, migration, and New York City during graduate studies.

   Qin Xiaoyou, Li Ke, Wu Anna, Qi Tingduo, and Astor Feng introduced
me to the complexities of practicing religion in China while I was an un-
dergraduate exchange student at Beijing University. I am also deeply indebted to Philip and Janice Wickeri, Franklin and Jean Woo, Myron Cohen,

Angela Zito, Bud and Millie Carroll, Don MacInnis, Edwin Fisher, Ruth Harris, Gail Coulson, Peng Cui'an, Li Yading, Gao Ying, Zhao Zhilian, Ji Tai, and many others who have shared their wisdom and friendship with me in this endeavor.

Jose Casanova and Ari Zolberg at the New School University graciously included me in their study of Religion and Immigrant Incorporation in New York, based at the International Center for Migration, Ethnicity and Citizenship, helping me place my work in the context of New York's immigrant history and diverse contemporary immigrant communities.

A crucial phase of my research was supported by a Dissertation Fellowship for the Study of Religion and Immigration from the Social Science Research Council, with funds provided by the Pew Charitable Trusts. My thanks go to Josh DeWind and the members of the SSRC Religion and Immigration Program who offered helpful critiques of my work and generously shared their research and findings.

The faculty and administration at Baruch College, CUNY, particularly my colleagues in the Deparment of Sociology and Anthropology, have provided a wonderful environment in which to complete this manuscript. Special thanks go to Glenn Petersen, chair of the department, and Myrna Chase, dean of the Weissman School of Arts and Sciences, for warmly welcoming a new junior faculty member, offering timely advice, and urging the completion of this book. Final revisions were also informed by students and faculty in the CUNY Honors College interdisciplinary seminar, "The Peopling of New York."

My deep appreciation goes to NYU Press, particularly to my editor, Jennifer Hammer, and the series editor, Peter Paris, for their clear and constructive suggestions for improving this book. John Kuo Wei Tchen and an anonymous reviewer also read my manuscript with great care and offered invaluable comments for deepening its analysis and sharpening its focus. Allison Reuling created the fine maps included in the text.

The completion of this book would not have been possible without the love and support of a small group of my most intimate family, friends, and advisers. It is with profound gratitude for their presence in my life that I give thanks to Qin Xiaoyou, a friend since I lived in Beijing in 1984 and my invaluable research assistant in New York's Chinese community; to my father, Tom, who inspired my curiosity about people; to my grandparents, Walter Brooks Foley and Mary Rosengrant Foley, who were the first in my family to live in Asia and travel in China; to Asher, whose timely insights helped me navigate the writing process; to Gennaro, Nick, Adel, Marco, Nina, and all my friends at the Metro who gave me a safe space in which to write and always saved a piece of baklava for me; to K Karpen, friend, collaborator, and spiritual guide; to Charlene Floyd, my academic soulmate and inspiration, with whom I have been exploring religious communities for nearly fifteen years; to Vicki Clark, my loved one these many years and mother of our son, who believed that I had a gift to teach; to my mother Frances-Helen, who took me to Hong Kong for the first time when I was seventeen and nurtured my interest in China; and to Thomas Luke, favorite son and inspiration for my creation, I thank you for the many sunlit afternoons filled with bike rides and ball games, ice cream and laughter—may there be many, many more in the days and months and years to come.

Finally, I must express my deep debt of gratitude to the members of the religious communities in New York's Chinatown and in Fuzhou, China, some mentioned here by name, others whose identities are disguised. Their willingness to share their lives and stories with me provides the primary material for this book and has been an unending source of inspiration on a professional and personal level. I trust that my retelling of their stories will in some small way repay the generosity they have shown me over the past years.

Map of China showing location of Fuzhou.

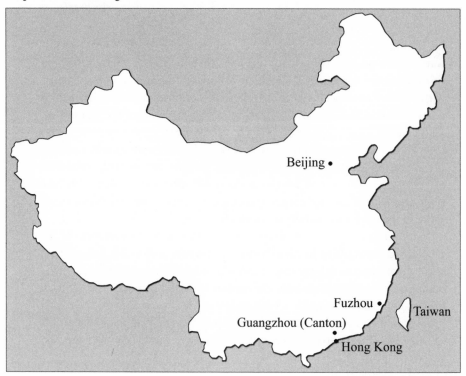

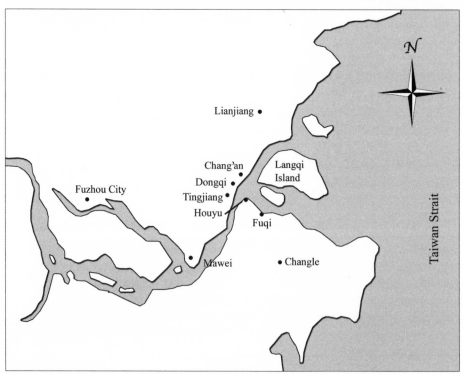

Detail of Fuzhou.

Introduction
Walking on Water

On a spring Sunday afternoon in 1999 I stood in the fellowship hall of the Church of Grace to the Fujianese in Chinatown, on New York's Lower East Side, eating lunch with about 150 recently arrived immigrants. Over a bowl of Fuzhou noodles, a young man named Li Lin told me the following story:

> We left from Changle City to the east of Fuzhou. It was March 11, 1993. I was twenty-one years old. I hadn't planned to go but a cousin of mine was going. So I went with him. The snakeheads [smugglers] in Changle sent us by bus to Wenzhou, twelve hours north on the coast. We waited in the mountains of Wenzhou one night and then were loaded onto an old fishing vessel the next evening. Somewhere north of Taiwan we were transferred to a Taiwanese cargo ship. One hundred and forty of us.
>
> It was April 12 before we reached Mexico. A Mexican boat came out into international waters to meet us. We changed ships and then when we were in sight of land small groups of us were put on motor boats for a speedy ride to shore. The Mexicans took us by bus to a safe place overnight and then north to the U.S. border the next day. There were twenty of us in the group, ten Chinese and ten Mexicans, plus two Mexican leaders. I couldn't believe the river at the border was so small. It was barely more than knee deep. But before we could cross that night, helicopters with spotlights appeared, searching for illegal immigrants. We lay still in the low underbrush until three or four in the morning when they disappeared and we made our way across the border.
>
> The van that met us was soon stopped by police. We all ran for our lives and managed to escape into the nearby mountains. One of the Mexican leaders had a cell phone and called for another car, which took us to Los Angeles. Chinese smugglers met us again there. We stayed for two

nights in a hotel full of illegal immigrants and flew the next day to Washington, D.C., where we waited until our relatives and friends were able to make the $20,000 payment for our journey.

We encountered many storms during that month at sea. It was an extremely difficult crossing. I wasn't sure we would make it. Many times I found myself singing old hymns I had learned in my childhood in the house church meetings my mother led. Sometimes in the early morning, if the weather was calm, I would go up on deck and sit in the ship's prow. The old hymns would come back to me. In the cross, in the cross, be my glory ever. I didn't really know what it meant. It just came flooding back out of my memory. When I started to sing, my entire being felt comfortable and safe. I had never had this feeling before, this feeling I had on the boat. At the time I didn't really know what the feeling was about. But when I got to America I realized that God had been present with me on that journey. Even though I grew up in a Christian family I hadn't really taken it seriously. But on the boat I finally learned how to pray, to pray with my heart, not just with my mouth.

Li Lin's story, like that of so many recent immigrants from southeast China, is a story of great hardship endured in the hope of making a better life. Like many of his compatriots, his journey connects religious communities and networks in New York and in China. For many immigrants, religious communities are an initial point of entry into U.S. reality. They are a place for reconnection with family and fellow villagers, for sharing news of home, for exchanging ideas about how to survive in this alien and exploitative environment, to give thanks to their particular deity for safe passage, and to make petitions for a successful continuation of the journey. They are also a place for organizing support for their religious communities—churches and temples back home.

When I got to New York I ended up finding a room right next door to the Church of Grace. My mother had told me to look for it but I didn't know where it was. I never imagined how wonderful it would be to find a church made up solely of people from Fuzhou, speaking my own dialect. When I went to church, all the intense pressures of the outside world fell away. My entire being would relax. And I felt warm and comforted. The church has really helped me a great deal. I wasn't a very serious Christian in China. But I'm very involved here. I've even become a member of the church's Board of Deacons. The Church of Grace is my home here.

Fuzhounese Immigrant Religious Communities in New York

Since the early 1980s, tens of thousands of Chinese from the towns and villages outside Fuzhou, in southeastern China, have made their way to New York. This massive international migration, spurred by economic restructuring in both China and the United States and facilitated by a vast and highly organized international human smuggling syndicate, has uprooted whole segments of Fuzhounese communities, dislocating people economically, culturally, and legally, and placing them in a receiving country for which they are unprepared and which is unprepared to incorporate them. The undocumented status of many of the new immigrants further complicates the picture.

Their primary destination is Chinatown, New York, a densely populated Chinese community on Manhattan's Lower East Side, where these new immigrants utilize kinship, village, and religious connections to begin their U.S. journey and survive in an unfamiliar environment. The street corners where East Broadway passes below the Manhattan Bridge are crowded with young Fuzhounese waiting for jobs to be posted in the myriad employment agencies. The jobs may take them temporarily across the United States to work in "all-you-can-eat" Chinese buffets or place them in garment sweatshops or on construction sites in the New York area. But for most recent Fuzhounese immigrants, New York's Chinatown is home base, the place they return to recuperate, reconnect with family and friends, and find their next job.

Over the past fifteen years, Fuzhounese immigrants have transformed dramatically the face of New York's Chinatown, supplanting the Cantonese as Chinatown's largest ethnic Chinese community and vying for leadership in the area's economics, politics, social life, and even language use. In many ways the Fuzhounese are to today's Chinatown what the Cantonese were before 1985. Cantonese first arrived in California in the 1840s, brought as low-wage laborers in farms, gold mines, and railroad construction before expanding to the East Coast after the completion of the transcontinental railroad in 1869. They have so predominated among Chinese in New York and in America in general that up until 1960 more than 50 percent of all Chinese in the United States originated in one single county of Canton—Taishan—on the province's southernmost coast (Hsu 2000). But since the 1980s the largest single source of Chinese migration to New York and the United States as a whole has been Fuzhou, making it essential to understand the Fuzhounese if one wants to understand New York's Chinatown today.

Like the Cantonese who migrated to Chinatown before them, the Fuzhounese have brought with them their religious beliefs, practices, and local deities. Over the past fifteen years, Fuzhounese have established a number of their own religious communities, fourteen by the end of 2002. These include Protestant and Catholic churches as well as Buddhist, Daoist, and Chinese popular-religion temples. In the complex economic, political, and social environment of Chinatown's ethnic enclave, these religious organizations have become central locations for a transient Fuzhounese population, where they can build a community, activate networks of support built on kinship, region, and faith, and establish links to their home churches, temples, and communities in China.

In this book we will examine the role of local New York religious communities in the Fuzhounese immigrant experience. What is their place in the immigrant incorporation process? How significant are the transnational religious networks being established between New York and Fuzhou in building boundary-crossing relationships and identities? How do these religious communities, despite their institutional fragility and the factionalizing conflicts in China and the United States, enable immigrants to construct systems of meaning?

In particular, we will explore the influence of Fuzhounese immigrant religious communities in the following spheres:

- Replicating and mitigating hierarchies of class stratification in Chinatown
- Shaping how Fuzhounese immigrants mobilize social capital necessary for survival
- Building active transnational religious networks between New York and Fuzhou
- Constructing alternative identities that resist the definitions of employers, smugglers, and the state
- Encouraging the search for meaning within the immigrant experience, reinforcing immigration as a process of self-understanding.

We will look closely at two Protestant congregations in New York's Chinatown.

The Church of Grace, independently established in 1988, now has a membership of over one thousand, a mailing list of two thousand, and activities that overflow its space in a renovated 1904 public bath house on Allen Street. Comprised exclusively of immigrants from the Fuzhou area and conducting its services and many activities in the local Fuzhou dialect of Chinese, this Protestant Christian congregation is a first stopping point for many new arrivals, a center for mutual aid and information exchange about New York and Fuzhou, and an access point for connections to home churches and communities in China.

The New York House Church split from the Church of Grace in 1998 over theological, political, and regional differences rooted in the dynamics of their home communities in China. The one-hundred-member congregation, led by a revered senior minister who suffered greatly for his faith during China's Cultural Revolution, locates its origins in the anti-Communist underground house-church network in China and, in particular, an indigenous Fuzhounese denomination commonly called the Little Flock.

We will also consider four additional Fuzhounese congregations—a Buddhist temple, a Daoist temple, and two Catholic parishes—which are included to reveal the diversity and complexity of religious practice in the Fuzhounese immigrant community, to reflect the common experience of religious practitioners in New York and China, regardless of their particular tradition, and to provide a broad gauge for examining the patterns by which Fuzhounese religious communities engage Chinatown's ethnic enclave and the global flows of labor and capital that swirl around them.

He Xian Jun Buddhist Temple is a small storefront temple that serves as a religious and community center for the 2,500 immigrants from Fuqi village (total population 4,000), a coastal village on the outskirts of Fuzhou that now features one of the most developed temple complexes in the region, thanks to nearly one million U.S. dollars raised by villagers in New York and sent home to honor religious sentiments and build community influence.

The Daoist Temple of Heavenly Thanksgiving, also a storefront, serves as a central religious, social, and economic coordination site for compatriots from Chang'an Village and neighboring Dongqi Village who now have a network of U.S. restaurants that solely employ fellow villagers, mostly undocumented workers. Members of this temple have also built a new temple in Chang'an and facilitate a transnational ritual process linking their home village deities, a spirit medium now living in the American Midwest, and their fellow villagers across the country.

Transfiguration Roman Catholic Church, one of the oldest religious institutions in Chinatown, is currently home to three generations of immigrants: Italian, Cantonese Chinese, and Fuzhounese Chinese. Transfiguration's Fuzhounese community struggles to integrate its primarily rural, pre-Vatican II Catholic traditions and beliefs into a modern multiethnic congregation in which it often feels marginalized by language, theology, politics, and class.

St. Joseph's Roman Catholic Church, located only a few blocks from Transfiguration, now houses a small but growing group of Fuzhounese immigrants who split from Transfiguration over theological and political issues related to the chasm between public and underground Catholics in China. Much of the energy of this ardently anti-Communist and pro-Vatican community is focused on addressing the persecution of Chinese Catholics in the Fuzhou area.

Religion and Immigration in Context

New York City has long been America's preeminent immigrant city—a title now shared with Los Angeles. Today the city's foreign-born population has reached 40 percent, a level unequaled since the last great wave of immigration peaked in 1910. Today's immigrants, however, are significantly different in a number of key respects. While newcomers from Ireland, Germany, Italy, and eastern Europe predominated in the nineteenth and early twentieth centuries, today's immigrants are much more ethnically diverse. In New York between 1990 and 1996, the top ten sending countries were the Dominican Republic, the former Soviet Union, China, Jamaica, Guyana, Poland, Philippines, Trinidad and Tobago, Haiti, and India (Foner 2001). This revival of immigration, which added 1.2 million people to New York City between 1960 and 1990 and another 1.1 million between 1990 and 1998, has been vital to the renewal of the city, replacing an almost equivalent exodus of established residents.

Today's newcomers are also significantly more diverse religiously than the predominantly Protestant, Catholic, and Jewish immigrants of one hundred years ago. While government census data do not track religious affiliation or preference, contemporary studies reveal dramatic growth among

Buddhists, Muslims, Hindus, Sikhs, Zoroastrians, Jains, as well as practitioners of Haitian Voodou, Cuban Santeria, Chinese Falun Gong, and other Afro-American and Afro-Caribbean religions. This growth noticeably expands and reinforces the fabric of religious pluralism that historically has been a key component of American life and central to the vibrancy of New York City.

Despite a wealth of material on Chinese immigration and the Asian American experience, only limited research has been published to date specifically addressing Chinese religious communities in the United States. Most of it focuses primarily on Chinese Christians in earlier immigrant generations (Cayton and Lively 1955; Palinkas 1989; Woo 1991; Chen 1992; Tseng 1999; Yung 1995; Yang 1999; Yoo 1999). Even less has been published about non-Christian Chinese religious expression.

While a number of studies have been conducted in New York's Chinatown (Wong 1982, 1988; Kwong 1996 [1987]; Yu 1992; Zhou 1992; Lin 1998; Tchen 1999), religion has received only passing mention or has been completely neglected. Even in Kuo's (1977) book on Chinatown's voluntary associations, the role of churches is covered in little more than one paragraph. In all, little attention has been given to the rich history and contemporary reality of Chinese religious communities and expressions in New York.

The watershed 1965 Immigrant and Nationality Act dramatically increased and diversified immigration to the United States. As part of the growing literature on post-1965 immigration, attention has turned recently to the role of religion in immigrant communities. As religious pluralism in the United States increases exponentially, the contributions and complications of religious diversity in the fabric of American life deserve even closer scrutiny. Increased attention to this central aspect of immigrant communities can only advance our understanding of the immigrant experience in the United States. Notably, work by Warner and Wittner (1998) and Ebaugh and Chafetz (2000) has drawn together collections of ethnographic case studies from Chicago and Houston, respectively, and begun to lay out an analytical framework for future research. Additional studies are currently underway in immigrant gateway cities including New York, Miami, Washington, D.C., Los Angeles, and San Francisco.

Fieldwork among Fuzhounese religious communities has required consideration of three issues not always at the forefront of other studies and which, when taken together, offer a unique contribution to this emerging body of literature.

1. A gap in the new literature concerns class issues in the immigrant experience. Scholars have examined issues of gender, transnationalism, second generation dynamics, and organizational structure, but little attention has been paid to the economic conditions of immigrants or to the role of religious communities in challenging or replicating existing class hierarchies in the United States. Chinatown's Fuzhounese religious communities are primarily comprised of garment shop, restaurant, and construction workers, many of whom are undocumented. The choice of this subject has required a more careful exploration of issues of class and religion because of the socioeconomic context in which these communities exist. In this book I examine these dynamics particularly in light of the problematic theory of the ethnic enclave often cited in contemporary literature on immigrant incorporation. This study's focus on the religious communities of poor immigrant workers will make a significant contribution to advancing our understanding of the immigrant religious experience.

2. It is also my contention that immigrant religious communities must be examined as embedded in global processes and transnational flows that transcend established notions of space and time while linking home and host countries. Only a handful of recent studies have taken this approach seriously (Brown 1991; McAlister 1998; Levitt 2001; Ebaugh and Chavetz 2002). In this book I have placed Fuzhounese migration and Fuzhounese religious expressions in historical and global perspective, allocating chapters to the political economy of both Fuzhou and New York's Chinatown, as well as the complex religious dynamics of Fuzhou that have in turn affected New York's Fuzhounese religious communities. My experience in conducting the fieldwork for this study has revealed to me the absolute necessity of providing this kind of in-depth context in order to understand today's immigrant religious communities.

3. Fuzhounese immigrants related to these communities consistently frame their experiences in religious terms, striving to understand what these life changes mean. The transition from life in China to life in the United States is a jolting one. It requires a drastic realignment of self-identity. The Fuzhounese move from being rural to urban dwellers, from being economically limited yet unencumbered to being deeply indebted, from being legal to being illegal. They must navigate both a seemingly impenetrable U.S. environment where they are racialized as Chinese and a highly stratified Chinatown where they are ethnicized as Fuzhounese. In the midst of this rupture, religious communities serve as important lo-

cations for constructing alternative associational networks, identities, and systems of meaning that place value on their faith, responsibility, and morality. By including the voices of Fuzhounese immigrants I seek to accomplish two goals. First, I hope their voices will shed light on the personal experiences of meaning-making and break through the dehumanizing influences of global capitalism and the exploitative ethnic enclave. Second, I intend to challenge the functionalist tendencies still prevalent in the social-scientific study of religion that so often examine the social role and function of religious groups and avoid this central theme of the search for meaning.

Outline of the Book

Most Fuzhounese immigrants of the past twenty years have started their U.S. sojourn in New York City's Manhattan Chinatown. In chapter 1 I explore the contemporary realities of this ethnic enclave and its controversial role in the incorporation of these new immigrants into the U.S. economy and culture. Portes and others (Wilson and Portes 1980; Portes and Bach 1985) have introduced the concept of the ethnic enclave as an alternative to the assimilationist narrative of immigrant incorporation. Zhou (1992) suggests that social solidarity in the Chinatown enclave allows immigrants to utilize cultural capital to enhance earning potential and upward mobility. This chapter considers how dense networks of social obligations engendered in the enclave, while they enable new immigrants to survive, may actually result in certain cultural, political, and economic disadvantages for the Fuzhounese immigrant workers. What looks like social solidarity among Chinese at one level may constitute a framework for coethnic exploitation at another level.

In chapter 2 I examine the historical and contemporary context of Fuzhou in an attempt to illuminate the root causes of today's massive outmigration. In addition to longtime patterns of Fuzhounese outmigration, I consider the effects of recent Chinese economic reforms and their connection to a globalizing world capitalist economy. Together, chapters 1 and 2 seek to describe the contemporary local context and global/transnational processes in which the Fuzhounese religious communities, described in chapters 3 to 6, are embedded.

Chapter 3 provides an overview of religion in Fuzhou, with particular attention paid to concepts of orthodoxy and heterodoxy in Chinese history, the role of heterodox sects in modern Chinese history, and the contemporary conflict between Falun Gong and the Chinese state. Chapter 4 explores the post-1949 history of Protestant and Catholic religious traditions in Fuzhou, including attempts by the state to establish new definitions of orthodoxy and heterodoxy and Christian responses. Chapter 4 concludes with descriptions of three strands of Protestantism prominent in the Fuzhou area that have direct connections to New York's Chinatown and the religious communities discussed in chapters 5 and 6.

In chapter 5 we examine the religious landscape of Chinatown. After describing the overall Chinese religious scene in New York and the religious complexities of Chinatown itself, the chapter specifically considers the development of four Fuzhounese congregations: the He Xian Jun Buddhist Temple, the Daoist Temple of Heavenly Thanksgiving, and Transfiguration and St. Joseph's Catholic churches. This analysis will provide a multireligious framework for analyzing the more expansive Protestant case study that follows.

Chapter 6 is an ethnographic study of two Fuzhounese Protestant churches—the Church of Grace to the Fujianese and the New York House Church, independent congregations recently founded by Fuzhounese immigrants and serving an exclusively Fuzhounese constituency immersed in the political, economic, and cultural context of the Chinese ethnic enclave.

In chapter 7 we examine the implications of these case studies of Fuzhounese immigrant religious communities for contemporary debates on the relationship between religion and immigration. Based on the fieldwork I conducted during the course of this study in Chinatown and in Fuzhou, it is my conviction that to fully understand the dynamics of New York's Chinatown as an ethnic enclave, one must consider religion. And to fully understand the dynamics of religion in New York's Chinatown one must place its religious communities in the context of local economic and political realities as well as transnational flows and global processes.

Fieldwork Methodology and Access

I began my fieldwork in Chinatown in the fall of 1994, conducting a limited survey of mainline Protestant churches. My primary finding was that Fuzhounese immigrants were not members of these congregations, which were comprised of earlier generations of Chinese primarily from

Guangzhou (often referred to as Canton), Taiwan, and Hong Kong. In the spring and summer of 1997 I conducted a more systematic survey of Chinatown's religious communities. A street-by-street walking tour of the neighborhood quickly identified newly emerging independent religious communities exclusively serving Fuzhounese immigrants. Interviews revealed close connections between these New York groups and home communities in China. No set pattern existed. Not every group exhibited as direct an involvement in the movement of people as the Daoist temple. But all served as a node of access to the networked webs of information, employment, housing, health care, and connection to China. These webs encompassed both New York's Chinatown and Fuzhou and were built on the continuous flow of people and money, both documented and undocumented, between the two locations.

In July and August of 1997 I traveled to Fuzhou and other cities in Fujian Province to test these initial findings. Though developing access to others in China is always a delicate process and usually quite time consuming, I discovered that introductions from New York friends, relatives, and congregation members opened unexpected doors. Furthermore, discussions of religious beliefs and traditions provided an avenue for initiating conversations about other, sometimes more sensitive issues.

My most intensive fieldwork was conducted between December 1998 and the spring of 2001. I initially focused on the Protestant Church of Grace, which, of all the congregations, was the most organized with regular programs and an identifiable leadership structure. Of all the congregations it was also the most welcoming to my inquiries. Over time, I expanded my contacts with the other congregations as well, conducting regular participant observation and interviews when possible. Leaders, both clergy and lay, and members have generously shared their stories of faith and migration, introduced me to their families and friends, and entrusted me with the responsibility of sharing their stories with others. I have attended rituals, festivals, religious programs, and administrative meetings. I have conducted hundreds of hours of in-depth interviews, visited people's homes—sometimes only a bed in a crowded tenement room—accompanied members to local hospitals and doctor's visits, accompanied asylum seekers to immigration court hearings, and attended weddings, funerals, Christmas parties, New Year's celebrations, and citywide evangelistic meetings. In three of the congregations I was allowed to administer written questionnaires, though only toward the end of my research after sufficient rapport had been established.

In July and August of 1999 I again returned to Fuzhou, this time even better prepared with personal introductions. I was able to visit many of the home churches and temples related to the immigrants I had been working with in New York, and the texture and vitality of Fuzhou's religious landscape began to come alive for me in ways that it had not done before. It is clear to me that the access afforded me on this trip and on a subsequent visit in March and April 2001 would have taken months if not more to develop in China without the intervention of my New York informants—if I would have been able to develop it at all.

For most Fuzhounese, the isolation of their religious groups from American culture beyond Chinatown mirrors their individual experiences and that of the Fuzhounese population as a whole. Few Fuzhounese have any meaningful ongoing contact with non-Chinese. In this context I was at first a great curiosity as a European-American who spoke Chinese, and continue to be so for newly arrived immigrants. Moving beyond curiosity, I became a source of information about the "world beyond." I was often asked to interpret events, describe people and places, and offer advice about everything from proper preparations for Y2K to how to program an overused photocopy machine's security code. At times I became a cultural broker, translating letters from the Immigration and Naturalization Service into Chinese, recording English-language practice tapes for members preparing for U.S. citizenship exams, locating a notary public, advising the board of deacons of the practices of other U.S. churches on issues from pastors' salaries to how to obtain a certificate of occupancy from the New York City Buildings Department. In the weeks after the September 11, 2001, bombing of the World Trade Center, I made numerous visits to a devastated Chinatown, riding my bicycle to circumnavigate the police blockades cutting off lower Manhattan from the rest of the city, and spending hours listening to workers' tales, translating English-language news broadcasts and interpreting events. All of these interactions built relationships of trust over time.

My visits to Fuzhou in 1997, 1999, and 2001 bridged many additional gulfs as I had the chance to visit people's hometowns, families, home churches and temples, and close associates. These experiences were never underestimated or underappreciated by the Fuzhounese in New York. The deepening of my rapport after these trips was striking.

I must also acknowledge the powerful desire of the members of these congregations to have their stories told, individually, as communities of faith and as the Fuzhounese people. The journey that they have undertaken has been arduous. Their existence in New York is often precarious. In hot, overcrowded garment sweatshops, in the backs of busy Chinese restaurants serving inexpensive food to the U.S. middle and upper classes, in the dangerous construction trades clearing and developing our country, Fuzhounese are building the American economy and nation with the very sinews of their bodies, laboring in a land and among a people that know them not, where their presence is not recognized by the country's immigration statutes. In the midst of this, Fuzhounese long for their contributions to be recognized and affirmed.

Like Li Lin, whose story opens this introductory chapter, recent Fuzhounese *toudu* or "steal across" the sea to the United States, braving wind and weather, immigration agents, human smugglers, and border patrols. All Fuzhounese, regardless of their legal status, have chosen to leave their homes and communities in search of a better life for themselves and their families, striking out from their coastal towns and villages, crossing the sea, walking on water, this time beyond Asia to the United States of America. The following pages tell their stories. For many, their faith provides a means of making sense of their journey, and their religious communities provide a means for surviving on often rugged paths. Where they have gone, they have taken their deities with them, immigrant gods accompanying a sojourning people. And where they have gone they have constructed religious communities as safe harbors in the storm, as islands of safety on their way to an unfamiliar shore.

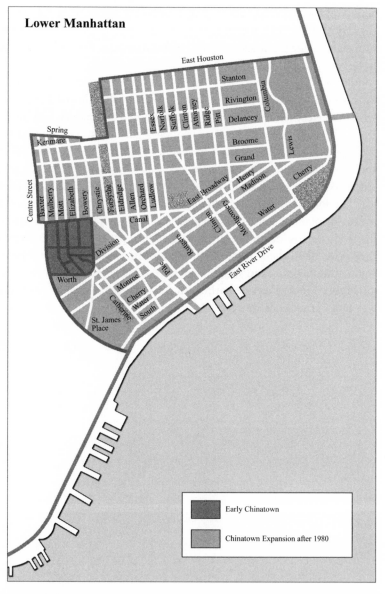

Map of Chinatown.

1

Chinatown and the Fuzhounese

On a clear cold day in Chinatown, the steam escapes from garment sweat-shops and rises from clouded windows up into the sky. Sunlight plays off the city and federal office buildings of Foley Square to the west and along East Broadway through the heart of Chinatown's new Fuzhounese neigh-borhood. As East Broadway, also known as Fuzhou Street, emerges from under the Brooklyn Bridge, Eldridge Street shoots directly north, its old ten-ement buildings lining a path that frames the glistening Chrysler Building in the midtown Manhattan distance. At the southern end of Eldridge Street stand the employment agencies—called "introduction halls" in Chinese—where Fuzhounese go to check the want ads posted on big boards: a restau-rant in Asheville, North Carolina, paying $1,500 a month plus room and board; another in Dallas, Texas; a construction site in midtown using nonunion labor paying $1,000 for two weeks work; a garment shop in Brooklyn paying by the piece; a canning factory in Pennsylvania. Nearby, a fleet of private vans offers to take passengers to the next city—Philadelphia, Boston, or Washington. On the corner, a crowd of young men and a few young women hang out smoking. Waiting for a job: the next step along this path to what they hope will be their American dream.

For most Fuzhounese immigrants, New York City's Manhattan China-town is their first stop in America. Here they connect with friends and fam-ily and home villagers. They find jobs. They eat Chinese food. They bunk in with fellow workers who fill the Lower East Side tenements. They visit tem-ples and churches to offer thanksgiving for safe passage from China. And they begin to piece together a strategy for finding their way through Amer-ican society. Popular estimates among the Fuzhounese themselves claim 300,000 immigrants from the Fuzhou region now make their home in the United States, with 60–70,000 in New York City at any given time. The Fukien (older transliteration of Fujian) American Association in New York City estimates that there are more than 150,000 new immigrants in the

United States from the city of Changle, near Fuzhou, alone (Hood 1997: 91). These figures are difficult to corroborate. Many such estimates are based on local population records in China that document the outmigration from each village, township, and city. No comprehensive demographic survey of the Fuzhounese community in New York City exists. Nor is it clear, given the high number of undocumented workers among the population and their high level of transience, that such broad-based surveys would be accurate.

The 2000 Census has identified 700,000 Asians in New York City, just under 10 percent of the population. Chinese are the largest group with 361,000 residents, followed by 214,000 South Asians and 86,000 Koreans. In the 1990s Chinese ranked third only to immigrants from the Dominican Republic and the former Soviet Union among New York City's new arrivals. Chinese have settled in three particular locations: Flushing, Queens, a middle-class Asiatown; Sunset Park, a multiethnic working-class neighborhood along the subway lines linking Brooklyn to lower Manhattan; and the earliest Chinese settlement, Manhattan's Chinatown, a complex ethnic enclave of tenement housing, restaurants, garment sweatshops, shopping districts, tourist attractions, and businesses.

Manhattan's Chinatown exists in the American popular imagination as one of the signature sights of New York City, spoken of in the same breath with the Statue of Liberty, the Empire State Building, the Brooklyn Bridge, Wall Street, Central Park, Little Italy, and the New York Yankees. The name, Chinatown, evokes images of crowded streets, curbside fish and vegetable markets, firecrackers on the Chinese New Year, cheap Chinese restaurants with whole roasted ducks dangling in windows, narrow alleyways, incomprehensible Chinese signs and sing-song Chinese language, mysterious gang violence, old ladies telling fortunes by the park, and old men playing dominos and mahjong. Tourists from across the United States and around the world flock to Mott Street to buy Chinese trinkets and sample Chinese food. New Yorkers brave the throngs on Mulberry and Grand streets to buy fresh vegetables, seafood, and meat. Overwhelmed visitors crowd under the golden arches of the Canal Street or Bowery McDonalds, an oasis of Americana in a sea of foreignness. These powerful stereotypes of Chinatown accentuate the exoticism of this ethnic enclave on New York's Lower East Side. They play upon the strongest orientalist tendencies of American cultural discourse, reinforcing the notion of Chinatown's marginalized otherness and setting this area and its inscrutable people apart from the rest of New York City and even the rest of U.S. culture.

These stereotypes tend to obfuscate and mystify the complex internal dynamics of Chinatown, dynamics that often pit Chinese against Chinese based on differences of regional origin, language, educational background, economic resources, political persuasion, and legal status. The new Fuzhounese immigrants who labor in the restaurants, construction sites, and hundreds of garment factories run by Chinese in the area and across the country are the most vulnerable to this intense stratification. For while Chinatown is a gateway into America for most Fuzhounese and the beginning of their pursuit of the American dream, for many Chinatown is also a trap, an ethnic enclave manufactured by the economic and political Chinatown elites to keep them isolated and thus vulnerable to labor exploitation.

Mr. Liu Zhu'en

Mr. Liu Zhu'en's experience is not unlike that of many Fuzhounese immigrants who have made their way to New York in the past fifteen years. Twenty-eight years old and an only child, he grew up in Tingjiang, where his parents still live, east of Fuzhou on the north bank of the Min River where it flows into the sea. In 1994, at the age of nineteen, he decided to leave Tingjiang and travel to America. He arranged the journey with a local snakehead (smuggler) for $24,000, payable upon safe arrival. Along with a group of young people from Tingjiang he traveled south by bus to a small town on the coast outside Guangzhou, where they were led onto a two thousand ton freighter commanded by Taiwanese smugglers. Altogether, 165 Fuzhounese from different towns and villages made the voyage. On the boat they slept on the hard wood floor and ate at most two bowls of white rice congee/gruel every day. Some days it was only one bowl. With so many people aboard, they were forced to use ocean water to shower. The smell would wash away, but afterward the salt would stick to their skin and itch and itch and itch. They had already "jumped into the sea." There was no turning back.

After seventy-five days on the boat, Mr. Liu and the others were transferred to a fishing vessel, where they passed one day and one night before reaching the shore of Mexico. One group at a time, the human cargo was to be transferred ashore and led across the mountains into Los Angeles. But after the first group had been gone for awhile, word came back that five of them had died along the way. They never found out why. The snakeheads became very agitated and moved the boat farther offshore to wait. That night was very cold and stormy. The seas raged around them and water poured into the boat. The passengers, unprepared for the cold, huddled together, shivering in the bottom of the boat, awaiting calm seas and a chance to disembark on dry land and make their way on the final stretch of the journey to America.

I wasn't on very good terms with my family when I left Tingjiang. In fact, I hadn't told anyone in my family that I was leaving. When we finally arrived in Los Angeles the smugglers wanted their money. Twenty-four thousand dollars. So I called home and told my family. My father couldn't believe it was me. He couldn't believe that I had already reached America. And he didn't really recognize my voice on the telephone. I think he thought it was a trick. So he asked the snakehead to let me get in touch with one of my cousins who was already in America so that they could see me and verify it was really me. But then the smugglers thought that I was trying to trick them. They told my father that they would kill me if they didn't get the money, and then they hung up. They began to beat me. They beat me with copper piping. They beat me on my back, on my legs, and on my chest. I will have the scars the rest of my life. I was beaten unconscious and left lying bloody on the floor. The next time I called home, thank God, my father had already made arrangements for the money, borrowing from friends and family in China and the United States. The plan was for my father to pay the snakeheads back in Tingjiang. But I could tell he still didn't trust them. I wasn't sure what was going to happen. That was a long night waiting to find out if he had actually paid. I was really scared. I didn't want to be beaten again. But he paid. After a week, the smugglers let me go and I headed to New York.

I was young and I had finally made it to the "Land of Beauty," as we call America. I wanted to get to work. At the beginning I found a good job in a restaurant. I worked very hard. The boss liked me and even raised my pay.

But after several months I came down with a very serious illness that affected my legs. I still think it had something to do with the beating by the snakeheads. This was the beginning of my great hardship in America. I had difficulty standing for any length of time. The pain was too intense. I couldn't keep a job. For more than four years this went on. I saw doctor after doctor. Both Western and Chinese. But because I was illegal and I didn't have any money I didn't have many choices. I went to emergency rooms when it was really bad, but I was always afraid someone at the hospital would turn me in. I went to many different Chinese health clinics. They were illegal just like me. But nothing seemed to work. It was so bad I started to think about how to kill myself. If life was going to be this hard I couldn't keep it up. For a while the pain subsided and I was able to work again. The doctors told me not to, but I didn't really have a choice. I needed the money to pay back my debts. But in March 1999 the pain came back. I couldn't stand up. It hurt to sit down, too. What was I going to do? I thought about going home to Tingjiang. But there was nothing for me there—not after five years away.

Miraculously in April 1999 I started to feel better, a little bit at a time. I think this was the work of God. I had been living next to the Church of Grace on Allen Street. The people there had been helping me, sometimes paying my medical bills, visiting me in the hospital, and praying for me. One day, when the pain was so bad I didn't know what to do, I went to the church and prayed. I asked God what to do. I gave my life to Jesus. I think that's when things started to turn around. I've decided to stay in America. The pain still comes and goes. But it's bearable most of the time. I'm able to work again. At least for short stints. But I'm not as strong as I used to be. These jobs in the restaurants are so grueling I can usually only work for a week or two. Then I have to take time off to rest. At least I don't think about committing suicide anymore.

Fuzhounese immigrants like Mr. Liu struggle for survival and success in New York amid intense isolation. Where possible, they utilize family, village, friendship, and religious networks to ease their way. But in many cases the informal safety net is inadequate in the face of the pressures and violence of the marketplace. Snakeheads demand their fees. Employers enforce long hours, skim tips, withhold wages. Undocumented workers fail to avail themselves of human services or refuse to complain of abuses for fear of deportation. In these conditions, a sojourn in the "Land of Beauty" may quickly become a torturous passage.

Ms. Chen Ru

While the earlier waves of Fuzhounese were predominantly men, often sent by their families to establish an economic beachhead in the United States, in recent years the number of women leaving Fuzhou has significantly increased. While many of them follow husbands or fathers who may have been able to achieve legal status or enough economic stability to pay for their snakeheads, many others strike out on their own or utilize networks of women relatives, as in the following story, to enter the U.S. labor market.

My name is Chen Ru. I'm nineteen. My mother died when I was a little girl—seven days old, actually. My father never was around much after that. He was always off gambling. I was basically an orphan. My paternal grandmother raised me in the countryside near Changle.

My father's sister came illegally to New York a number of years ago. She's still illegal but she has a very good restaurant up on the Upper West Side of Manhattan. When I was younger she would send money back to support me and my grandmother. She's been trying to get me to come to America for several years.

Finally in 1999 I decided to come. I made arrangements with a snakehead in Changle. There are lots of them around—all looking for business. I agreed to pay him U.S. $50,000. Within a week I was on my way with a fake U.S. visa in my fake Chinese passport. I boarded the plane in Fuzhou with two other girls from Changle. We changed planes in Shanghai. Our flight went to the Philippines, where I waited for nearly a month. From the Philippines we were sent by plane to Los Angeles. I knew we would never make it through immigration so I hid in the women's bathroom in the airport. But late that night they found us. I was held in an INS detention center in Los Angeles for a month. I called the local snakehead in L.A. He worked with a lawyer to get me out on bail until my hearing. I'm not sure how they did that but these snakeheads have really good relationships with lawyers. Maybe they claimed political asylum or religious persecution.

As soon as I got out they put me on a plane for New York. I never showed up at the court in Los Angeles. The INS has never tracked me down.

My aunt lent me the U.S. $50,000 to pay the smugglers. I worked in her restaurant in New York for a while and I lived in her little apartment. But I didn't want to be a burden on her, so I started to go to the employment agencies in Chinatown to see what kind of work I could find. There are a lot of them all over Chinatown, but especially on East Broadway. Employers from all over the U.S. post jobs, long term and short term, mostly in restaurants. I took a job at a Chinese buffet restaurant advertised in Miami. They put me on a bus the next day. I worked there for three months living in the back of the restaurant. The money was pretty

FIGURE 1 Fuzhounese men look for jobs at Manhattan Chinatown employment agencies.

good but I missed my aunt, so I came back to New York for a while. Now I'm working in another Chinese buffet restaurant in Washington, D.C. The owner is nice and we all live in an apartment next to the restaurant. I'm working hard.

It's not easy being in America. People try to take advantage of you sometimes, especially as a woman. Even relatives. My uncle even asked special favors from me in return for a place to stay when I was out of a job for a while. So I stay close to a group of young women. We're all friends from the church. We pray for each other. And we help each other out as much as we can—finding places to stay, jobs, stuff like that.

In three or four years I should be able to pay off the loan from my aunt. I know I'm not here legally. There's nothing I can do about that. But I do have to pay off this debt.

The stories of Liu and Chen are typical of many young Fuzhounese, particularly those smuggled into the United States, who arrive with a dream of making a living better than they had in China, only to find themselves struggling every day to survive. Chinatown provides an initial point of entry, a place to find jobs, places to stay, doctors, and phone cards to call home. With no legal status, however, they have little access to the mainstream economy. Even many of those with legal status lack basic English-language skills or awareness of U.S. culture. For them the point of entry provided by China-town and the extended Chinese ethnic employment networks that have spread across the United States may have no means of egress.

History of Chinese in New York

Fuzhounese are but the latest Chinese to immigrate to New York and the lat-est strand in the complex web of relationships stretching between China and New York City. When Henry Hudson sailed into New York Bay in 1609, his expedition was financed by the Dutch East India Company in the hopes of finding a much-longed-for sea route to the riches of China and India. By the eighteenth and nineteenth centuries, Chinese luxury items such as porcelains, teas, and silk arriving on British clipper ships that had sailed around Africa's Cape of Good Hope had already become status symbols among New York's rising merchant and political elite. As the nation at-tempted to establish itself on the world economic stage after the American Revolution, New York's merchant class emulated its former colonial masters and turned to the China trade. On February 22, 1784, the *Empress of China* set sail from New York Harbor packed with Spanish silver coins and 57,687 pounds of ginseng, a highly sought-after medicinal tuber in China that grew wild up and down the eastern coast of America. The ship returned to New York fifteen months later with a prized cargo of porcelains, silks, teas, and other luxury items. Its voyage inaugurated direct links between the United States and China, drawing together merchants in the port cities of New York and Guangzhou (Canton). While trade with China was legally limited to the port of Guangzhou, the emerging Sino-U.S. trade succeeded in linking thousands of people picking tea in the hills of Fujian Province and harvesting ginseng along the American coast into a network of trade and an ongoing process of cross-cultural interaction that would develop over the next two hundred years (Tchen 1999).

Trade between the two countries gradually increased in the nineteenth century as the United States continued its economic rise. When the British forced open China's ports in the Opium War (1839–1842), New York mer-chants quickly joined in, replacing the dwindling ginseng trade by shipping opium into China and transporting indentured coolies ("bitter labor" in Chinese) to the Caribbean and South America. Their dramatic profits fueled not only New York's expanding economy, but also the vast array of cultural institutions established by the city's merchant elite in the nineteenth century (Tchen 1999).

The first Chinese ventured to New York in the early 1800s as sailors, cooks, and stewards on the ships plying the U.S.-China trade. Most of those who stayed settled in the multiethnic Five Points neighborhood in lower Manhattan, located near the burgeoning maritime commerce of the East River piers and populated by Irish, German, and Polish immigrants, freed African Americans, and later Italians and Eastern European Jews. The teeming Five Points neighborhood, while providing a landing place for the city's new immigrants, also became known as one of the most notorious slums in American history. According to Charles Dickens, writing after a visit to New York in 1841, "Here, too, are lanes and alleys, paved with mud knee deep; underground chambers, where they dance and game . . . hideous tenements which take their name from robbery and murder; all that is loathsome, drooping and decayed is here" (cited in Anbinder 2001: 33). The housing and health conditions were truly terrible and became the focus of reform movements led by Jacob Riis and others later in the century. But the extensive intermingling of people and cultures in the very heart of this booming international commercial center also represented a microcosm of the pluralism that has been a key to the fashioning and sustaining of New York City.

By the mid-1800s a number of Chinese-run boardinghouses emerged on lower Baxter Street to accommodate these Chinese seamen as well as others from the failed California gold rush and some from coolie labor in Peru and Cuba. Chinese street peddlers sold cheap hand-made cigars and rock candy. Chinese tea merchants marketed their wares to New York's middle and upper classes. Restaurants catering to the Chinese "bachelor society" gradually enticed other New Yorkers. Later, the hand-laundry trade, which by the 1880s was being vacated by upwardly mobile Irish women, would grow into one of the most significant occupations among Chinese for a century. By 1869 it is estimated that sixty to seventy Chinese were regularly living in lower Manhattan, with many others passing through New York and its harbor (Anbinder 2001; Yu 1992).

New York's Chinese population began a steady expansion in the 1870s. Chinese workers had come to the West Coast of the United States from southern China, mainly Guangdong Province (Canton), from the 1840s, first as cheap labor for large mining companies during the California Gold Rush, then as agricultural workers, and later to build the western spur of the transcontinental railroad through the Sierra Nevada Mountains. While many were brought to the United States as indentured laborers, others were middle-class young men seeking their fortunes with enough money to buy passage on a ship and to get started in America. By 1875 there were 105,000 Chinese laborers in the American West.

Despite this rich history of contributions to building American society, antipathy toward the Chinese ran deep, exacerbated by the economic recession of the 1870s. They became targets of xenophobic politicians, journalists, and working-class mobs who branded them the "yellow peril" for taking jobs away from American citizens. They were humiliated, ostracized, and hundreds were beaten and killed. Chinatowns—urban concentrations of Chinese—began to emerge during this time as safe havens to escape the racism, violence, and economic discrimination directed against them by white Americans. By the 1870s, spurred by the completion of the transcontinental railroad and continuing intimidation and discriminatory legislation in the American West, many Chinese began moving east of their own accord. Others were brought across the country as unwitting strike breakers in labor disputes, continuing a pattern of exploitation by American industrialists.

Discrimination against Chinese heightened in the 1870s and was codified in 1882 when the U.S. Congress passed the Chinese Exclusion Act, the first and only federal immigration law to ban immigration of people of a single nationality. This act, in place until 1943, restricted the ability of Chinese immigrant laborers to enter the United States legally for over sixty years during the height of great European migration of 1880 to 1924. Combined with other federal legal action denying citizenship to all but whites and blacks, the Exclusion Act had a profound effect on the self-understanding of Chinese laborers in the United States, locking in a sojourner status and ensuring that the identity of Chinese in the United States remained firmly rooted in China and linked to family, lineage, and home village (Kwong 1996 [1987]; Hsu 2000).

Despite these restrictions, Chinese continued to creatively build links between China and the United States. Students, diplomats, and businessmen retained the right to enter the United States. Other Chinese bought passports from Macau, a Portuguese colony, which were available at consulates in mainland China. Among the working classes, ongoing connections, while more difficult, continued, including remittances and return migration, encouraging a continuation of the flow of people. It is estimated that tens of thousands of Chinese, particularly from the southernmost counties of Guangdong, migrated overseas in open defiance of both U.S. and Chinese legal restrictions, pursuing their dreams of striking it rich on "Gold Mountain." Their stories, lived out as sojourners on the legal, economic, and social margins of U.S. society, in predominantly male bachelor communities, laboring in restaurants, laundries, and groceries, foreshadow the experiences of their Fuzhounese compatriots one hundred years later (Hsu 2000).

By the late 1800s the Chinese were joined by Italians and Eastern European Jews, replacing Irish and Germans in the Five Points area and continuing the complex layering of immigrant experiences and cultures on New York's Lower East Side. The Italians were largely poor farmers from southern Italy. The Jews were escaping religious persecution. Many of the Chinese were fleeing anti-Chinese violence on America's West Coast. And while Chinese never came close in number to the hundreds of thousands of Italians and Jews arriving in New York each year at the turn of the century, by 1900 a clearly identified community of two thousand Chinese, mostly men, had settled in the area of Pell, Doyer, and lower Mott streets.

Chinatown began a steady expansion in the 1940s, 1950s, and 1960s. By 1945, four thousand Chinese inhabited the area. The Chinese Exclusion Act was repealed in 1943 in recognition of China's participation on the side of the Allies during World War II. In addition, the U.S. government granted citizenship to all those who had served in the U.S. armed forces and allowed limited family unification under the War Brides Act. A separate, though low, immigration quota for Chinese was set at 105 per year. By 1953 the Chinese population had expanded to 15,000 with thousands of new immigrants arriving annually, many admitted under special legislation for refugees fleeing Communist mainland China through Hong Kong.

New York's Chinatown grew more rapidly still after 1965, when the U.S. government passed the Immigration and Nationality Act. The previous laws gave preference to nationalities already represented in the U.S. population, thereby ensuring continued strong immigration from northern and western Europe. The new law, expanded in the 1970s, substituted a flat quota of 20,000 immigrants for every country, without regard to race and nationality, and included special provisions for reunification of families. A total of 32,831 Chinese lived in New York City in 1960. That number grew to 238,919 by 1990 and 361,000 in 2000. In Manhattan's Chinatown, the Chinese population grew from 11,578 in 1960 to 94,487 in 1990 (Lin 1998: 108). Though the detailed 2000 Census data were not available at the time of writing, all indications are that, with the massive Fuzhounese immigration since 1990, the Chinese population of Manhattan has increased significantly, though some of the increase may be masked by their undocumented status.

Chinatown Today

Today, Manhattan's Chinatown has expanded well beyond its early borders, pushing north through Little Italy, east through the Jewish settlements of the Lower East Side, and south into government housing projects and toward the Brooklyn Bridge. It is a densely populated area crowded with tenement housing, restaurants, stores, businesses, and community organizations of all varieties. Chatham Square stands as a symbolic crossroads of today's Chinatown. Located near the key intersection of old Five Points, the area around Chatham Square has been known for nearly two hundred years as a central location for newly arrived and poor immigrants. From Chatham Square, Mott Street runs north through the heart of the original Chinatown section. Parallel to Mott, the Bowery conjures images of poor unemployed men and their flophouses and Christian missions. To the west, Park Row runs directly toward City Hall and a concentration of municipal and federal office buildings, including the U.S. District Court House whose grand exterior stairs feature prominently in many U.S. motion pictures. East Broadway runs eastward, anchoring the new Fuzhounese district.

Two statues stand in Chatham Square, constructed by competing political elites in Chinatown and symbolizing the stark political and cultural differences between Chinese immigrant generations. One, of Confucius, was erected in 1984 by earlier immigrants from Hong Kong, Canton, and Taiwan. Its construction was organized by the Consolidated Chinese Benevolent Association and largely paid for by the Taiwanese Nationalist government as a sign of respect for the traditional Chinese culture that had been destroyed under the mainland Communist government, particularly during the Cultural Revolution. The second statue, constructed in 1997 by Fuzhounese individuals and civic associations at a cost of $200,000, is of Lin Ze Xu, the famous Chinese patriot from Fujian Province who led the Chinese resistance to the British importation of opium into the port of Canton in the 1840s. The Lin statue, two feet taller than the Confucius statue, stands facing East Broadway, the main Fuzhounese thoroughfare in Chinatown.

From Fuzhou to New York

The earliest Fuzhounese immigrants arrived in New York in the 1940s: a few sailors who jumped ship after arrival and a few hundred who were granted residency for serving in the U.S. Merchant Marine during World War II. New York's Fuzhounese population grew slowly over the next three decades as seamen who had escaped from China to Hong Kong in the 1950s made their way to the United States and chose to stay on illegally. Attempts to re-unify their families in the 1970s in New York provided an early stimulus for the extensive smuggling network that exists today, as Fuzhounese worked through Chinese travel agencies to procure the documents and tickets for relatives who had been able to leave China for Hong Kong to make the on-ward passage to the United States (Kwong 1997a: 28).

Opportunities for Fuzhounese outmigration expanded as China launched its economic reform program in the late 1970s and opened to overseas investment. Those with relatives in Hong Kong and Macau at-tempted to "visit" or to get temporary permission to work. If allowed out by the Chinese government, they stayed, gradually bringing their families to join them. In turn, those in Hong Kong and Macau began to look for ways to relocate to New York, often overstaying tourist visas obtained in order to visit "relatives" in the United States. At the same time, overseas Fuzhounese networks were drawn into the establishment of the human smuggling en-terprise.

By the mid-1980s a growing number of rural Fuzhounese were seeking to follow their compatriots abroad. New York was not the only option as Fuzhounese networks also extended to Japan, Australia, and Europe. But New York was for many the most attractive. News of economic opportuni-ties, even for undocumented workers in the restaurant and garment indus-tries, had reached Fuzhou, and remittances from New York had begun to flow into hometowns and villages. Some few utilized family reunification clauses in the U.S. immigration laws after their relatives had attained U.S. legal status. Others utilized human smuggling networks in the Fuzhou area that were rapidly expanding with support from opportunistic Taiwanese crime syndicates already deeply involved in the global smuggling trade. Some Fuzhounese were smuggled to the United States directly by air either from China or after exiting to Hong Kong. As the air routes became more carefully monitored, smugglers utilized sea routes, often to Mexico, where Fuzhounese immigrants and their snakeheads crossed the border alongside

Central American immigrants and their "coyotes." Chinese smugglers continued to adapt their routes to best evade U.S. government border control
efforts, becoming ever more creative and brutal while charging ever-in-
creasing smuggling fees. The average smuggling fee in 1988 was $22,000 and
by 1993 had increased to $30,000 (Chin 1999). Fuzhounese interviewed in
this study reported paying fees between $50,000 and $60,000 in late 2002.
Undocumented immigrants are typically held by snakeheads upon arrival
in the United States until friends and family pay the full smuggling fee.
Those unable to raise the funds may be beaten, their families in China may
face extortion, or the unfortunate immigrant may be forced into service to
the snakeheads in criminal activities, including prostitution. Even those
who successfully borrow the smuggling fee from family and friends are
under incredible pressure to repay the debts, which may carry interest as
high as 25 percent annually. Even working long hours and living frugally,
new immigrants are lucky to pay off their debts in five years (Kwong 1996
[1987], 1997a; Chin 1999).

Chen Qiang

*My family made all the arrangements. My uncle's friend knew someone
who knew a snakehead and they set everything up. We flew from Changle
airport to Hong Kong, then to Cambodia, Hong Kong again, Holland,
then Brazil. From Brazil we were put on a fishing boat, which put us
ashore on the U.S. Virgin Islands. We were all detained there and claimed
political asylum. Since I wasn't eighteen yet they sent me to a Children's
Home in Georgia until we could find a sponsor for me.*

*To tell you the truth, I never really thought much about coming to
America. I had been going to high school. Then all of a sudden my parents said I was going to America. They said there wasn't much of a future
for me in China. No way of making a living. In the beginning I really did-
n't want to come. I didn't have a very good impression of America, only
what I had seen on TV. Lots of bad things. Lots of violence. How many
people were killed each month. That's the kind of news we got from the
TV. But I was being sent to make money.*

*Finding a sponsor to get me out of detention in the Children's Home
was a big problem. I don't have any relatives or friends in the U.S. So I
needed to find someone I could pay to be my sponsor. I was looking. My
family was looking. Even the INS was looking for us. Finally, a worker in*

a garment shop run by the daughter of my uncle's friend agreed to sponsor me. I gave her $3,000.

I wasn't really that worried when I was in the Children's Home. Life there was pretty good. It was only after I was released that I got worried. Find a place to stay. Find a job. Food to eat. How to get through the day. I had to rely on myself. I didn't have any friends. It was very hard. When I first got to New York my uncle's friend helped me find a place to stay for a while. I had to find my own work. I went to the employment agencies. I've been working in restaurants, mostly doing deliveries on a bicycle.

Plus when I got out of the Children's Home my family had to pay the snakeheads $48,000. We've paid them, but now we owe our relatives and we're paying them back with very high interest. So it's a lot of pressure on me now to make money and send it back. I send back as much as I can and they pay off the debts. Most months I can send at least $1,000. But that's a disaster! Definitely not enough. Other people who are waiters can make $2,000 a month. If you speak English you can take phone calls and make more. At best I can only work as a busboy right now. I only use a little bit of money to live on. I eat in the restaurant and live in the restaurant if I can. Otherwise I stay wherever I can find a place to lie down. At a friend's. At the church.

I give ten percent of what I make to the church to say thanks for all their help. I've given a lot of books to their library and I bought the church a new computer. I need a little bit to live on, buy clothes, buy some fruit, pay my transportation on the Path train to New Jersey where I work. If I could make more I could pay my debts back faster. If I could make $2,500 I could send $2,000 back to my family.

Someday I hope I can move up to busboy, then waiter, then to reception, and then finally to open my own restaurant. Fuzhounese in America all have this hope. They don't speak any English. They have a huge problem with their legal status. So they dream of working their way up and someday owning their own restaurant.

Chinatown and the Fuzhounese:
Six Contemporary Immigrant Waves

The vast majority of Fuzhounese immigrants to the United States have come in the past twenty years. The Fuzhounese religious communities considered in this study are comprised primarily of these immigrants who have

TABLE 1.1
Fuzhounese Immigrant History

Arrival	Characteristics	U.S. Legal Status
Before mid-1980s	Residence outside China prior to arrival in U.S.	Legalization under 1986 IRCA
Mid-1980s to 1989	Smuggled, rural, poor	Legalized under provisions of 1989 and 1990 executive orders
To present	Young, smuggled	No legal status
To present	Both urban and rural, all ages	Immigrated legally under 1965 INA, especially under family unification provisions
To present	Children born and raised in U.S.	Legal by birth in U.S.
To present	Children born in U.S., raised in China	Legal by birth in U.S.

arrived since 1980, 82 percent since 1990. Interviews and surveys reveal that among this group several compressed waves or generations comprise recent Fuzhounese immigration history (see table 1.1). An analysis of these waves sheds light on the stratification within the larger Fuzhounese community and within religious communities as well.

The first contemporary wave of Fuzhounese began to arrive in the late 1970s and continued through the early 1980s. Many of them came to the United States by way of an intermediate Fuzhounese community, most frequently Hong Kong, but also Macau and Singapore. Some of them arrived legally, most did not. Many arrived with enhanced financial and social capital. For instance, many came having learned Cantonese along their way, easing their transition into a Chinatown that was then, though no longer, heavily dominated by Cantonese speakers. Fortuitously for these immigrants, all were able to regularize their immigration status, either with a green card or citizenship as a result of the amnesty granted undocumented workers under the 1986 Immigration Reform and Control Act. In turn, they were able to utilize family unification provisions of the 1965 Immigration and Nationality Act to bring immediate family members to the United States, initiating a continuous chain of legal migration.

A second wave began to arrive in the mid-1980s through 1989. This group, whose passage was provided largely by smugglers, began to empty the smaller towns and villages outside Fuzhou. These immigrants were largely rural poor willing to take a risk to improve a difficult life. Many of those who arrived prior to 1990 legalized their status as a result of two executive orders from President George Bush. The first, after the Tian An Men Square uprising in 1989, permitted all Chinese students in the United States to adjust their immigrant status. The second, in 1990, gave "enhanced consideration" to applications for asylum based on threats of forced abortion or coerced sterilization. After successfully normalizing their immigration status, like the previous wave, these immigrants too were able to pursue reunification with family members legally.

The third wave began in the 1990s and continues today. Increasingly, this is comprised of young immigrants who come to the United States without legal documentation and by means of human smugglers. They arrive significantly indebted to the snakeheads and, unless they have family connections who are willing to advance payment, remain indebted for years. Save for the limited number who successfully apply for political asylum, all remain undocumented, outside the mainstream, working in the informal economy. They are the most easily exploited segment of the Fuzhounese immigrant population.

A fourth wave of immigrants parallels the third in time sequence, spanning the 1990s. But this wave benefits from the earlier legalization of their relatives. These immigrants are of all ages, including children, siblings, and parents of earlier immigrants. They arrive with legal status and are able to engage U.S. society as such. This fourth wave, chronologically, is not monolithic but is comprised of two distinct segments. One segment includes relatives from Hong Kong or sometimes Macau or Singapore, reuniting with their family. These immigrants, particularly the young people, are urbanized and often well educated by the public school systems in those countries. They arrive with added advantages for survival and success in the U.S. environment, including English and Cantonese language skills, advanced education or expectations of such, and a basic introduction to the skills needed in the urban economy. Most of these immigrants enter directly into the U.S. educational system, either in high schools or colleges, particularly the City University and State University of New York systems.

The other segment of the fourth wave is also comprised of legal immigrants arriving by virtue of family reunification provisions of the immigration law, but from the rural areas outside Fuzhou. These immigrants come with little preparation for success in the mainstream U.S. economy, educationally or linguistically, having completed at most junior high school and speaking little English, if any, and imprecise Mandarin. Despite their legal status, the older immigrants in this group, mostly parents of earlier immigrants, remain largely isolated in their family groupings. And despite their legal status, the young immigrants are often relegated to the ethnic enclave economy in Chinatown or its extension through the network of Chinese restaurants that crisscrosses the country.

A fifth wave of the Fuzhounese immigrant community is comprised of children born in the United States who are growing up here. They are U.S.-educated and speak English as a first language. They grow up in distinctly Chinese homes, but they are the second generation, a transitional group that is also steeped in U.S. culture. Among the Fuzhounese, this group is small but growing, mostly under ten years of age.

A sixth wave, largely invisible to the public, if not to the Fuzhounese themselves, is made up of children born in the United States but sent back to China as infants. As depicted in the story of Mr. Lu Jianguo later in this chapter, these children are often born to struggling Fuzhounese workers who came here illegally and remain without status. By virtue of their U.S. birth, they are automatically citizens; although raised in China by grand-parents or other family members, they carry U.S. passports. Because of their parents' poverty and lack of U.S.-based support networks, however, they cannot be raised in the United States. Their future status and its effects on their parents will bear careful watching.

This categorization of immigrant generations and predicaments of the Fuzhounese community provides a framework for understanding the structural stratification of the larger Fuzhounese population and, of partic-ular concern to this study, the Fuzhounese religious communities of New York's Chinatown. The attributes described among Fuzhounese immigrants as a whole exist in parallel within the religious communities. And within the churches, differential access to power and authority often parallels the broader social and legal conditions of the membership.

Immigrant Stories

Life histories gathered during the course of this study, such as those of Li Lin, Liu Zhu'en, Chen Ru, and Chen Qiang as well as those that follow, re-flect the diversity of experiences among Fuzhounese living in New York's Chinatown today and illustrate the marked stratification even within this most recent group of Chinese immigrants. Fuzhounese are rich and poor and in between. They are documented and undocumented. They are smuggled in. They have come through family reunification. Varied legal statuses, educational backgrounds, language abilities, financial capital, and social networks frame their ongoing struggles. These life histories capture both the logistics and the emotions of the immigrant journey and the New York immigrant life. Touching upon a number of the immigrant waves previously described, these stories disclose the pain and suffering as well as the hopes and dreams of these adventurous and often courageous sojourners in a strange land. They also reflect the inequality and differentiation that exists within the Fuzhounese community.

Mrs. Chen Huibing

Mrs. Chen Huibing was born in Fuzhou City in 1945. Her family was relatively poor, which turned out to be to their advantage during the political campaigns of the 1950s and 1960s, as anyone considered to be of privileged class status was criticized and targeted for reform and reeducation. She worked as an elementary school teacher in China. She and her husband, who was born in 1936, were married in 1969 at the height of the Cultural Revolution.

My family had always been Buddhist in China. But there had been so much sickness for so long in my family and our prayers to the gods weren't working. When a neighbor woman told us about Jesus we began to pray to him and the illnesses went away. My mother was the first one in our family to become a Christian, in August of 1985. I became a Christian in 1986. We started a church in my mother's home. My husband and I lived there too. Every week people would come to pray and read the Bible. We registered it with the local religious and government authorities. After that, once a week, the largest church nearby, Flower Lane Church, would send a sister to preach. I left Fuzhou in 1992 to come to America. Since then our house has been torn down as part of the urban renewal. But our church meeting has moved to the home of another sister.

I came legally to the U.S. My husband's older brother sponsored us. I came for my children. If we hadn't come, they wouldn't have been able to come. I work in a garment shop sewing clothing. The first shop I worked in was run by a Jewish man but he retired and moved away. The one I'm in now is run by a Chinese man from Canton. I make about six or seven hundred dollars a month, sometimes less. We work when the shop has an order. They call me at home and tell me to come in. Sometimes it's seven days a week, 12–14 hours a day. Sometimes it's only three or four days a week. It's very unpredictable. It depends on the orders. I get paid by the piece for the sewing: six cents for each T-shirt, seven cents for a shirt with hood and zipper, nine cents for a shirt with five buttons, seven cents for a long dress, and eight cents for pants with a zipper and two pockets.

My husband has been very ill the last couple of years and unable to work regularly. When he works we make over $1,000 a month. When he doesn't we rely on my salary alone. Our rent is $380 a month. We share a three bedroom apartment with two other families. Each family has one bedroom. We share one living room, one kitchen and one bathroom. When my husband is not working our budget is very tight. We don't have any extra money to send home to support my mother or my daughter and family who are still in Fuzhou. They must take care of themselves.

My son came to the U.S. last year. We had applied for a visa for him in 1992 but it took seven years. He works in a restaurant about twelve hours away from New York. We don't see him very much. He has a wife and two children back in Fuzhou. His youngest child, a son, was born after he had arrived in America. He is very sad not to be able to see his little boy.

Mr. Lu Jianguo

My name is Lu Jianguo. I'm thirty years old, married and have two children. I'm from Fuqi, a pretty poor village on the southern bank of the Min River. There's not much farmland. Most of the income comes from fishing. My family was always very poor. I've been eating bitterness since I was born. If you don't have money people can't stand you. There were times when we didn't really have enough to eat. I only went to school until I was ten. We were so poor I had to go to work. I can read a little bit but not too much. There's no way we could make it better there. My older brother left in 1986 and was smuggled into America. He got his green card in 1989 after Tian An Men, June 4th. I came in 1992. I paid the smugglers twenty thousand dollars. I had to pay it off over time once I got here, plus a lot of interest. We spent sixty days on the boat coming. I'm not sure where we landed, because I don't speak any English. Maybe somewhere near Boston. Then the snakeheads brought us to New York.

My wife came over around the same time as I did. She was also smuggled in. She's not from my village. I'm not sure where she's from. I've never been there though I think it's nearby. I've never really been anywhere in China. We met here in New York and got married here. I couldn't have married in China. I was too poor. My wife is at home. She just gave birth. So she isn't working. I can't find any work right now either. We're living on our little bit of savings. She works in a garment factory. She's very brave and strong. She works until one or two o'clock every morning. Sixteen or eighteen hours a day. Most women do. She'll look after the baby for a while and then go back to work.

We live in a three bedroom apartment, three families, each with one room. We're all from Fuzhou. We have to take care of ourselves. Nobody looks after us. If you get sick there isn't anybody to help. Each family pays $400 a month for the apartment.

Maybe when my daughter grows up my wife and I can go back to China and my daughter can petition for us to come legally. I have two children. One here in New York. One in China. The one in China is one year old and is being raised by my wife's parents. I paid someone I knew $1,000 to take her back to China. That's the way it works usually. A woman I knew took her back. The baby had her own passport, so it was not a problem. She was born in the U.S., so she's a U.S. citizen. We got her a passport. I took her to the airport. I don't think I had ever cried before. But I did when I sent her back to China. Why? She was only seventy days old, [he cried] when I sent her back. But I don't have any money. I can't take care of her here. So many Fuzhounese are like this. To send a child away to grow up with grandparents in another country ... it's very bitter. We are all working too. And to have a baby in the apartment making so much noise would disturb everyone. And my wife needed to go back to work too. Two daughters, a baby here, and a one-year-old in China. I haven't seen a picture in a long time. They say she has a bad temperament so they can't get a picture of her. I want her to come back to America, but I don't know when we'll be able to work it out.

Fuzhounese Differences: Wider Stratifications

The stories of Liu Zhu'en, Chen Ru, Chen Qiang, Chen Huibing, and Lu Jianguo clearly illustrate the complexity of the Fuzhounese community in New York. While the range of immigrant experiences includes some who have been quite successful, it also includes many individuals who are extremely desperate financially and emotionally. These marginalized individuals are central to making the Chinatown ethnic enclave function, but they exist on the edge of survival. For behind the steamy garment-shop windows and bustling restaurants lies the stark reality of impoverishment and exploitation. These immigrants have come to America in search of economic stability for themselves and their families, but what many have found is grueling labor and an uncertain future. The remainder of this chapter will examine the differences among the Fuzhounese reflected in the life histories within a broader pattern of stratification found in Chinatown and among Chinese immigrants as a whole.

Just as Fuzhounese immigrants comprise a variety of waves, so too does the larger Chinatown community, with immigrants from Hong Kong, Taiwan, south Asia, and many parts of mainland China. And Chinatown's stratification exists not only within these waves but between them. Kwong (1996 [1987]) suggests the terms "Uptown Chinese" and "Downtown Chinese" to describe the Chinese community's internal differentiation along class lines. Uptown Chinese immigrate to the United States with skills needed by the U.S. economy. They may be students, business owners, or professionals. With these skills they are better able to integrate into U.S. society and tend not to live in Chinatowns, though they may have businesses there. Downtown Chinese usually immigrate to the United States with limited financial and social capital. They comprise the working class, employed in restaurants and garment shops. They live in urban Chinese settlements, like Chinatown, speak limited English, and, in the case of many Fuzhounese, may not have legal status, leaving them isolated from the mainstream economy and society and highly vulnerable to economic exploitation.

Stratification is an issue for all immigrant groups in America, not only the Chinese. Legal immigrants to the United States include professionals, entrepreneurs, laborers, refugees, and asylum seekers. And in recent years large numbers of undocumented workers have arrived, not only from China, but also from Mexico, Russia, Central America, the Caribbean, eastern Europe, and even Ireland. Labor migrants, legal and undocumented, in search of menial and largely low paying jobs, have come to represent the majority of immigrants to the United States (Portes and Rumbaut 1996). The differences in legal status and in social and financial capital available to these immigrants mean that immigrant communities with common national origins are not monolithic but, like the Chinese, are often distinguished by significant internal stratification.

Analyzing Ethnic Stratification:
The Ethnic Enclave Model

In recent years scholars have formulated a number of frameworks for understanding inequality among various immigrant groups and the implications of this inequality for the economic formations in major cities and contemporary processes of immigrant incorporation. Of particular theoretical importance to this study of Fuzhounese immigrants in New York's Chinatown is the groundbreaking work done by Portes and Bach (1985) and later Portes and Stepick (1993) on the development of an ethnic enclave among Cubans in Miami, which they see as an emerging model for immigrant incorporation in today's global cities.

In *Latin Journey* (1985) Portes and Bach record a case study of a new ethnic formation in the Cuban community in Miami, a formation they call an "ethnic enclave." The history of Miami since the 1950s is a history of successive waves of immigration and the resulting impact on Miami politics, culture, and economics. The 1959 Cuban Revolution brought entire groups of privileged Cubans to Miami, fleeing the collectivization and nationalization underway in Castro's Cuba. A later wave of poorer refugees arrived from Cuba in the 1980 Mariel boatlift (Portes and Stepick 1993; Card 1990).

Portes and Bach argue that the success of Miami's Cuban immigrants derives from the establishment of an ethnic enclave in which they utilize networks of ethnic solidarity to mobilize needed cultural or social capital. According to their definition, the enclave consists of

> immigrant groups which concentrate in a distinct spatial location and organize a variety of enterprises serving their own ethnic market and/or the general population. Their basic characteristic is that a significant proportion of the immigrant work force works in enterprises owned by other immigrants. (1981: 291)

In further developing the concept in *Latin Journey*, Portes and Bach argue that the two most essential and influential characteristics of enclaves are

> (1) the presence of immigrants with sufficient capital, either brought from abroad or accumulated in the United States, to create new opportunities for economic growth, and (2) an extensive division of labor. (1985: 203)

Portes and Bach suggest that this formulation usually occurs through two successive waves of immigration of the same group. First, an entrepreneurial class is successfully transplanted from home to a receiving country. This class grows. Its economic activities expand and diversify. When the second wave of immigrants arrives, the entrepreneurial class can offer them opportunities virtually unavailable to immigrants entering other labor-market sectors. The enclave's economic structure, they argue, enables immigrants to achieve upward social mobility. Using culturally based social networks, language, common history, and traditions, immigrants are able to find better-paying jobs, more promotion opportunity, and greater ability to use education and skills in the ethnic enclave than they are in the "dead-end jobs" of the secondary labor market of the dominant economic structures.

Indeed, despite low wages in the enclave, workers stay in subordinate jobs in order to take advantage of "paths of mobility unavailable on the outside" (Portes and Bach 1985: 204). In Portes and Bach's scenario, as immigrant firms expand, so do openings for coethnics at the supervisory and managerial level as well as opportunities for ownership and self-employment. In this model, the prosperity of the community is built on close-knit family and kinship networks, where both enclave entrepreneurs and workers are bound by and benefit from ethnic solidarity—mutual obligations, trust, and loyalty—which constitutes a form of social capital absent beyond the enclave boundaries. Portes and Bach portray the Cuban enclave as a favorable alternative to the secondary labor market for new immigrants.

A New Immigrant Narrative

Urban ethnic neighborhoods are not new. But in presenting the ethnic enclave concept, Portes and Bach are offering a very different immigrant narrative than those of the past. Instead of seeing immigrant concentrations as a place of transition—a place to move away from in order to get better jobs and opportunities—they are suggesting a new and extremely optimistic possibility for the incorporation of new immigrants into the U.S. economy. Cubans in the Miami enclave have jobs in the enclave itself. These jobs, suggest Portes and Bach, are in fact better-paying jobs than those available outside in the secondary labor market. And because they are within the Cuban enclave, lack of English language skills is not a barrier to employment. Cuban employers are able to retain motivated workers who are willing to work hard in order to have the opportunity to learn the trade themselves and advance within the firm as foremen and supervisors. Eventually they hope to utilize ethnic connections within the enclave to open up their own business and become self-employed. In this narrative, Cuban immigrants can move from the status of humble immigrants without skills and without capital to achieve self-employment and ownership inside the enclave and accomplish this within one generation. If true, this is indeed a new trajectory and suggests a framework for reconceptualizing notions of class, mobility, and assimilation within immigrant communities.

Applications of the Ethnic Enclave Model

The concept of the ethnic enclave is hard to generalize, as even Portes and Bach admit (1985: 38). In describing the Cuban ethnic enclave, they lay out several defining characteristics. The ethnic enclave is not an ethnic neighborhood. It is primarily focused on ethnic economic activity. The enclave has an entrepreneurial class possessing the capital necessary for the establishment of ethnic businesses. And the enclave has a diversity of employment arising from the growth of these businesses, which in turn offers opportunities for upward mobility both to supervisory and management positions and even to ownership and self-employment.

These are very unique conditions. First, immigrants with professional and entrepreneurial skills, especially those with individual capital, have some degree of mobility in the mainstream American economy. They are often not willing to be stranded in an immigrant enclave to work and perhaps live alongside the poor and unskilled. Second, to maintain the diversity of job opportunities that will allow participants in the ethnic enclave to achieve self-ownership and self-employment, firms cannot grow too large. In small communities, monopolies in any particular sector would severely inhibit options for self-ownership and self-employment. All told, the scenario—in which immigrants with capital and entrepreneurial skills start businesses large enough to hire workers but not too large to monopolize the enclave—seems extremely rare.

Perhaps there are very few immigrant communities that would satisfy the criteria. In *Latin Journey*, Portes and Bach detail only two other examples, the Japanese and Jewish immigrant communities arriving in the United States during the 1890–1914 period. Both are noted for their tightly knit communities that were not exclusively residential.

They were instead economic enclaves, areas where a substantial proportion of immigrants were engaged in business activities and where a still larger proportion worked in firms owned by other immigrants. . . . For the entrepreneurially inclined, networks based on ethnic solidarity had clear economic potential. The community was (1) a source of labor, which could be made to work at lower wages; (2) a controlled market; and (3) a source of capital, through rotating credit associations and similar institutions. (1985: 38)

Using these parameters, can the ethnic enclave model detailed by Portes and Bach in the Cuban community in Miami be generalized to other immigrant communities?

Other studies have examined the possibility of applying the ethnic enclave model to the immigrant experience, for example Dominicans and Colombians in New York (Gilbertson 1993; Gilbertson and Gurak 1993), Chinese in California (Sanders and Nee 1987), and Chinese in New York (Zhou and Logan 1989; Zhou 1992). Each of these studies has raised further questions about the success of the ethnic enclave and failed to provide affirmation of Portes and Bach's original claims (Guest and Kwong 2000).

Min Zhou and John Logan (1989, later expanded in Zhou 1992) attempt to apply the ethnic enclave concept to New York's Chinatown, an area with many similarities to Miami's Cuban enclave. Yet their findings produce mixed results. Zhou and Logan suggest that for Chinese immigrant men, labor market experience, education, and English-language ability, or human capital, have the same positive effects on wage earnings within the enclave as they would outside of it. However, they find that "human capital returns for men are not greater within the enclave than outside" (1989: 819).

Zhou and Logan's analysis of women's experiences reveals that despite the increased importance of women in the Chinatown enclave economy, both as consumers and workers (primarily in the garment industry), the key predictors of women's earnings were hours logged and occupation, not human capital. They found a total absence of human capital effects and no measurable earnings returns on previous human capital. Why? Zhou and Logan identify certain status-based obstacles for women working within the enclave, including occupational segregation by gender, women forced to play triple roles as mother, wife, and worker, and jobs requiring higher education that are consistently reserved for men. They conclude that Chinese cultural notions of male supremacy reinforce gender discrimination in the ethnic enclave. The authors suggest that further research must be conducted to determine "to what degree the positive functions of the enclave for men are derived from the subordinate position of women" (1989: 818). While Portes and Bach's criteria for an ethnic enclave seem to be met in New York's Chinatown, their Miami findings appear to be difficult to replicate.

Though the quantitative findings for the success of the Chinese ethnic enclave are mixed in the 1989 study, in her book *Chinatown: The Socioeconomic Potential of an Urban Enclave* (1992), Zhou relies heavily on cultural explanations to make the case for the positive returns of participating in the enclave economy. Following Portes and Bach's notion of ethnic solidarity, Zhou argues that in Chinatown the "economic behavior of enclave participants is not purely self interested, nor is it based on strict calculation in dollars." The enclave benefits entrepreneurs who receive profits in large part from the low wages paid to labor, but in return also incur obligations to the workers. The enclave benefits the workers who, while "willingly exploited," are given opportunities for training in occupational skills that may improve future employment (1992: 14). Chinese immigrant laborers are willing to work for substandard wages, a fact Zhou attributes directly to three factors: a Chinese cultural work ethic, a positive comparison to poorer wages in China, and a willingness to make sacrifices in the short term in order to derive benefits in the future. In the case of Chinese women in the enclave, Zhou argues "their behavior must be understood in the context of Chinese culture which gives priority not to individual achievement but to the welfare of the family and the community as a whole" (1992: 14). Despite the mixed results of her 1989 study, Zhou argues that whatever women may lose for themselves becomes a significant contribution to the family as a whole.

Ethnic Stratification and the Manufacturing of Ethnic Solidarity

In his work on the political economy of New York's Chinatown, Peter Kwong challenges the suggestion of predominantly positive effects of ethnic solidarity in the ethnic enclave and questions the claims that it is a promising channel for moving recent Chinese immigrants into the mainstream economy and society as portrayed by Portes and Zhou:

> Chinese are attracted to Chinatown because of employment opportunities. However, job availability should not be confused with easy upward mobility, nor should it be seen as the result of ethnic solidarity. Employment in

ethnic enclaves is the product of America's post-industrial economy in which American businesses have shifted their production to immigrant communities that provide cheap and unorganized labor. (1996 [1987]: 203)

Chinatown's enclave economy is not primarily a system of mutual support, but in essence, an unregulated free enterprise zone operating within a globalized world economic system based on flexible accumulation (Harvey 1990) and exploiting disadvantaged Chinese immigrants, particularly recent Fuzhounese arrivals. Garment shops and restaurants operate six days a week, ten to twelve hours a day, and pay as little as two dollars an hour, offering no benefits. And recent waves of illegal immigrants from Fuzhou have driven wages down farther still. While these wages are comparatively higher than in mainland China, the working conditions in China's free enterprise zones are so horrifying they should never be duplicated here. Furthermore, many illegal immigrants would not choose to work for these wages or under these conditions, but they have no options beyond the enclave. Many are under intense pressure and sometimes coercion to pay off their debts to smugglers who brought them into the United States or to family and friends who provided the bridge loans. Many are lulled into a false sense of potential upward mobility by the Chinatown economic and political elite, which Kwong suggests manufacture ideas of "ethnic solidarity" in order to entice coethnics into exploitative labor relations and to retain their loyalty.

Kwong's introduction of the terms uptown and downtown Chinese emphasizes the importance of a class analysis for understanding the intense stratification present in New York's Chinese community, an ethnic group often referred to as a "model minority." The more positive interpretations of the benefits of ethnic solidarity and the ethnic enclave risk ignoring the key internal dynamics of the ethnic community and economy in which Chinatown's economic elite, who also double as an informal political structure, build and maintain an exploitative environment with the tacit approval of the outside governments at the city, state, and federal levels. Without seeing the differentiation of the elites and working class, as well as the differences among Chinese ethnic groups and within them, it is hard to understand the dynamics of Chinatown society. The introduction of issues of class and stratification is crucial for understanding the position of Fuzhounese immigrants within the Chinese community as well as the internal dynamics of the Fuzhounese religious communities in this study (Kwong 1996 [1987], 1997a; Guest and Kwong 2000).

Conclusion

This study reveals the complex dynamics at work in the Chinatown ethnic enclave. Clearly, ethnic solidarity exists and recent immigrants use it to mobilize the financial and social capital necessary for entering the United States and surviving in a highly stratified environment. Fuzhounese immigrants, particularly undocumented immigrants, are extremely creative actors working to manipulate a system stacked with disadvantages. In ingenious fashion, these newcomers to New York employ language and kinship affinities, hometown and family networks to find jobs, housing, health care, child care, and legal advice. As we will see, Fuzhounese religious communities are central as sites for constructing and reconstructing networks of ethnic solidarity and accessing available financial and social capital as immigrants make their way along an often precarious journey.

At the same time, this isolated ethnic enclave is a trap for many Fuzhounese who, marginalized by language, culture, and class from both the mainstream U.S. economy and the Chinatown elites, have no way to escape. As Chen Qiang so eloquently states:

Someday I want to take my mind and really enter American society. This is an American place. There are not a lot of Chinese in America. But being in this Chinese environment in Chinatown is like being in jail. If you go out you can't speak English. If you want to travel, you don't know where to go. Life here is so much worse than in most of America. Being in Chinatown is just like being in China! So I would like to be able to get out into American society. I need to learn English. If only I had the opportunity! I'd like to go to school. But that's probably unrealistic considering how much money I have to pay back.

The analysis of inequality and exploitation within the Fuzhounese community and the Chinatown enclave presented in this chapter provides an important piece of the framework for understanding the internal dynamics of the religious communities considered in later chapters. Fujianese religious communities play a significant role in the lives of their constituents.

They are central points in the global flow of these migrant laborers and they are key actors in mitigating some of the harshest effects of Chinatown's ethnic enclave. But we can also see that these Fuzhounese religious communities are deeply embedded in the enclave, in its inequalities, and in its stratification.

Who are the Fuzhounese and why do they come to New York? The following chapter examines the political economy of contemporary Fuzhou and its history of outmigration and interaction with the global economy. By placing contemporary Fuzhounese migration in the context of generations of Chinese who have sought economic opportunity overseas, chapter 2 establishes another key framework for understanding the role of Fuzhounese religious communities in the migration experience.

2

Fuzhou
Diasporic Traditions

For centuries, Fuzhou's people have reached beyond the borders of China to seek their fortunes and protect themselves against the vagaries of natural disasters, political upheavals, and economic crises in their country. As a result, today Fuzhounese can be found throughout east and Southeast Asia (Hicks 1993). The current migration of Fuzhounese to New York continues a long-established strategy for self-preservation and economic enhancement employed not only by the Fuzhounese but also by communities all along China's southeast coast (Ch'en 1940).

Fuzhou, capital of Fujian Province on the southeast coast of China, has been a leading port city for centuries not only for coastal China but for south and Southeast Asia as well. Eighty-seven years before Columbus's famous voyage on the *Niña, Pinta,* and *Santa Maria* and two hundred years before the Dutch settled Manhattan Island, a seven-foot-tall admiral named Zheng He set sail from Fuzhou in 1405 with a fleet of 317 ships and 27,870 sailors on an imperial-sponsored trading mission to the south seas of Asia, the Middle East, and down the east coast of Africa, enhancing the connectedness of the era's "world system" (Frank 1998). The British named Fuzhou among the first five treaty ports forcibly opened to Western powers after China's defeat in the Opium War of 1839–1842, and as such it was one of the first places opened to foreign missionaries. In China's contemporary history, Fuzhou was declared one of China's first special economic zones, designed to lead the nation into the post-Mao era of reform and openness to the outside world.

The current migration to New York diverges from earlier Fuzhounese outmigrations in a number of key respects. In the Fuzhou metropolitan area today, domestic economic reforms and opening to foreign investment have led to significant economic growth throughout the 1990s, yet the unprecedented magnitude of current migration has emptied the surrounding towns and villages of their younger generations. While Fuzhounese have often been attracted by job opportunities abroad, the pull of an international labor market extends the Fuzhounese diaspora beyond Southeast Asia across the Pacific Ocean to the United States and in some cases, Europe, and establishes complex social and economic networks between host and home communities. In one of the most striking developments, highly organized international human smuggling syndicates enable much of this outmigration to occur.

Fuzhou Today

Fuzhou, whose population is now nearing six million, is a bustling industrial sprawl that is quickly leaving behind its centrally planned socialist economy of the past forty years and moving into a more pivotal role in China's domestic economy as well as the global economy. A sleepy, midsize port city in the late 1970s and early 1980s, Fuzhou has expanded significantly since then, exemplifying coastal China's rapid economic growth over the past twenty years. The first impression of the visitor at the turn of the twenty-first century is that everything is under construction. The air is thick with construction dust that lingers over the city, hemmed in on three sides by mountains, before being swept away periodically over the Pacific Ocean. The narrow tree-lined streets have been widened. Dilapidated two-story wooden structures housing stores on the ground level and cramped dwellings on the second have been demolished, replaced by apartment blocks and high-rise office towers. A fleet of red taxis now plies the thoroughfares where fifteen years ago only public buses and bicycles held sway. Newly middle class business people discuss banning bicycles from the main streets to eliminate the nuisance they pose to automobile traffic. While port cities such as Guangzhou, Xiamen, and Shanghai have outpaced Fuzhou's expansion, Japanese and Taiwanese investment in Fuzhou has increased significantly in the 1990s and joint venture, export-oriented industries have boomed in the city and its suburbs. After years of isolation, Fuzhou is returning to the more prominent position it previously has held in the Chinese domestic economy and global economic affairs.

Fujian Province, located on the southeastern China coast, is bounded to the south by Guangdong, to the north by Zhejiang, and to the west by Jiangxi. Fujian is isolated from much of inland China by mountain ranges

FIGURE 2 Old fishing boats and new houses in Tingjiang.

both north and west. This geographic isolation has helped maintain Fujian's peripheral status vis-à-vis the Chinese central government for most of its history. Another mountain range sharply divides the province between inland mountainous areas and the coastal regions. Ninety-five percent of the province is either hilly or mountainous. Only 5 percent is flat and ideal for farming. The rest is farmed through intensive terracing and irrigation. Transportation and communication between inland and coastal regions has historically been facilitated by several major river systems that cut through the mountains (Rawski 1972: 59–61).

The greater Fuzhou area includes three cities and six counties. Most of the undocumented Chinese in the United States originate from within this larger region, particularly from Changle City, Mawei District, Tingjiang Township, and Lianjiang County. The city of Fuzhou sits on the edge of Fujian Province's coastal plain, surrounded by mountains to the north, south, and west. The Min River travels from the province's northwest through Fuzhou before opening into a wide estuary and flowing past hundreds of small islets along the jagged coastline and into the Taiwan Straight. Fuzhou lies thirty miles inland from the ocean. It occupies approximately the same latitude as Miami, Florida, with a subtropical climate averaging 67° F and summers filled with monsoon rains.

FIGURE 3   Farmland in Houyu on the southern banks of the Min River.

The roads running out of Fuzhou toward the coast are lined with factories, industrial parks and foreign investment-oriented free-trade zones as
they pass through the city and its suburbs. But farther to the east along the
banks of the Min and southeast toward Changle, the four- and six-lane
highways pass farmland and fishing boats along with half-empty towns and
villages full of vacant new homes built with overseas remittances. It is the
towns and villages along this coastal plain that produce the flood of tens of
thousands of immigrants now populating New York's Chinatown and toil-
ing in restaurants, garment shops, construction sites, and factories across
the United States.

When asked, immigrants in New York say they are from "Fuzhou." In reality this refers to the larger Fuzhou region and not to Fuzhou City itself. Of
the 343 who responded to surveys conducted in Chinatown's Fuzhounese
Protestant churches and a Buddhist temple during this study, only twenty,
or 5.8 percent, identified Fuzhou City as their hometown. Eighty-five percent are from the less developed and more rural areas along the coast.

Despite strong economic growth in Fuzhou City, including increased industrial production, particularly for export, the same economic opportuni-

ties have not extended to the coastal areas. Farming pays at best U.S. $600 a year. The fishing industry is failing. There is little other local industry and only a few service-sector jobs have emerged in restaurants and stores opened with overseas remittances. Interviews conducted as part of this study revealed that in these towns and villages casual labor may earn between $50 to $100 per month.

While some coastal residents migrate to Fuzhou City to work in its expanding economy, these opportunities pay only $1,800 a year and hold little promise of long-term stability. As documented by Solinger (1999), China now has upwards of 100 million internal migrants comprising a massive floating population moving from rural to urban areas in search of wage labor. In China today access to the social safety net, including housing, education, and health care, is predicated upon a system of household registration—*hukou*—which ties Chinese to their place of birth. Outside one's registration area, access is difficult or impossible to establish. As of late 2001, the Chinese government has begun a gradual reform of the *hukou* system. But while more flexibility exists in the system today than twenty years ago, the ability to legally change residency is limited for many rural dwellers who have scarce financial resources and few personal connections. As a result, rural residents choosing to migrate to a city may provide the labor necessary

FIGURE 4 Fishing trawlers at anchor as viewed from Fuqi Temple.

to fuel China's urban economic expansion, but they have been forced to live outside the social safety net and denied their full rights of citizenship.

Over the past fifteen years, outmigration to New York has developed as the main economic strategy for people in Changle and north along the Min River (Chin 1999). The word on the Tingjiang street, for instance, is that with hard work even an undocumented worker can earn nearly $2,000 a month in the United States. While this may be true for some, it does not account for the grueling hours and difficult work conditions that make these jobs impossible to sustain physically for long periods of time. Still, many calculate that they will be able to earn far more by migrating to the United States, even after paying exorbitant smuggling fees, than they would by remaining in China. As a result, most young people do not work. They rely on remittances from relatives already established overseas and wait for their turn to emigrate. One consequence is that most local farmland is no longer tilled by local farmers. It is rented out to other Fujianese who have migrated down from the province's mountain regions, or to migrant workers from Sichuan Province whose depressed interior economy has made Sichuanese a major component of the floating population throughout China.

Diasporic Traditions

Interacting with the global economy and sending its sons and daughters abroad is not an anomaly in Fuzhou's history. Rather, it represents a repetition of an age-old pattern. Fuzhou, according to Chinese records, was established in 207 B.C.E. by the duke of Fu-yue as his capital city. Some accounts suggest that as early as 1,900 years ago, Fuzhou's port received ships from Southeast Asia. Economic development and population growth in this frontier region were relatively slow until the middle of the Tang dynasty in the eighth century, when the province grew rapidly from marginal status to being one of China's most heavily settled and economically prosperous.

> The emergence of an Indian Ocean trading ecumene in the seventh and eighth centuries, coinciding with and no doubt prompted by the emergence of messianic Islam at the western end of the littoral, led to a major expansion in the total volume of the Indian Ocean trade and brought a new wave of traders to the Chinese ports. By the turn of the eighth century the traders of the Persian Gulf had tied together east and west into an un-

broken network extending from the shores of Africa all the way to the coast of China. (Clark 1990: 40)

By the eighth century, large communities of Arab and Persian traders could be found in Guangzhou and Yangzhou, and their trading routes took them along the coast of Fujian.

By the beginning of the Song Dynasty (978–1279), Quanzhou in Fujian had become one of the major ports of call of South Seas traders. Reports from the era note Quanzhou traders frequenting ports around the South China Sea, including Vietnam and Borneo. Merchants from Quanzhou and Fuzhou were also involved in northbound trade to Korea and Japan. By 1087 Quanzhou was established as an official superintendency (legally sanctioning the trade) and soon surpassed Guangzhou as China's leading port (Clark 1990). By the late thirteenth century, Marco Polo would visit Fujian. Of Fuzhou he remarked on the large number of ships loaded with goods. And of Zaitun (Quanzhou), "It is indeed impossible to convey an idea of the number of merchants and accumulation of goods in this place, which is held to be one of the largest ports in the world" (cited in Clark 1990: 51).

One of the most famous figures in China's long history of international commerce was Admiral Zheng He (1371–1440?), a Chinese Muslim eunuch from Yunnan Province. Over a twenty-eight-year period from 1405 to 1433, under the sponsorship of the Ming emperor, Zheng He commanded huge fleets that visited thirty-seven countries from Southeast Asia to India, the Persian Gulf, and the east coast of Africa. A recent theory suggests that on one of his voyages he may have circumnavigated the globe one hundred years before Magellan. Thousands of Fujianese merchant traders accompanied these trading missions. Fuzhou served as one of the primary ports for organizing their maritime supplies, logistical support, and repairs. According to the chronicles of the Ming Dynasty, at each stop over the course of seven voyages—in Taiwan, the Philippines, Vietnam, Cambodia, Thailand, Java, Sumatra, Ceylon, India, and Persia, across Southeast Asia and around the Indian Ocean—Zheng He's fleet encountered the far-reaching networks of overseas Chinese from the southeast provinces which had at that time already been in formation for hundreds of years and which still provide the framework for the vast overseas Chinese network in Asia today.

Mercantile connections along Fujian's coast made possible a remarkable integration between urban coastal markets and rural agriculture. Trading up and down the east coast of China and deep into China's river networks,

Fujianese maritime merchants were able to circumvent the treacherous trade routes over the mountains. Through the resulting China-wide trade networks, the farmers of Fujian's hinterland could sell their goods far beyond the traditional market networks to all of China and even to the entire Indian Ocean littoral. Fuzhou, at the eastern end of the Min River system, served as a central transfer point between hinterland and domestic and international markets.

Beyond the boundaries of China, Fuzhou's port was also deeply integrated into a global trading regime centered around Asia. Zheng He's voyages are illustrative of China's pivotal role in an intricate global economic system which scholars suggest dates to at least 1250 c.e. and perhaps earlier. China held a leading position in production and export, including tea, fruit, drugs, cotton, tobacco, arms and powder, copper and iron products, quicksilver, zinc, and cupronickel. China was unrivaled in porcelain ceramics, and few other countries could compete with its production of silk, either in quantity or quality. Silk, China's largest export, was sold mainly to other Asian buyers but also for the Manila-Americas trade operated by Spanish galleons (Frank 1998; Abu-Lughod 1989).

At times, Chinese international trade and migration have been circumscribed by the Chinese central government. In the early stages of the Qing Dynasty (seventeenth century) the new rulers placed severe restrictions on trade and travel in order to consolidate their authority over the loyal remnants of the predecessor Ming Dynasty, many of whom had escaped to Fujian, Taiwan, and even Southeast Asia. Most recently, after 1949 the Communist Party gradually introduced restrictions on internal mobility and external contacts, peaking in severity during the Cultural Revolution (1966–1976) when contact abroad was seen as counterrevolutionary activity. Throughout such periods of intense restriction, however, the role of the Fujianese in the maritime aspects of China's internal economy has allowed them to maintain access to opportunities for international trade and travel. Sailors from Fuzhou, even during the height of the Cultural Revolution, were involved in the transportation of goods along the China coast, including Hong Kong.

Western Imperialism and New Engagements

From the sixteenth to the mid-nineteenth centuries, the establishment of the European trade regime and European colonies in Asia provided a strong pull for Chinese outmigration. European plantations and land development required intensive labor, and many from southeast China, including Fuzhou, followed already-established overseas networks to reach these new labor markets. With the loss of the Opium War in 1842 to the British, China entered a new era in which its encounter with the outside world suddenly became complicated by the interjection of foreign powers onto Chinese soil.

The Opium War erupted as a result of a severe trade imbalance that had developed between China and the British over the previous two centuries. China exported silk, porcelains, tea, spices, and many other luxury goods to the West but severely restricted imports, at one point closing all ports except Guangzhou to foreign trade and requiring merchants to pay any trade deficit in silver.

By the 1830s the frustrated British hoped to change these policies and introduce large quantities of opium grown on their poppy plantations in India to the limited but growing opium market in China, thereby shifting the trade balance in their favor. The Chinese resisted under the leadership of the Fujian scholar-official Lin Zexu. They confiscated close to three million pounds of raw opium, and flushed it into the sea. The British, with vastly superior naval power, soon occupied Guangzhou and sent an expeditionary force to the capital in Beijing. There the emperor was forced to sign the first of a series of unequal treaties promising indemnification for losses, agreeing to accept opium as payment, and allowing Britain and later other Western powers access to certain treaty ports. Within these treaty ports the Western powers were to be allowed free trade, extraterritorial legal rights, and the freedom for missionaries to evangelize. Thus, after a period of relative isolation, the southeastern coast of China, and the port city of Fuzhou in particular, were officially reopened as a hub for international trade and commerce and nodes of access for the Chinese to the global economy and for foreigners to the Chinese domestic economy.

Of particular interest for our study, the signing of the unequal treaties heralded the arrival of the first Western Protestant missionaries on China's soil. Fuzhou became one of the primary destinations. The first Protestant missionaries, sent by the American Board of Commissioners for Foreign Missions (ABCFM), an interdenominational agency spearheaded by the Congregationalists, arrived in Fuzhou in 1847. The U.S. Methodist Episcopal Mission was established in 1848 and the British Anglican Church Missionary Society Mission in 1850. These three groups would form the backbone of Protestant foreign mission work in Fuzhou in the nineteenth century. They were joined by the Young Men's Christian Association in 1905 and the YWCA in 1913.

Fuzhou proved a difficult assignment for these early missionaries. They were not welcomed by the Chinese, who saw them as part of the larger foreign incursion. In addition, health problems were rampant, and quite a few missionaries and their children died or were forced to return home. Missionary work was also severely affected by political affairs. Missionary letters from Fuzhou note the decision to evacuate all foreign church workers twice in the nineteenth century, once because of the Chinese Taiping Rebellion and once because of the armed conflict between the French and the Chinese.

Despite Fuzhou's sizable population, nearly 600,000 in the mid-1800s, Chinese conversion to Christianity happened slowly. The first Chinese converted only in 1856, nine years after the launch of the ABCFM mission. By 1880 the Anglicans could claim only 3,556 converts and the Congregationalists only 215 (Dunch 1996: 39, 42). One significant factor lay in the Chinese perception of missionaries as compatriots of the foreign imperialists who were forcing opium into China by means of military might. Nor was this perception enhanced by the missionaries' reliance on the terms of the unequal treaties as well as on Western merchants and government consular officials for assistance with communication, transportation, legal protection, and even currency exchange. According to missionary H. W. Worley,

Foochow [Fuzhou], perhaps more than some other centers, felt the moral incongruity of the message of the missionary who came in the wake of the opium ships. This was still more augmented by the fact that in the early days of the mission in Foochow no satisfactory means of forwarding money to the missionaries had been found. The only way of getting local currency, without taking a trip all the way to Hong Kong was to go to the opium ship which anchored off the mouth of the river and there exchange drafts on New York for Mexican silver dollars. No missionary could make the trip from Foochow, thirty miles down to the mouth of the river, visit and opium ship, and come back again with a bag of silver dollars, without the fact being known to a very wide circle of Chinese. In view of this circumstance and connection it is not so surprising that the mission grew so slowly, but that it grew at all. (Cited in Lacy 1948: 43–44)

Revolutions and Renewed Exodus

The nineteenth and twentieth centuries have been periods of tremendous upheaval for China, and this upheaval has had significant implications for the history of Chinese immigration and of Fuzhou. The Opium War with the British was only the first of five wars of foreign aggression during this time, concluding with eight years of Japanese invasion and occupation (1937–1945). In addition, five revolutionary civil wars tore the country apart from within. The massive Taiping Rebellion lasted from 1850 to 1864. The Republican Revolution of 1911 brought an end to the severely weakened Qing Dynasty. The incomplete Nationalist Revolution of 1925 to 1928 sought unity against foreign imperialism. The Nationalist Party and the Communist Party fought from 1945 to 1949 for control of the country. And of course Mao's Cultural Revolution shook China from 1966 to 1976. In addition, numerous smaller uprisings added to the turmoil of the period (Fairbank 1986: x).

Despite these military, political, and economic upheavals of the nineteenth and early twentieth centuries, Fuzhou continued, and at times expanded, its extensive interaction with world commerce. Fuzhou's primary commodity for export during much of this time was its famous Wu Yi tea, and clipper ships from Britain and the United States filled Fuzhou's Pagoda Anchorage loading their shipments. By the peak of the tea trade in 1903, 40 million pounds were shipped from Fuzhou annually (Gardella 1994). Even with the dilatory effects of the Japanese occupation of Fuzhou and its surrounding region in the 1930s and the intense civil war between the Communists and Nationalists that saw tens of thousands of Fujianese Nationalist sympathizers flee to Taiwan in 1949, Fuzhounese continued to engage in commerce beyond China's borders.

By 1940 there were more than 8.5 million overseas Chinese and nearly 3 million of these were from Fujian Province. Most were from the southern portion of Fujian, but 300,000 were from the northern region, particularly Minhou and Fuqing, both south of Fuzhou, and Minqing and Gutian to the north and west. Ninety percent of the overseas Chinese in Southeast Asia were from Fujian and Guangdong Provinces, and of all Fujianese overseas, 95 percent were in Southeast Asia, highlighting the strong connections between Fujianese and the Southeast Asia region. In the later part of the nineteenth century, just as contract laborers were being organized in south China, particularly Guangdong Province, to work in the farms, mines, and railroad construction on the U.S. West Coast, so too were large-scale contract labor groups being organized in Fujian to supply the rapidly expanding labor needs of the European colonies in Southeast Asia. Local Fujianese middlemen recruited farmers for Malaysia and Vietnam. So many Fuzhounese laborers were imported to Sarawak, Borneo, that the city of Sibu came to be known as Little Fuzhou. At one point, several hundred Fuzhounese were even recruited to work in the mines in Mexico (Hicks 1993).

From the annals of Santu, an island in Shansha Bay north of Fuzhou with a large emigrant population, we learn the following:

> During the period 1851–1875, while the British were encroaching on Burma and when the French annexed Annam (Vietnam), they very often obtained assistance from the people of Santu-ao. Thus, as prohibition on emigration had been lifted and residents of the homeland were constantly emigrating, their power expanded and they were used by foreigners. . . .
>
> At the beginning of the Kuanghsu Period (1875–85) Ch'iu Chung-po from Hsin-an bought several steamships and travelled to Penang, Singapore, Hong Kong, Swatow [Shantou], Amoy [Xiamen] and so forth. People who were prepared to take risks in the hope of making a quick fortune took passage on these and travelled to Southeast Asia, so that wasteland thrived instantly. . . . In the latter years of Kuanghsu (1899–1908), when the national government declined and people's moods deteriorated, there was a seemingly endless surge of migrants taking their families to the archipelago of Southeast Asia. (Hicks 1993: 231)

While the large-scale contract labor groups became less prominent by the turn of the twentieth century, Fujianese outmigration continued as entrepreneurial merchants and individual laborers utilized overseas Fujianese regional, village, and kinship networks to escape China's economic and political turmoil and seek a better life for themselves and their families back home. As they do today, remittances from overseas Chinese played a crucial role in providing for economic survival and stability for kin and community in Fujian.

The flow of immigrants out of China gradually slowed after 1949, as did the flow of remittances from overseas Chinese into the mainland, as the new government of the People's Republic of China initiated a series of reforms and campaigns to bring the country under central control and restricted contacts with the outside world. Communist scrutiny of Fujian was particularly intense because of the province's close proximity to Taiwan, the new home of the defeated Nationalist government. In 1949 thousands of Fujianese who were loyal to the Nationalist Party or had served in the Nationalist military fled to Taiwan, often leaving family behind, rather than face retribution from the victorious Communists. Various military raids from Taiwan into Fujian during the ensuing thirty years only served to reinforce this anxiety. Largely cut off from its overseas connections throughout the period of 1950 to 1980, the Fujian and Fuzhou economies lagged behind the rest of the country. The situation was only exacerbated by the mainland government's reluctance to invest in a "front-line" province so close to Taiwan. Industrial development was particularly affected.

Post-1978: Economic Reform and Reconnecting to the International Economy

In the late 1970s, the Chinese government moved rapidly to reestablish its legitimacy with the Chinese people after the disastrous Cultural Revolution. After the death of Mao Zedong (1976) and the fall of the Gang of Four, China's new paramount leader, Deng Xiaoping, instituted a series of economic reforms beginning in December 1978 that would transform rural and urban life as well as foreign relations. Decollectivization gradually returned land to farmers through the family responsibility system. Farmers regained control of crop management and labor allocation, and many families began to diversify their economic activities into rural industries and marketing. With the loosening of restrictions on household registration, labor mobility gradually increased and sizable numbers of the rural population moved to the city to seek wage labor (Zhou 1996). Urban reforms included the weakening of the work unit (*danwei*) as the sole unit for economic activity. Urban private enterprise began to emerge as a response to chronic underemployment and limited earning possibilities within the work unit (Lieberthal 1995).

After its self-imposed international isolation of the 1960s and 1970s, China awoke to find that it lagged far behind other Asian economies, including the smaller Asian "tigers" such as Hong Kong, Taiwan, Singapore, and South Korea, not to mention Japan. Deng's Open Door Policy, inaugurated in the early 1980s, sought to rectify this situation by creating at first four special economic zones (SEZs) along the southern and southeastern coasts of China. These SEZs, comparable to export-processing zones in the globalization literature, were designed to entice foreign corporations to invest capital and transfer modern technology in return for cheap labor and land, tax breaks, and a stable social environment.

Fuzhou was one of the first SEZs opened in China as the government attempted to build upon its historic role as a dynamic port city and on its position as a borderland with Taiwan. Along with SEZs in Xiamen in southern Fujian and Shenzhen directly between Guangzhou and Hong Kong, the Chinese sought to open an investment corridor in southern and southeastern China that would be attractive to overseas Chinese, particularly those in Hong Kong and Taiwan. While Fuzhou's economic growth lagged behind both Shenzhen and Xiamen in the 1980s and early 1990s, in recent years direct overseas investment has increased significantly, with many Taiwanese companies shifting production into the Fuzhou SEZ. Economic ties to Japan are under reconstruction as well. With direct trade and transport links beginning to open between Fujian and Taiwan, the investment and economic integration of the two economies should continue at an increased pace.

Overseas Chinese have provided the primary link between SEZs and the global economy. In China as a whole, only 7 percent of foreign investment in the early 1990s came from the United States and 5.8 percent from Japan (Castells 1998: 295). Seventy-one percent of the $116 billion pledged for investment in China between 1979 and 1992 came from Hong Kong and Taiwan. Chinese investors from Hong Kong and Taiwan used *guanxi* (relationship) networks, particularly looking for relatives, friends, people from the same place of origin (*tongxiang*). Initial investments focused on building the necessary infrastructure to support international connections (hotels, business services, airports, roads, and property development). Once these were established through Hong Kong and Taiwanese capital, investments began to flow from overseas Chinese all over the globe, including New York, California, Canada, Australia, Kuala Lumpur, Jakarta, Manila, Bangkok, Penang, and Singapore (Castells 1998: 297).

In spite of this tremendous investment and development in Fuzhou and along the coast of China, outmigration has resumed on a massive scale. With the end of the Cultural Revolution and the institution of economic reforms in the Fuzhou area, outmigration was seen by many as a form of family economic diversification necessary after the instability of the past thirty years of political campaigns and centrally planned economic policies. Residents began to reactivate kinship and village networks for outmigration, particularly to Hong Kong and Macao and later the United States, as well as

Australia, Japan, and parts of Europe. The stories of Ms. Li Bao'en and Ms. Jiang Ruxi highlight the motivations and strategies of Fuzhounese people during this period.

Ms. Li Bao'en

My name is Li Bao'en. I was born in a village south of Changle in 1950. My father was a sailor and left China in the 1950s when I was a little girl and went to Hong Kong to work. He sent money back to the family whenever he could.

My husband and I were married in 1971. He was from Changle, which was at the time a county seat. I moved there to be with him. Unfortunately, being a village girl I couldn't legally move my official residence permit [hukou] to a town or county seat like Changle. It made it very difficult. And when our children were born they were given rural hukou, not urban ones. Life became even more complicated trying to get them health care and education. Much of the time they lived with my mother in the village.

We decided if we could get outside of China we could establish an overseas residency permit. First, my husband applied to go to Hong Kong where my father was. He waited eight years with no success. Most of the time if you wanted to go out to Hong Kong you had to go through the back door, bribe someone, or have some personal connections in the government. We didn't have the right guanxi. Finally in 1980 he applied to go to Macau. Nobody wanted to go to Macau! The economic situation was pretty bad there, unlike Hong Kong. But in 1980 all you needed was a letter from a friend in Macau saying you were a relative and inviting you to come work. Within three months his application was accepted. He went first. I followed a couple of years later and the kids came several years after that. He worked on the dockyards at first doing hard labor as a coolie. He didn't make much money, but what he could save he sent back to us. He was trained as an electrician in China and he gradually moved into that work and construction too.

My husband got a visa to work in the U.S. in 1991. Then he petitioned for me and the kids and we came in 1992. We have a nice house in Flushing, Queens, but I come into Chinatown often to shop and to do things at my church. My two kids have graduated from college now, one of them with a degree from the City University of New York. That's really important to us since neither one of us went beyond high school in China. We brought my mother out to live with us two years ago. She misses her friends but it's easier for us to take care of her here. I send money back sometimes to help out people or groups that I care about, like my old church. But we don't plan to go back to live in China. There's nothing for us there now. We've both become U.S. citizens. We're planning to stay. And the rest of our family, brothers and sisters and my husband's parents, will probably come join us.

Ms. Jiang Ruxi

Ms. Jiang Ruxi was born in Fuzhou City in 1958, but she was sent by her family to live with her grandmother in a small village south of Changle to avoid the unrest of the Cultural Revolution. When she finished high school in 1976 her parents, who did have personal connections, arranged for her to go to Hong Kong to *tanqin*, visit relatives. She remained in Hong Kong to work until 1984. Her older brother followed. Through other family contacts he then went to work in Japan, where he married and continues to live with his wife and three kids. After eight years in Hong Kong, Ms. Jiang decided to try her luck in the United States.

In 1984 I came to New York as a tourist and just stayed after my visa expired. I was able to get my U.S. citizenship after the amnesty in 1986. I've been working in garment shops since then. I live and work in the Chinese area in Sunset Park, Brooklyn. But I just do it to make money. I can make more here than in Fuzhou.

With my U.S. passport I can come and go when I feel like it. I try to visit my older brother in Japan once a year and usually the whole family gets together in Fuzhou once a year. I own a five-story building in downtown Fuzhou that I rent out to a Japanese restaurant and a couple of businesses. My younger brother rents the top floor for his business. He went to Japan in 1986 to go to college. Now he has an import/export business. A lot of Japanese want to invest in Fuzhou. It's a Special Economic Zone. Labor is cheap. And business conditions are pretty good. Whatever they want, my brother can arrange. He is even designing some Japanese restaurants in Fuzhou for Japanese investors.

Some people think all Chinese must be poor. But we're not. There are people in Fuzhou who make a good living. Especially people who have business with the Americans or Japanese. I like it in Fuzhou. It's my home. I like it here in America, too.

Fuzhounese Emigration and the Chinese Diaspora

When asked to describe the Fuzhou area and Fujian Province, residents frequently reply,

> *Shan duo, Di shao.* The mountains are plentiful, the land is sparse.
> *Di shao, Ren duo.* The land is sparse, the people are plentiful.

This reality, they then explain, lies at the root of the Fuzhounese tradition of outmigration. When population outstrips the land's ability to produce food or human and natural disasters strike, Fujianese people take to the sea. "Fuzhounese are very brave," I was often told. "They have been emigrating for thousands of years, trying to find better work and a better life." In the minds of the people of Fuzhou, their tens of thousands of compatriots in the New York area are but the latest wave of daring outmigrants leaving behind family and home to seek prosperity on another shore.

The history of the overseas Chinese has recently been popularized by Sterling Seagrave's *Lords of the Rim* (1995). His stories of China's overland trade routes with the Middle East and Europe, Buddhist missionaries in the Americas before Columbus, the seven-foot-tall admiral, Zheng He, and the establishment of overseas Chinese communities throughout Asia stir the imagination. The history of the overseas Chinese is long and complex, as is the mythology surrounding it.

Today there are more than 28 million overseas Chinese in Southeast Asia, most of whom have originated in China's southeastern coastal provinces of Fujian, Guangdong, and Zhejiang. Significant Chinese communities can be found in Indonesia (7.2 million), Thailand (5.8 million), Malaysia (5.2 million), Singapore (2 million), Burma (1.5 million), the Philippines (0.8 million), and Vietnam (0.8 million). In many of these countries, Chinese control crucial segments of the economy.

> Though they make up little more than three percent of Indonesia's population of more than two hundred million, ethnic Chinese are the nation's trading class, from shopkeepers to billionaire managers of multinational conglomerates, and they control as much as seventy percent of Indonesia's private economy. They are also among the country's young and well-educated professionals, own many of its factories and form the backbone of the distribution network for food and other commodities. (Mydans 1998)

Estimates suggest that overseas Chinese form a network with U.S. $2.5 trillion in economic activity in 1996, second only to the national economy of the United States and ahead of Japan (Kwong 1997b: 74).

Over the past fifty years significant scholarly research has been conducted examining the experiences of overseas Chinese, focusing on their relationship to the Asian economy and to their homeland China, and their role in China's economic development (Purcell 1965 [1951]; Skinner 1957; Pan 1990; Ong and Nonini 1997; Ong 1999; Wang 1991, 1998). Additional research has focused on China's emigrant communities (Ch'en 1940; Watson 1975; Woon 1984; Hsu 2000). In his classic work, *Emigrant Communities in South China: A Study of Overseas Migration and Its Influence on Standards of Living and Social Change* (1940), Ch'en Ta focuses on the effects of outmigration on villages in southern Fujian and northern Guangdong provinces. James Watson (1975) also turned his attention to an emigrant community, conducting a multisited research project examining the Man lineage in the New Territories of northern Hong Kong and its migrant outposts among restaurant workers in London. Foreshadowing dynamics in Fuzhou's rural emigrant communities, Watson states:

> Until approximately fifteen years ago, San Tin was a traditional peasant community with an economy based on agriculture. By the early 1960's however, the villagers had ceased farming and San Tin was converted into an emigrant community with an economy almost totally dependent upon remittances. Eighty-five to ninety percent of San Tin's able-bodied men now work in Chinese restaurants scattered throughout the United Kingdom and other parts of Western Europe. (1975: 2)

Madeline Hsu's recent study, *Dreaming of Gold, Dreaming of Home* (2000), examines the Chinese diaspora as it extends to the United States. The people of Taishan County, southern Guangdong Province, were the primary source of Chinese immigrants to the United States between the 1840s and 1960s. Until 1960, more than 50 percent of all Chinese in the United States came from this one county. Hsu examines the migration process, Taishanese life in America, the transnational linkages constructed across the Pacific, and the impact of these ties on the home community in China. Her work reveals the ways in which an earlier period of economic globalization in the 1800s—including expansion of trade, transportation, and communication networks—made work in the United States an employment option and enabled regular exchange of people, remittances, and information between families separated by the Pacific Ocean. Hsu focuses on the remarkable ability of Taishanese to mobilize ties of family, kin, and village to circumvent and manipulate extremely harsh U.S. immigration laws even during the period of Chinese exclusion, 1882–1943. She also considers the limited ability of nation-states, in this case China and the United States, to control immigration, two characteristics notable among contemporary Fuzhounese migrants as well.

One of the most prominent contemporary theorists of overseas Chinese is Aihwa Ong who, in her monograph, *Flexible Citizenship: The Cultural Logistics of Transnationality* (1999), and in a volume coedited with Donald Nonini, *Ungrounded Empires: The Cultural Politics of Modern Chinese Transnationalism* (1997), declares that earlier scholarly frameworks are inadequate for understanding contemporary realities of overseas Chinese. Ong and Nonini suggest a new rubric, Chinese transnationalism, "a culturally distinctive domain within the strategies of accumulation of the new capitalism—both Chinese and non-Chinese—emerging over the last two decades in the Asia-Pacific region" (1997: 4). Ong and Nonini state that a fundamental goal of their work on Chinese transnationalism is "reconceptualizing the relationship between the study of Chinese identities and the place-bound theorization of a pre-global social science, implied in such terms as territory, region, nationality and ethnicity" (1997: 5).

The activities of today's transnational overseas Chinese, they argue, must be viewed as a Chinese strategy of accumulation within contemporary globalized capitalism in which the speed of all aspects of economic activity has increased dramatically and the importance of geographic space in determining mobility and flows of capital, goods, services, and even labor has decreased, an effect which Harvey (1990) calls space-time compression. Seemingly following Castells (1996), they argue that the world is no longer made up of cores and peripheries, but is a "polycentric global capitalism" with "multiple nodes of geopolitical and economic power" (1997: 14). Chinese transnationals are playing a pivotal, nodal role in the new flexible capitalism that has emerged in Asia-Pacific since the 1970s and creating new kinds of social organization in this changing environment.

Fuzhounese in Ong and Nonini's Framework

How do these discussions apply to the recent waves of Fuzhounese immigrants? Does the notion of transnationalism provide a useful framework for understanding the Fuzhounese religious communities considered in this study? Ong and Nonini's narrow focus on the transnationalism of Chinese elites has led to a failure to account for class stratification within the Chinese diaspora. Where do recent Fuzhounese immigrants, particularly undocumented immigrants, fit into Ong and Nonini's framework of Chinese transnationalism? Are they transnational Chinese? In their book's opening paragraph, Ong and Nonini retell the highly publicized story of the *Golden Venture*, which ran aground off Long Island in 1993 with its cargo of 286 smuggled Chinese immigrants. But rather than focus on the lives of these immigrants, Ong and Nonini use this incident to reflect on the smugglers as Chinese business people functioning within a global capitalist framework. The *Golden Venture* incident illuminates for them "the global scope of many Chinese businesses, their historical roots in diaspora, their operational flexibility and spatial mobility, and their capacities to circumvent disciplining by nation-states" (1997: 3).

With this perspective, Ong and Nonini define these undocumented immigrants as Chinese transnationals by virtue of their having been acted upon by transnational forces, processes, and flows, in particular a transnational Chinese smuggling syndicate. Their framework gives little consideration to the possibility of the immigrants themselves acting as transnational agents. For while undocumented Fuzhounese are affected by the global economy and transnational regimes of flexible accumulation, they are not only commodities transported by the smuggling networks. Fuzhounese choose to utilize these networks, to actively participate, to become migrants.

Undocumented Fuzhounese immigrants do not fit the model of Chinese transnationalism described by Ong and Nonini. But business people from Taiwan, Hong Kong, and other Asian countries, mainland economic and political elites, and power brokers in smuggling networks do. Even some early Fuzhounese immigrants who have regularized their immigration status are moving beyond the isolation of the Chinatown economic enclave.

But the experiences of individual Fuzhounese and of the religious communities considered in this study suggest that even undocumented Fuzhounese, despite structural marginalization from many legal forms of transnational behavior, still seek out ways to be actively involved in their communities, both in New York and in Fuzhou. In their book *Nations Unbound* (1994), Linda Basch, Nina Glick-Schiller, and Cristina Szanton Blanc pioneer the theoretical application of the concept of transnationalism. In one of their earliest formulations they write:

We define "transnationalism" as the processes by which immigrants forge and sustain multi-stranded social relations that link together their societies of origin and settlement. We call these processes transnationalism to emphasize that many immigrants today build social fields that cross geographic, cultural, and political borders. Immigrants who develop and maintain multiple relationships—familial, economic, social, organizational, religious, and political—span borders we call "transmigrants." An essential element of transnationalism is the multiplicity of involvements that transmigrants sustain in both home and host societies. (1994: 7)

Are Fuzhounese "transnational" immigrants within this broader framework? Their remittances support family members and build family homes.

Contemporary studies of U.S. immigrant communities, studies which are largely unrelated to studies of overseas Chinese, have built upon and expanded Glick-Schiller's theorizations of transnationalism, examining the creation of transnational social fields (Mahler 1998), transnational migrant circuits (Rouse 1991), and the layering of transnationalisms from below, including everyday practices of individuals and groups, with transnationalisms from above, including global institutions and the state (Smith and Guarnizo 1998). Others have explored the question of what exactly is new about the patterns of the new immigrants (Foner 2000; Portes, Guarnizo, and Landolf 1999). But as with much of the immigration literature, the literature on transnationalism, with a few recent exceptions (Brown 1991; McAlister 1998; Levitt 2001; Ebaugh and Chavetz 2002), has consistently ignored the role of religious networks and communities in the migration process and the process of building and maintaining transnational social and economic ties.

The Fuzhounese communities examined in this study illustrate how transnational ties are built and maintained and their significance for the lives of immigrants. Many Fuzhounese may not be able to travel back and forth between the United States and China. Their legal status in the United States and the Chinese governmental system may not allow many of them to participate politically in either place. But through social organizations such as religious communities and village and regional associations they do find means to participate across the Pacific. They send money to build churches, temples, and ancestral halls. Through them they receive regular news from home. Through them they cooperate to channel funds into religious activities and community-based development projects in China.

For Fuzhounese, this transnational participation may have many motivations. Interviews suggest that one powerful consideration is the possibility for these marginalized struggling workers, many of whom are undocumented, to create alternative patterns of citizenship both in the United States and in China. Structurally marginalized from full citizen participation both in the United States and in China, through their transnational activities, circumscribed as they may be, Fuzhounese immigrants attempt to negotiate alternative strategies for participation and for survival against the rigors of New York's ethnic enclave and the restrictions of the immigration laws of the state.

Why They Leave

With economic opportunities expanding in the Fuzhou region over the past decade, why have so many Fuzhounese chosen to embark on this danger-filled and expensive journey to the uncertain conditions awaiting them in New York? Here are eight reasons.

1. Fuzhounese leave to make money, more money than they can make at home. The expanding economic opportunities accompanying foreign investment and industrial growth of Fuzhou City in the 1990s have had limited impact on Fuzhou's rural areas. Incomes in rural areas or from factory jobs, described earlier in this chapter, cannot compare to anticipated U.S. earnings (Chin 1999: 17).

2. Rural workers migrating to Chinese cities in search of work have been structurally disadvantaged by the restrictions of the household registration system (Solinger 1999) and, in Fuzhou, an employment registration system limiting legal employment to city residents. Rural Fuzhounese may have chosen to be undocumented workers in America, rather than undocumented workers in a Chinese city.

3. By the mid-1980s remittances from Fuzhounese in New York were already transforming rural towns and villages. Beautiful four-story homes were being built and ancestral halls reconstructed. With Fuzhou's urban and rural economic improvements still a number of years in the future, the lure of rapid economic advancement and the desire to maintain "face" (*mianzi*) or appearances within the community led fellow villagers to consider outmigration as a strategy (Kwong 1997a).

4. Changes in U.S. immigration laws allowed many early immigrants to legalize their status and bring family members to the United States

through the family-reunification provisions of the 1965 Immigrant and Nationality Act. Also important were the Immigration Reform and Control Act of 1986, which granted amnesty to undocumented immigrants who could prove their arrival before 1982 and the executive orders of President George H. W. Bush, which in 1989 granted legal status to Chinese students in the United States after the Tian An Men Square massacre and in 1990 eased restrictions on applications for political asylum based on China's population control policies. Later immigrants regularly claimed political-asylum status if they were apprehended after arrival in the United States, or they waited for the next amnesty, assuming that each new U.S. president would issue such an order, as both Presidents Reagan and Bush had.

5. Rural Fuzhounese extended the time-honored tradition of deploying family members beyond the local area as a means of family economic diversification, this time reaching beyond China and across the Pacific Ocean. In light of the political and economic upheaval of the previous era in China and the uncertain prospects for the future, outmigration seemed a rational strategy for economic enhancement.

6. The rapidly expanding human smuggling network made transportation to the United States readily available. Snakeheads were and are still ubiquitous in the Fuzhou region. A 10 or 20 percent down payment on the total fee, which by 2002 had surpassed $60,000, would start their journey to America. Being good business people, snakeheads promoted their services with tales of Fuzhounese economic success in New York.

7. At the turn of the millennium, the towns and villages east and southeast of Fuzhou are no longer poor. Remittances have continued to flood back into the Fuzhou area, invested particularly in housing construction and support of families. Beyond the creation of a limited number of service and construction industries, however, these remittances have had little substantive effect on the local economy. With few local opportunities for economic advancement and significant numbers of fellow villagers already in the United States, younger generations have begun to see outmigration as an obvious career choice—almost an extension of the family business.

8. One of the most significant factors in Fuzhounese immigration is the seductive and powerful pull of the U.S. labor market. The demand of the U.S. economy for low-wage, low-skilled workers, coupled with the U.S. government's inconsistent enforcement of labor and immigration laws, draws Fuzhounese workers to New York. Illegal immigration,

including Chinese immigration, can only be understood in light of this economic reality. Fuzhounese participate in a global labor market. As long as the demand continues, undocumented workers will continue to cross national boundaries to fill the jobs. Ironically, harsh immigration laws and border enforcement have little positive effect on this flow. Instead they raise the costs of smuggling and make undocumented workers even more vulnerable to smugglers and U.S. employers.

Tingjiang: Widow's Village

On June 20, 2000, fifty-eight Chinese died in the back of a sealed, refrigerated tomato truck traveling from Belgium to Dover, England. These immigrants, many from Tingjiang and neighboring areas, were smuggled from Fuzhou to England by a Fuzhounese crime syndicate. Apprehended by the Belgian police in April, they were later released and given an order to leave the country. Their Chinese smugglers eventually loaded them onto the truck and sent them on their way. Tragically, the refrigeration unit had been turned off and the occupants slowly suffocated. Only two survived.

Tingjiang is in many respects typical of the emigrant communities around Fuzhou. Local residents suggest that as many as 80 percent of the men between twenty and forty years of age have gone abroad in the past ten years, mostly to New York. Many of the young women have gone abroad as well. More are preparing to go at the next opportunity. Among the teenagers and children of Tingjiang, interviews revealed that some had not seen their father or mother for ten years. English academies have proliferated and are full of these young people preparing to go to America. One ancestral temple conducts daily English classes led by a Fuzhou university graduate. "Why are you studying English?" "To go to America!" they replied. "Why should I stay here?" one young woman asked. "My whole family—father, mother, older brother—are already in New York City. My grandparents will go later if they want to. I will leave soon. I want to make money too!"

On June 26, 2000, the *New York Times* published a callous article about Tingjiang entitled "Chinese Town's Main Export: Its Young Men." Noting Tingjiang's nickname, "Widow's Village," given because all the young men have gone abroad to work, leaving their wives and families behind, the article states:

But don't weep for Tingjiang. It is an unabashedly prosperous place, peppered with lavish multistory tile houses, some with elevators and pools. The kids wear Gap clothes. Cell phones are a standard accessory. And its widows are only widows in the Sunday football sense: Tingjiang's missing men are still very much alive—almost all working illegally in restaurants and on construction sites, thousands of miles away, in the United States.

The story of the Fuzhounese deaths in England and others like it reveal that the apparent prosperity of Fuzhounese emigrant communities masks a much more complex and discouraging reality for Fuzhounese immigrants. Not all of them are alive and not all of them are well. The passage to the United States, or more recently to Japan, Australia, and Europe, organized by international smuggling networks is often grueling and hazardous. And employment, once located, is often long and arduous. New York's Chinatown is full of Fuzhounese looking for work, which they often can do for only a limited duration because they cannot endure the physical hardship of sixteen-hour days and seven-day work weeks sleeping on the kitchen floor of a restaurant. The Lower East Side's tenement houses, built for earlier generations of European immigrants, are hazardously overcrowded. The pressure on bodies and minds can be extremely heavy.

While towns and villages like Tingjiang are filled with Nike tennis shoes, Gap T-shirts, and ubiquitous cell phones, these superficial status symbols do not tell the story of economic disparity within the community, or the poverty, the family separation, the physical and mental illnesses of many. The current Fuzhounese migration may renew centuries-old patterns of outmigration. But it is occurring in an intensified global economic context and is intimately tied to an internationalizing labor market hungry for low-wage, exploitable workers, which, while having some similarities to the Southeast Asian regional labor market of the late nineteenth and early twentieth centuries, now connects Fuzhou to the other side of the world and is facilitated by a multi-billion-dollar human smuggling industry.

Conclusion

In the modern history of China religion has frequently been an avenue for engaging issues of social inequality and stratification. Religion has been intimately tied to many of the social movements over the past two hundred years that have addressed the economic and political dislocations of their times. In some respects, religion has been a language people can use to talk about their suffering, among other things, rising to the forefront at particular moments of history and connecting profoundly to certain historical processes. The following two chapters will examine the situation of religion in modern Chinese history as well as its particular formations in the Fuzhou area. They will help provide a framework in which to understand the theological and political context from which New York's Fuzhounese religious communities have emerged and the dynamics influencing their institutional polity and practice today.

3

Religion in Fuzhou
An Overview

A religious revival is sweeping Fuzhou and the entire Fujian Province. Beginning in 1979, religious practices have been reestablished and religious traditions reinvented, recovering from the devastating effects of the Cultural Revolution and returning religious activities to a prominent role in both urban and rural life. Buddhist temples, family ancestral halls, Daoist shrines, Protestant and Catholic churches are rising in cities, towns, villages, hillsides, and rice paddies across the greater Fuzhou region. Economic liberalization has increased local discretionary expenditures, and overseas Chinese have flooded the area with funds, filling local temple and church coffers and revitalizing traditional cultural-religious practices such as village festivals, funeral and wedding ceremonies, grave building and sweeping, feng-shui (geomancy), and fortunetelling. Although recent evidence suggests the pattern is spreading across China, this extraordinary renaissance of ritual activity has been most intense in southeastern China, particularly in Fujian, Zhejiang, and Guangdong provinces (Pas 1989; Dean 1993, 1997, 1998; Yang 2000).

The Chinese government recognizes five official religions: Buddhism, Daoism, Catholicism, Protestantism, and Islam. Local popular religious practice, which is the predominant expression in rural China, does not fit any of these categories, however, and is still considered to be "feudal superstition." The state seeks to limit these practices by circumscribing legal religious activities within officially registered religious sites that must be aligned with one of the five recognized religions. China's religious policies and their often inconsistent implementation continue to evolve in response to this rapidly shifting religious landscape. According to a Changle government official interviewed in early 2001:

The development of religion in our area has far outpaced our government's ability to deal with it. For instance we now have 100,000 Christians in a total population of 680,000 in Changle. Ninety percent of them are Catholic, mostly meeting in unregistered locations. These are very high percentages in China. We are racing to keep up. So obviously we are going to make mistakes.

The religious revival currently underway is enriching the religious diversity of the greater Fuzhou region. This rapid expansion of religious organizations and practices, however, may at times mask the ongoing deep conflict between religious organizations and the Chinese state that is deeply embedded in the nation's history. The surprising emergence of Falun Gong onto the national Chinese stage in the late 1990s and the Chinese government's equally rapid moves to suppress it provide a contemporary example of the deep fault lines that continue to exist between the state and religion.

Sources of Religious Diversity in Fujian

The roots of Fuzhou and Fujian's religious diversity lie deep in the history of the province on the borderland of the Chinese empire. Throughout China's history, Fujian has been a refuge from famine, overpopulation, political repression, and military disruption. Each new wave of immigrants has brought with it spiritual practices, religious beliefs, and particular deities that have been added to Fujian's richly textured religious fabric. As China has reopened to the outside world over the past twenty years, overseas Chinese have reinforced this fantastic religious diversity. Emigrants, particularly those in Taiwan and Hong Kong, who left Fujian, often before 1949, have helped rebuild ancestral halls, restore graves, and reconstruct temples, many of which were destroyed or severely damaged during China's Cultural Revolution (Lin 1993).

Since the 1990s, the tens of thousands of Fuzhounese working in the United States have channeled significant resources back home. Just as Fuzhou's overseas garment and restaurant workers remit hard-earned savings to build new homes for children and aging parents, roads for the local village, and shops for the local economy, so too do they underwrite the building and rebuilding of religious edifices in their hometowns and support professional and lay religious practitioners and activities. It is quite common for Fuzhounese workers who have arrived safely in America to express their gratitude to the divine power which guided them to these shores by returning a portion of their earnings as an offering of thanksgiving (Langfitt 2000). Though many will not be present for ceremonies and rituals in their home communities, they hope their gifts will enhance their good fortune as well as their status in the community.

Since 1980, the Chinese government has reinstated its constitutional provision of freedom of and freedom from religion. While applied unevenly across the country, the gradual reimplementation of this fundamental policy has created a religious environment significantly more relaxed than the antagonism and repression in the 1950s, 1960s, and 1970s. With the rapidly receding influence of official Marxist-state ideology, religion has raced into the vacuum to reclaim a central role in public discourse of ultimate meaning and values, a discourse ever more vibrant as the rapid pace of socioeconomic change compels a reconsideration of what matters in life. Because of Fujian Province's history of distance from the central Chinese government, coupled with the emerging influence of Fuzhou's overseas Chinese population, the possibilities for religious activity in the Fuzhou area have been particularly expansive.

Fuzhou City's Religious Scene

In Fuzhou City, with a population nearing six million, religious practices are deeply woven into the social fabric, and temples and churches are sprinkled broadly across the city. While large-scale public rituals are discouraged by the local Religious Affairs Bureau and Public Security Administration (Dean 1997) religious activity is rapidly expanding in officially registered religious sites and in unregistered locations, such as in Christian house churches. For example:

- The expansive Western Zen Buddhist Temple occupies prime real estate in the western section of the city of Fuzhou, its recent restoration funded by a wealthy adherent living in Singapore. The air is thick with incense and bundles of paper money immolated to appease ancestors and bring good luck to the worshiper.
- The spire of the Protestant Heavenly Peace Church, rebuilt with funds drawn largely from overseas Fuzhounese Methodists in Asia, rises on the hillside of the Cangshan district of Fuzhou City just

across the Liberation Bridge, its presence highlighted by a neon red cross.

Other religious sites are more humble in location and adornment, standing on quiet back streets or down narrow, winding *hutong*, Chinese alleys:

- In a tiny storefront where Mrs. Chen conducts her ceremonies, the faithful come to consult a local deity, the Heavenly Emperor Ye. Plied with tea and cigarettes, Ye possesses Mrs. Wang, a spirit medium, and through her entranced voice advises the petitioner on prospects for luck, wealth, male children, and how to avoid misfortune.
- Behind a fast-food restaurant on August 17 Road North stands a thousand-year-old courtyard holding the city's only mosque. The imam, recently arrived from Gansu, a distant western province of China, has been sent by the All-China Islamic Council to minister to Fuzhou's approximately two thousand Muslims, descendants of Muslim traders who called upon Fuzhou and Fujian Province's ports centuries ago. No one, save the imam, comes to the mosque for prayers as most of the Hui minority population, as Muslims are described ethnically, continue only a few cultural traditions that have little religious substance.
- On a narrow shelf high on the wall in her kitchen, Mrs. Wu keeps a small altar to the kitchen god and burns incense daily to ask for its protection. Her husband is a recently converted Protestant. Her mother is a devout Buddhist. Mrs. Wu walks a careful line to keep harmony in the household.
- Outside the officially registered Protestant and Catholic churches, many of Fuzhou's Christians gather in dozens of house churches, meeting in the living rooms of the faithful, unwilling to "cooperate" with Christians in the public churches, who are viewed as working closely with the Chinese government.

Mr. Dong's Buddhist Supply Store

In a small storefront in an old-style two-story wood structure on August 17 Road South in the heart of old Fuzhou, Mr. Dong operates a religious supply shop, one of many along that stretch of the road that supports the ritual needs of the religious revival occurring in Fuzhou and in the surrounding towns and villages. Business is brisk. Mr. Dong's first customer of the morning runs a similar shop on the eastern edge of Fuzhou City at the foot of Drum Mountain, where a large Buddhist temple complex and monastery are among Fuzhou's main tourist attractions. The customer buys thirty copper altar candlesticks wholesale for his shop, ties them precariously onto a board on the back of his motorcycle and speeds away. The next customer, from a village south of Fuzhou, buys a more varied selection of goods for a new ancestral hall that his family has constructed. Mr. Dong specializes in copper goods. His shop is full of copper candle sticks, incense bowls, and statues of the Buddha and the bodhisattva goddess Guan Yin. But the store, like most of the religious supply shops that line both sides of the street, carries a wide variety of all the paraphernalia needed for Chinese Buddhist, Daoist, and popular religious rituals. Candles, red wooden drums, paper money, and incense fill the counters and shelves inside his dark and musty stall. Outside hang colored lanterns, lettered signs, and even a few costumes for ritual performers.

Mr. Dong's father, born in 1915, had operated a religious supply store for many years until it was closed down at the beginning of the Cultural Revolution in 1966. His father reopened the store in 1989 and Mr. Dong left his job at a government-run food supply company to work with him. He had been earning fifteen dollars a month plus subsidies for housing, health care, and his daughter's education. Now his store, which after his father's death in 1997 he runs with his wife, clears about $500 a month after taxes and expenses. Four of his six siblings are in private business now; two of them— his youngest sister and oldest brother—are in religious supplies.

Mr. Dong, a Buddhist himself, goes to the local temple on the first and fifteenth day of every lunar month and on major holidays, as is Buddhist custom. There he burns paper money, paper clothes, and paper goods to honor and appease his ancestors, provide for them in the underworld, and ward off any ghosts that may endanger his own well-being. Although the shop he owns supplies ritual goods to religious organizations and practitioners throughout Fuzhou and its surrounding towns and villages, Mr. Dong does not consider himself to be a religious specialist, either formally or informally. Religious professionals must formally register with one of the five local religious associations and with the government's Religious Affairs Bureau, but his only relationship to the government is as a private business owner. He is also skeptical about the claims of others to religious specialization.

FIGURE 5 Morning prayers at a Fuzhou temple.

There are religious specialists around. They come to buy supplies at my store, from all over the area. But to be effective they must have a special connection to the Buddha or the bodhisattva. To luck. To Fate. Not everyone can be one. Unfortunately, not all of them are legitimate.

Religion in the Greater Fuzhou Region

Outside Fuzhou City the religious landscape becomes even more complex and more intimately connected to the massive outmigration to the United States. Driving east along the northern bank of the Min River one passes town after town in which large visible new religious edifices have been constructed.

- In Tingjiang the Kangzhuang Protestant Church has built a five-hundred-seat sanctuary, a five-floor dormitory, a kitchen that can prepare food for one thousand, and an education building.
- Clearly visible across the river from Tingjiang to the south stands the Houyu Protestant Church, newly constructed, vividly painted in yellow, and prominently located on a steep hillside. Both of these

congregations have relied on members in America to provide the financial support to construct the buildings and to support the lay workers who organize their programs.

- In Dongqi Village, a five-minute car ride east of Tingjiang, the Huang family has rebuilt its ancestral hall, also relying on remittances from Huang family members in the United States. The building, with a beautifully decorated courtyard, serves as a family-run and oriented community center. Older family members fill the back rooms playing mahjong. A classroom on another side of the courtyard is filled with fifteen teenagers studying English in preparation for going to America.
- Rising on a hill at the back of the next village to the east, Chang'an, the Daoist Temple of Heavenly Thanksgiving, is a testimony to the successes of its members. Nonexistent ten years ago, this temple now climbs four stories against the hill in this nearly empty village, culminating in an altar to the Emperor of Heaven with a commanding view of the village below and of the Min River to the south.
- In Fuqi Village, south of the Min River near Houyu, a new road is being built with funds from the Fuqi Village Temple, a sprawling

FIGURE 6 Fuqi Temple main hall.

mountainside complex including a seven-story pagoda, constructed over the last thirteen years with remittances from Fuqi residents in New York. The temple's leader lives in New York and travels back to Fuqi at least once a year for special ritual ceremonies.

- Further south of the Min River and east of the newly classified city of Changle, the road to the new Fuzhou airport passes an eighty-foot-tall, red brick, gothic-style Catholic church built illegally by an underground Catholic congregation relying on remittances from New York. The building was constructed in plain view from the highway and only blocks from the local police station. Today it stands empty, however, and its twin towers tilt sadly. Days of dynamiting have nearly destroyed it in a government-ordered crackdown against religious structures that were constructed in the area without proper building permits.

- In a town south of Changle, the official Protestant church, a concrete hulk with a two-tiered sanctuary balcony and a four-story education building, built largely with funds from overseas, is a short distance away from an unofficial house church and evangelist training center also supported by parishioners now in America. The training center was closed and its leaders dispersed after a vitriolic conflict between two leaders spilled over into the Protestant church and forced public security and government religious authorities to intervene. The Protestant church attracts slim congregations now on an average Sunday. The leaders of the training center quietly continue their work, but from other locations.

Problematic State Definitions of Religion

The Chinese government has attempted to organize all legal religious activity under the rubric of the five officially recognized religions, each with its own national, provincial, and local, quasi-independent, state-authorized associations. Drawing upon European constructions of the notion of religion (Asad 1993) filtered through a Marxist lens, this formulation is extremely problematic. Catholicism and Protestantism, for instance, despite both being branches of Christianity, are classified as separate religions based on their particular histories in China. Both have grown rapidly in recent years, adding additional levels of complexity to their local and regional expressions that are not easily represented or managed by the state-authorized associations. Islam also has a unique and complicated historical trajectory in China and a dynamic political and social role in contemporary events. Much has been written about the diversity of Chinese Muslims, particularly about the appropriateness of categorizing them as a single ethnic or religious group (Gladney 1998; Dillon 1999). Buddhists and Daoists probably outnumber the other religious groups, but their memberships have never been successfully estimated as a result of a lack of membership records and blurred distinctions between Buddhism and Daoism, not to mention their intimate integration with Chinese popular religion at the local level. For instance, while a local temple may legally register as either Buddhist or Daoist, its symbols and rituals often include elements of both and are intertwined with popular religious beliefs.

To attempt to understand religion in China, particularly the Buddhism/Daoism/popular religion spectrum, as several distinct doctrinal systems is to impose Western constructs of "religion" onto a significantly different set of circumstances. In reality, these expressions cannot be categorized so neatly. China's religious landscape is and has been much too complex, and the boundaries between Buddhism, Daoism, and popular religious expression are fuzzy at best. A temple may include statues of the Buddha, the bodhisattva Guan Yin, a local Daoist deity, and even altars for family ancestors.

To a large degree, the state's religious categories are inadequate for descriptive or analytical purposes. The categories and the structures established for maintaining them do serve, however, as key tools in the state's system for defining what religious activities and beliefs are appropriate or inappropriate, legal or illegal, orthodox or heterodox. At many times in China's history the interaction of Chinese Daoist, Buddhist, and popular religious practices with the state has proven particularly problematic.

Defining Religious Orthodoxy and Heterodoxy

The distinction between "orthodoxy" and "heterodoxy" in Chinese religious practice has been highly scrutinized by China scholars (Overmyer 1976; Naquin 1976; Jordan and Overmyer 1986; Madsen 2001) as a key analytical framework for understanding the relationship of religion and the state. *Zheng* (straight) or *zheng dao* (straight path) are Chinese terms that have been translated as "orthodoxy." *Xie* is most commonly rendered as "heterodoxy." The term *yi duan* or "heresy" is sometimes used within religious

FIGURE 7   Temple festival, Fuqi Village.

traditions as a less serious way to describe internal theological differences that lack external political ramifications. In the past, China's Confucian scholar-officials considered the *zheng dao* to be true Chinese culture and the many heterodox beliefs and practices to be impure deviations. Despite the changed political and religious dynamic of post-1949 China, these hotly contested and negotiated terms are still deployed to demarcate acceptable and unacceptable religious beliefs and practices, not only in the eyes of the Chinese state and its officially sanctioned religious organizations, but also within religious traditions to draw distinctions between different theological, ritual, or political stances. For example, Protestants consider Catholics to be *yi duan* because of their veneration of Mary. Underground Catholics consider Catholics in the open churches to be *xie* because they have renounced their primary allegiance to the pope as a condition of their recognition by the Chinese state. Buddhists decry Falun Gong as *xie* to clearly distinguish themselves from this widespread practice, which has been denounced by the government.

Heterodoxy as Threat to the State

Historically the Chinese state has viewed religion warily and has consistently attempted to absorb it into the religious hierarchy of the State Cult, headed by the emperor, coopting religious beliefs and practices into the state orthodoxy. This has not always been successful. Throughout China's history, heterodox sects have challenged the authority of the state and the emperor's Mandate of Heaven, his cosmic/divine right to rule. Heterodox religious activities in the contemporary era have significant historical antecedents. Several heterodox sects, often though not exclusively drawn from folk-Buddhist traditions, generated significant peasant-based and millenarian tendencies that threatened the social order of the Chinese state during the nineteenth century. This was a time of transformation in China marked by the precipitous decline of the Qing Dynasty and the encroachment of European imperialism. The traditional institutions of Chinese government failed to respond adequately to the changing elements of the economic, political, and social environment. The Qing—of Manchu descent rather than the majority Han nationality—were viewed in certain circles as foreign usurpers of the kingdom and were targets of attempts to overthrow the government. Famine and poverty were rampant in many parts of the country. When China's territorial integrity was compromised by Western powers through a series of unequal treaties, the government's power and authority were further undermined so that the Qing position declined rapidly.

The Eight Trigrams rebellion in the fall of 1813 was a loose network of religious sects, belonging to a three-hundred-year-old millenarian religion, sometimes called the White Lotus Sect whose primary deity was known as the Eternal and Venerable Mother. These sects carried out simultaneous uprisings in several cities in north China, including Beijing.

Like other popular folk-Buddhist sects of the Ming and Qing periods (still popular in some places in China), the White Lotus was a salvation religion. Unlike Confucians, who considered this world to be basically good and improvable if the people underwent proper moral cultivation, folk-Buddhist sects believed the world to be hopelessly corrupt. Only supernatural intervention could save it. The unsuccessful Eight Trigrams rebellion was only one of many uprisings undertaken by these sects during their three hundred years of history and it was typical of regular outbursts of peasant protest that were expressed through a religious sect and a millenarian ideology (Naquin 1976; Madsen 2001).

The best-known peasant-based millenarian movement of the nineteenth century, and the most deadly and protracted in Chinese history, was the Taiping Tianguo, or the Heavenly Kingdom of Great Peace of 1851–1864. Hong Xiuquan, founder of the Taiping, believed that God the Father had called him to save humankind and that Jesus was his Elder Brother. Furthermore, God had ordered him to overthrow the current Qing Dynasty and set up a new order of brotherhood and sisterhood among God's children. With an army of 60,000 by 1851, the Taipings surged into central China, making Nanjing their Heavenly Capital in 1853, slaughtering all the resident Manchus in the process as an act of purification and ethnic cleansing. The ensuing fifteen-year civil war resulted in the deaths of as many as twenty million Chinese and extensive destruction of property, with more than six hundred cities changing hands, often with massacres. The Qing finally reasserted control in 1864 (Fairbank 1986; Spence 1990, 1996).

The Boxer Uprising (1898–1901) focused on the eradication of Western influence in China, taking particular aim at Christian missionaries and converts and calling for an end to the special privileges enjoyed by these groups under the terms of the unequal treaties. The Boxers, peasant-based and millenarian, drew their strength from a combination of martial arts and spirit possession, which they believed would bring them magic invulnerability. In June 1900, the Boxers entered Beijing and Tianjin, killing Christians, looting and laying siege to the capital's foreign legation, only to be defeated by an international Western army (Fairbank 1986; Esherick 1987; Spence 1990).

Troubling Characteristics of Heterodox Sects

Many of the characteristics of these heterodox sects that were particularly troubling to the Chinese state in the nineteenth century are characteristics that still concern the Chinese government. They are at the root of its various efforts to circumscribe religious activities today. Madsen (2001) lists the following:

1. The millenarian sects focused on radical salvation. Confucian scholar-officials considered this not only intellectually wrong but also politically dangerous. People who truly believed the end of the era was imminent might be inspired to revolt against the established social order.

2. Salvation was immediate and physical, not only long-term and spiritual. Heterodox sects therefore attracted and held people through exorcisms, promises of superhuman feats achieved through martial arts, and magical healing practices—especially through *qi gong*, an element of traditional medicine. These sects claimed to address concrete problems and so threatened the state's preeminent role in managing society.

3. As voluntary associations, these sects challenged the predominant community social structure based on kinship. Anyone could join these sects and immediately achieve equal standing through proper ritual behavior. All members could achieve salvation, regardless of family, lineage, or village connections.

4. The voluntary associations extended beyond the normal geographic boundaries of local communities, building networks across long distances that had previously been monopolized by the state and enabling popular communication and action on a translocal basis.

5. Millenarian sects drew members from a cross section of Chinese society, including all economic and social strata—a radical leveling practice in a highly hierarchized society.

6. These largely rural sects, often separated from religious specialists by great distances, relied heavily on lay leadership, another significant leveling factor. These lay leaders included many women, adding another egalitarian challenge to a society dominated by patriarchal structures and practices.

Falun Gong

The current conflict between the Chinese government and Falun Gong is but the latest chapter in the ongoing saga of tension between the state and heterodox religious sects in China. On April 25, 1999, Falun Gong exploded into public view as 10,000–15,000 practitioners gathered quietly and unannounced in Beijing outside the central government offices to present a mass appeal requesting government acceptance of their practice. Publicly introduced in China in 1992 by Mr. Li Hongzhi, after seven years Falun Gong boasted 100 million followers, 39 general instruction offices, 1,900 ordinary instruction offices, and 28,000 practice sites (Schechter 2000: 41).

Falun Gong, which can be translated as "Practice of the Dharma Wheel," is a type of *qi gong*, a central element of traditional Chinese medicine. Like other forms of *qi gong*, Falun Gong aims through meditation and exercise to place its practitioners in a proper relationship to the cosmic forces that circulate within the body and through the world. Practicing these exercises is believed to bring physical health and spiritual enlightenment.

In the movement's early days, Li Hongzhi, along with many other *qi gong* teachers/masters, was associated with the official China Qi Gong Research Society. Through it the Falun Dafa Research Society was established to provide a formal link for his teachings to the *qi gong* network. The society allowed him to create training centers and contact locations to propagate his teachings. In 1994 a conflict arose between the Qi Gong Research Society and Li over the size of fees he should charge for his lectures and teachings. Refusing to raise his rates, Li left the society in 1995, placing himself outside the officially sanctioned network of practitioners.

Despite or perhaps because of the movement's phenomenal growth since 1992 and the organizational effectiveness of its April 1999 demonstration, by the summer of 1999 the Chinese government branded it *xie jiao*, that is, heterodox, calling it an evil cult and declaring that it must be smashed for the safety of the Chinese nation and the Chinese people. In Fuzhou, 260 practitioners were arrested immediately after the banning. In the years since, political study sessions have continued in schools and work units, describing the heretical teachings of Falun Gong and warning of its dangers to personal well-being. In 2001 the national Religious Affairs Bureau published a book on heretical teachings and unorthodox practices, focusing on Falun Gong but including heretical teachings in other religious traditions as well. Official religious organizations are quickly following suit, attempting to define their legally recognized groups as orthodox, in distinction to heterodox groups like Falun Gong. The Fujian provincial Protestant organization, based in Fuzhou, has opened an "antiheterodoxy office" to propagate to the grassroots the official understanding of Falun Gong and other unorthodox groups.

This tension between Falun Gong and the state reflects historic patterns. Folk-Buddhist sects, like Falun Gong, Madsen argues, have often blended smoothly with ordinary folk piety, in this case melding into the widespread morning meditation activities and pervasive *qi gong* medical practices. But under some circumstances—famine, poverty, or government repression— these sects may rise up in massive rebellion. Such "fluid changeability" has traditionally affected the Chinese government's response to these groups and continues to do so today. Despite Falun Gong's largely peaceful nature, the government mistrusts its ability to create alternative networks of power, communication, and mobilization. It mistrusts Falun Gong's leveling tendencies in light of China's growing economic disparities. And it mistrusts Falun Gong's emphasis on salvation outside the officially sanctioned framework for resolving social problems. The Chinese state has consistently attempted to restrict such "heterodox" movements. Its severe attacks and political mobilization against Falun Gong are only the latest example. But in many cases the restrictions have only served to make it more likely that the apocalyptic dimensions of these sects may come to the fore.

Conclusion

The future of Falun Gong and its relationship to the Chinese state remain to be seen. Despite a nearly four-year campaign against it, Falun Gong shows no signs of disappearing. Demonstrators from across China, many from rural areas, continue their almost daily displays in Beijing's Tian An Men Square, despite beatings, arrests, and imprisonment. The self-immolation in 2001 of Falun Gong practitioners in Beijing reveals the intensity of belief among many followers and the lengths to which some will go to resist the state's restrictions and pursue an alternative path to salvation. The rapid spread of the movement to dozens of nations and millions of people has only raised the stakes for the Chinese government, which now has identified Falun Gong with another grave danger, external interference in internal Chinese affairs.

Falun Gong is not widespread in the Fuzhou area. Nor is its manifestation in New York particularly relevant to the immigrant Chinese communities considered in this study. In fact, many of its U.S. adherents are not even Chinese. But Falun Gong is the most talked about religious movement in China today. For many Chinese it helps people cope with the economic dislocations and political uncertainties of the present period, a role the state reserves exclusively for itself. Most significantly for the purposes of this ethnography, Falun Gong provides a salient contemporary example of relations between religion and the state in China, an example that illustrates many of the dynamics described in the succeeding pages.

4

Religion in Fuzhou
Spotlight on Christianity

The religious revival sweeping Fuzhou extends both to Catholic and Protestant Christians. On its journey from Fuzhou to the ocean, the Min River passes town after town with prominently displayed, newly constructed churches. To the southeast, the Changle area is dotted with towering new church buildings. Nationally, Protestants are estimated at over 15 million (though some outside partisans suggest numbers as high as 100 million), and Catholic membership is estimated at 4 million in registered churches and between 8 and 10 million in unregistered churches. The number of Christians continues to expand in the greater Fuzhou region. The Changle area alone is estimated to be home to 100,000 Christians, nearly 15 percent of the total local population. Remittances from the faithful working in the United States are funding this explosion of new religious edifices and underwriting the massive expansion in religious activities. But relations between Christians and the government continue to be nettlesome, as do relations within the Christian communities. These difficulties involve fundamental disagreements about the role of the state in regulating religion and painful divisions among believers with varying theological and political views.

This chapter focuses on post-1949 developments in Fuzhou, with particular attention given to the negotiation of Catholic and Protestant identity and institutional structure in relation to the state apparatus during the Communist era. It analyzes the reasons why the Chinese government continues to be wary of Christian churches and their potential for resistance and rebellion. Discussions of heterodoxy and orthodoxy, applied to Buddhism, Daoism, and popular religion in the previous chapter, are here extended to include Protestants and Catholics. As this chapter reveals, outside China's urban areas Protestant and Catholic Christianity is relatively free-form and volatile. It is largely lay led, egalitarian, and millenarian, finding salvation outside the established social structure in much the same way as earlier heterodox sects in Chinese history (Madsen 2001). Its extensive reliance on women as evangelists radically expands established gender roles. Its growing networks transgress established kin, village, and regional boundaries and in many cases intentionally challenge the state's authority to control mobility and communication, not only within China, but with Christian groups beyond China's borders. Remittances and the regular transnational movement of overseas Fuzhounese, while encouraged by government authorities for their positive contributions in many areas of Chinese social life, complicate the government's efforts at control and regulation in the religious sphere.

Histories of specific Protestant communities presented in the latter half of the chapter serve two roles: first to expose the painful divisions that exist within the Protestant communities along political and theological lines; and second, to reveal the way in which these varying theological and political views lead to different strategies for negotiating the state-imposed categories of heterodoxy and orthodoxy. The exploration of Christianity's complex expressions and conflicts in the greater Fuzhou region will provide essential background for understanding the highly conflictive dynamics of Fuzhounese Christian congregations in New York City.

Christianity in China: An Overview

Protestant missionaries first arrived in Fuzhou in the late 1840s following China's defeat in the Opium War. The Jesuit missionary Giulio Aleni had come to Fuzhou much earlier, in 1625, though his interaction was limited largely to the scholar elite of the time (Zurcher 1990). It was only with the nineteenth-century work of the Spanish Dominican order that Catholicism began to take root among the Fuzhounese masses. Protestants and Catholics in Fuzhou and in China as a whole have followed two distinct trajectories and are considered to be two separate religions by constituents and government officials alike. This is reinforced by linguistic differences resulting from the inability of early Protestant and Catholic missionaries to agree on common terms for fundamental Christian concepts. So, for instance, Catholicism is known as the Teachings of the Heavenly Lord (Tian Zhu Jiao), and Protestantism is known as the Teachings of Christ (Ji Du Jiao). Both traditions, however, have since 1949 spawned groups that refuse to comply with state regulations, choose to operate independent of state-authorized religious institutions, and often openly defy the state's requirements for orthodox, religious activities. Internal theological and political differences have in turn spurred debates within each tradition about purity and pollution.

A thorough review of the rich history of Protestants and Catholics prior to 1949 is beyond the scope of this book. Suffice it to say that despite the special privileges granted to missionaries by the series of nineteenth-century unequal treaties, and despite the educational, economic, and legal benefits of conversion, the growth of Christianity among the Chinese population remained limited. Many Chinese viewed Christians as part and parcel of Western imperialism, and as nationalistic resistance intensified, Christians were frequent targets. Christianity grew slowly in the Fuzhou area up to 1949, for the most part only among the educated classes (Dunch 1996).

The situation changed radically for Christians after the Communists' victory over the Nationalists in 1949. China expelled all foreigners, predicated on its fundamental nationalistic commitment to return sovereignty to the Chinese after more that one hundred years of Western imperialism. The new government moved expeditiously to expel missionaries, to nationalize church-affiliated schools and hospitals, and to sever all ties, financial and otherwise, between Chinese Christians and their institutions overseas. By the end of 1950 all Protestant and Catholic missionaries had left Fuzhou. Administration of the large network of schools, colleges, hospitals, and social service agencies (like the YMCA) had been taken over by the government. Christian churches were left to survive on their own.

The Communist Party also moved to establish "mass organizations" to bring disparate social entities into one "united front" for rebuilding China. Activities of all five recognized religions were consolidated under the guidance of the Communist Party's United Front Work Department working through the government's Religious Affairs Bureau. Over the next few years, national associations were formed for each religion. The new Chinese constitution guaranteed freedom of religious expression, but under certain clear conditions. Principle among these was *aiguo, aijiao* or "love the country, love the church," a requirement that patriotism—building a socialist nation—be a central tenet of any legal religious organization. A second condition was self-sufficiency, especially independence from foreign influence. The mass organizations served the functions of promoting these principles of the new orthodoxy, providing formal relationships between religious groups and state and party structure, and encouraging the participation of Christians in society.

Catholics in Post-1949 Fuzhou

For Catholics, the reorganization demanded in the 1950s created serious structural and ecclesiastical problems that continue to plague contemporary church-state relations. As participants in the Patriotic Association, Chinese Catholics were forced to renounce allegiance to the pope and the Roman Catholic hierarchy. No longer, for instance, would the Vatican be allowed to appoint bishops for the churches in China. The Chinese Catholic Patriotic Association (CCPA), working in close consultation with the Religious Affairs Bureau, would assume that responsibility.

Not all Catholics were willing to accommodate to these new patterns. Complicating matters, the Vatican declared that all Catholics participating in the Patriotic Association would be excommunicated. Many Catholics, and Protestants as well, concluded that those Christians who participated in the government-promoted mass organizations had apostatized themselves and could no longer be trusted as true Christians. Catholics unwilling to participate in the officially recognized churches in many instances formed house churches outside the government network. As the Patriotic Association was being established at the local and regional levels, the government proceeded to imprison clergy and laity who refused to cooperate or who were considered to have allegiances outside China. As resistance continued, arrests and persecution increased. In Fuzhou, for instance, Bishop Zheng Changcheng, appointed by the Vatican in 1951 to replace the departed missionary bishop, was arrested in 1955 and imprisoned for twenty-nine years, returning to Fuzhou only in 1984 after years of labor reeducation on a farm in Jiangxi Province. He was then kept under house arrest until 1989, when at the age of seventy-eight he was allowed to resume his leadership of Fuzhou's Catholics.

After its formal establishment in 1957, the national CCPA denounced the Vatican and without the Vatican's authorization commenced the autonomous election and consecration of bishops. By 1962, forty-two bishops had been chosen and consecrated by bishops connected with the CCPA, including a replacement bishop for Fuzhou. From the point of view of the Vatican, these consecrations were "illicit" but "valid," a subtle theological distinction. Because the consecration rituals were carried out in the proper manner, the bishops were truly bishops; when they administered the sacraments, the sacraments truly conveyed God's grace. But because Rome had not approved their consecration, the bishops and their followers were acting disobediently.

> ... Under normal circumstances ... a good Catholic should not attend a Mass or go to a confession conducted by one of these illicit bishops or anyone associated with them, have a marriage blessed by them or receive any of the other sacraments from them. Catholics who did would commit a mortal sin, and if they did not repent, they would go to hell. Whatever the mix of motives that led some priests and bishops to participate in the CCPA, most ordinary Catholics seemed to have shunned these collaborators. An underground Church grew up, consisting of congregations who risked punishment by meeting secretly with priests who had refused to cooperate with the Patriotic Association. (Madsen 1998: 38)

Protestants in Post-1949 Fuzhou

The history of Fuzhou's Protestant community, and particularly its experience since 1949, is essential for understanding the complex political and theological dynamics that inform and differentiate New York's Fuzhounese Protestant churches. In 1949 there were six denominations in Fuzhou: Methodists, Anglicans, Church of Christ in China (of the Reformed tradition, including Congregationalists and Evangelical United Brethren), Seventh-Day Adventists, and two indigenous Chinese groups, the True Jesus Church and the Christian Assemblies (also commonly known as the Little Flock). A September 1950 national meeting in Beijing, convened by Premier Zhou Enlai and attended by four Protestant representatives from Fuzhou put in motion the establishment of the national Protestant Three-Self Patriotic Movement (TSPM; self-government, self-support, and self-propagation), and in the fall of 1950 a Fuzhou TSPM office was opened. These principles were a radical shift for many churches that had relied heavily on foreign financial support and personnel. Over the following years in Fuzhou a number of struggling congregations merged, consolidating activities within existing denominations and reducing the number of churches from sixty-four to thirty-six. The Protestant TSPM was formally constituted during the First National Christian Conference in 1954. The national Chinese Catholic

Patriotic Association was formalized in 1957, and local bodies were organized across the country.

For Protestants in most of China, the reorganization proposed by the Chinese government and formalized at the national TSPM conference in 1958 required a relinquishing of denominational structures and institutional patterns and a merger of all Protestants under the TSPM banner. This was by no means a simple task. In 1949 there were close to one million Protestants in China, approximately one-half of one percent of the total population. They were related to twenty-three major denominational groups, representing both indigenous organizations and foreign mission boards. Including those working in Christian institutions, there were about ten thousand professional Chinese church workers and almost four thousand foreign missionaries. Shanghai, which had always been the center of Chinese Protestantism, had 141 places of worship in 1950. Throughout China there were 322 Protestant hospitals, more than 240 schools, 13 Christian colleges, and 210 seminaries and Bible colleges (Wickeri 1988: 117–118).

In an example of both the uneven application of religious policy and the relatively relaxed approach to religion by the Fuzhou City and Fujian Provincial authorities, after the 1958 national TSPM conference mandated unification of Protestant denominations, Fuzhou's churches never merged. Instead, they retained their separate operations until 1966, when all were shut down over the course of a month as the Red Guards launched the Cultural Revolution. According to the head of Fujian Province's TSPM at the time, "We were never asked by the government to merge so we never did." Each denomination maintained independent activities and organization. The Methodist denominational structure continued, for example, though some of its practices were altered by changing social policy. For instance, the Methodist practice of rotating ministers periodically among its churches was ended because the implementation of the household registration system restricted people's ability to move from place to place. Until they were closed in 1966, the Methodist offices in Fuzhou were side by side with the offices of the TSPM.

Although the various denominations avoided consolidation under the TSPM in Fujian Province, their experiences were quite different. For example, cooperation increased between the three largest denominations—Methodist, Anglican, and Church of Christ in China—under the auspices of the TSPM. But the three smaller denominations, each with its own distinct theology and church polity, resisted even limited cooperation.

Difficult Christians: The Little Flock

Not all was smooth sailing for Fuzhou's Protestants during the 1950s. The Little Flock encountered particular difficulties. Many of its leaders had openly supported the failed Nationalist cause in the civil war, fearing the atheist ideology of the Communist Party. After 1949, many of these leaders were targeted by the new government as counterrevolutionaries. When many within the Little Flock opposed the Communists' signature land reform campaign in 1950–1951, the confrontation with the government escalated. Many Little Flock leaders and members were arrested and imprisoned, sentenced to varying terms of "re-education" to assist in their conversion to socialist principles.

The Little Flock was founded in Fuzhou in 1922 by Watchman Nee (Ni Tuosheng) as a completely indigenous and autonomous Chinese Christian movement. By 1949 it had grown to include over seven hundred congregations and meeting points with 70,000 members, primarily in China's coastal provinces, rivaling in size even the largest denominations introduced by missionaries. By 1949 the Little Flock, marked by an ardent nationalism and rejection of missionary influence, along with other indigenous sects and churches such as the True Jesus Church (founded in 1917) and the Jesus Family Church (1921) accounted for fully 25 percent of all Chinese Protestants (Wickeri 1988).

The Little Flock traces its theological and organizational origins to the Exclusive Brethren Movement in London, England. Margaret E. Barber (1869–1930), originally a missionary of the English Anglican Church, arrived in Fuzhou in 1899 and taught in a mission school for seven years before returning home. In 1911, Barber, known locally as He Shou'en, returned to Fuzhou after being strongly influenced by the Exclusive Brethren. Along with her twenty-year-old niece, M. L. S. Ballord (Li Shouling), Barber established a Bible school and training center on the Min River southeast of Fuzhou, where she had a profound influence on the early leaders of the Little Flock movement and on Christian communities throughout the area (Guo 1997).

Watchmen Nee was born in Fuzhou in 1903, a third-generation Christian from an Anglican family. As a student at the Anglican Trinity College high school in Fuzhou in 1920, Nee underwent a powerful conversion experience at a revival led by a Shanghai evangelist, Dora Yu. Nee followed Yu to Shanghai but returned to Fuzhou a year later. In 1922 Nee and the brothers Wang (Wang Zai and Wang Lianjun) were baptized in the Min River and launched the Little Flock movement, which spread rapidly in Fuzhou and the surrounding towns and villages. In 1923 Nee moved down the Min River to Ma'xian, where he lived and studied the Bible with Barber and read extensively, including books by members of the Exclusive Brethren (Kinnear 1973).

Nee's later teachings and the organizational form adopted by the early Little Flock reflected the insights gained through Barber and the Brethren. Nee argued persuasively for autonomous and independent local churches. He believed there should be only "one church in one locality" identified simply by its geographic location. Nee urged Christians to return to the pure and simple forms of Christian living and fellowship evidenced in the New Testament's early Christian communities. He called Christians to a deep personal experience of salvation and rejected a professional clergy. On these principles, Nee railed against foreign mission activity and denominational hierarchies. He encouraged his followers to abandon the established denominational churches, which he believed had become lukewarm in their faith and degenerate in their organizational structure. Entire congregations began to pull away from their mission denominations and the Little Flock expanded rapidly. As a result, the majority Protestant community often accused the Little Flock of sheep stealing.

In 1928 Nee relocated to Shanghai, where he built a three-thousand-seat assembly hall in the heart of the city. Little Flock churches spread quickly from Fuzhou throughout Fujian Province, neighboring Zhejiang Province, and inland from Shanghai in the 1920s and 1930s. A series of internal conflicts roiled the Little Flock as the number of churches grew and leaders attempted to coordinate work and assert doctrinal positions. In 1947, for instance, Nee declared that the Fuzhou Assembly would be known as the Little Flock's "Jerusalem," contradicting the principle of one church per locality in favor of creating a center for coordinating evangelistic work across China. Other Little Flock leaders strenuously resisted. Growth continued in the Communist period until Nee was arrested in 1952 and charged with a series of crimes against the state, culminating in public trials in 1956. Sentenced to fifteen years in prison, he died in a labor camp in 1972, a martyr for the faith in the eyes of his constituents.

Since 1979, Little Flock congregations like those in Tingjiang and Houyu discussed later in this chapter, have reemerged and continue to flourish, fueling much of the significant growth of Christianity in Fuzhou and in rural areas of Zhejiang and other provinces. Yet many Little Flock members today still bear the scars of their confrontation with the government, and the network of Little Flock churches carries its institutional memory. A fundamental distrust of the government was concretized, and members withdrew further from contact with the TSPM-related churches and leaders. A network of home meeting points developed outside the sanction of the state and grew during the Cultural Revolution. Today that network has grown rapidly and extends throughout much of China. Church leaders in Fuzhou estimate that more than half of local Protestants may be related to the Little Flock. While some urban Little Flock churches have in recent years registered with the government as official religious sites, they have done so largely to reclaim former Little Flock church buildings and properties and to exact certain promises of protection from the government—not in any hope of useful cooperation. Even these limited efforts at interaction with the religious and state authorities have provoked severe attacks within the Little Flock community. Drawing on their particular history of conflict with the state in the 1950s and the collective experience of Christians during the Cultural Revolution, the vast majority of Little Flock congregations in rural areas operate as house churches and remain fiercely independent of the state and antagonistic to its efforts to monitor and regulate them.

While the Little Flock is not organized beyond the local church as a denomination with a hierarchical structure, a clear network among congregations exists. Despite government regulations prohibiting Christians from traveling from one locality to another to proselytize, Little Flock Christians regularly exchange visits with other congregations across China, sharing information, training local leaders, and maintaining an extensive intracongregation network. And despite government prohibitions against professional visits from Christians outside the mainland, it is not uncommon to find Christians affiliated with Hong Kong and Taiwan Little Flock groups visiting local Little Flock congregations, speaking and training, especially in the areas of children's activities. It is worth noting that these international Christian networks are not unique to the Little Flock. Many Chinese Christian churches in the United States, Hong Kong, and Taiwan regularly send delegations to Chinese house churches to preach, deliver religious educational material, and distribute financial assistance.

Difficult Christians: The Home of Grace

Another indigenous strand of Chinese Protestantism with deep roots in the Fuzhou area, the Home of Grace, has regularly fallen outside the state's definition of orthodoxy and run into conflict with religious and public security authorities. The Home of Grace bases its theology and practice on the teachings of the famous Fuzhounese evangelist John Sung (Song Shangjie: 1901–1944). After Sung's death, his followers spread out around China to establish training centers to continue Sung's unique methods of Bible study, his ardent call to repentance of sin, and his emphasis on daily devotional prayer. Mrs. Dong, who had studied with Sung during his final years of life in Beijing, established a center in Fuzhou city in 1945, quickly attracting many followers, including Mrs. He of the Changle area. After 1949, Mrs. Dong and Mrs. He moved the Home of Grace to Changle and continued their work in the tradition of John Sung until, unwilling to participate in the newly established Three-Self Patriotic Movement and charged with being counterrevolutionaries, they were stopped by the Communists during the 1950s.

John Sung was born into a poor family in a small village outside the town of Hinghua, four hundred miles south of Fuzhou. His father was a Methodist minister in this area, heavily influenced by American Methodist missionaries, and a leader in the Methodist work that included churches, an orphanage, boys' and girls' high schools, and Bible schools for men and women. Reportedly an impetuous and brilliant young man, by age thirteen John Sung was traveling with his father and preaching in the towns and villages of Fujian Province. Trained in the Methodist schools in Hinghua, he was encouraged by a woman missionary to attend Ohio Wesleyan University (OWU). There he completed a bachelor's degree, a master's of science, and a Ph.D. in physics and chemistry between 1919 and 1926. Relentless in his studies and working full time to support himself, Sung also found time to engage in certain social causes of the time, including efforts to challenge racial discrimination in university policy and U.S. law through the OWU International Students Association.

Sung graduated with honors from OWU. Both the prestigious Yenjing University in Beijing and Harvard University offered him positions. But still unclear about his career path, Sung accepted a scholarship to study religion at Union Theological Seminary in New York, home to many of the major figures in the "social gospel movement," for example, scholars such as Henry

Sloan Coffin, Harry Emerson Fosdick, and Henry Van Deusen. The social gospel movement emphasized the Christian scriptures' call to a life fully engaged in the social issues of the time. Sung immersed himself in his studies and in his personal search, much as he did at OWU. His inquiries took him far afield from his mission-church beginnings. At one point he translated the *Dao De Jing* into English and spent significant time exploring Eastern religious texts and traditions. But he was not satisfied by these pursuits. In February 1927, as his biographer Leslie Lyall (1964 [1954]) reports, Sung had a spiritual awakening and returned to his early Christian roots, which were sunk deeply in the soil of personal piety, prayer, and Bible study. The next day he burned his class lecture notes and his theological books as "books of demons." He began fervently to call upon his fellow students and teachers to repent of their sins and return to the true God. Fosdick, then president of Union, fearing Sung was mentally destabilized from years of intensive study, convinced him to accept admittance to a sanitarium for psychopathic patients. There he stayed for six months, much of the time against his will, until he was finally released under the condition that he would return immediately to China. This he did, throwing his American diplomas, medals, awards, and fraternity keys into the sea as his ship approached the China coast.

In later years Sung would recall the six months in the sanitarium as having profoundly shaped his religious beliefs and practices. His mental hospital had become a theological college, he said. He read the Bible more than forty times beginning to end. With direct guidance from God, he developed his trademark form of Bible study. Called "turning the wheel" (*zhuan lunzi*) it calls for reading eleven chapters a day and is based on the theory that all the chapters of the Old Testament find a counterpart in the chapters of the New Testament.

After returning to China, Sung devoted himself to itinerant revival preaching and became one of the foremost evangelists of his generation in China. His preaching style, which some have compared to U.S. evangelist Billy Sunday, was theatrical. Sung would dash from side to side on the stage, sweating profusely, sometimes jumping into the congregation to exhort his listeners, at times standing atop the communion rail to drive home his points. His message at revival meetings challenged his listeners to experience the life-changing power of the Holy Spirit, to repent of their sinful ways, to engage in daily Bible study using his method, and to practice fervent daily prayer. He placed an emphasis on family, home-based worship and suggested organizationally dividing village churches into groups of ten for mutual support. In the 1930s, as war with Japan made evangelistic work in China more difficult, Sung made seven trips to southern Asia to conduct revivals among overseas Chinese from Fujian and Guangdong. His stops included Taiwan, Hong Kong, the Philippines, Singapore, Malaysia, Indonesia, Borneo, Thailand, and Vietnam, where he was particularly welcomed by overseas Fujianese.

Sung's charismatic performances inspired audiences by their energy and vitality. In contrast, his daily adult life was beset by a series of physical ailments, ranging from boils to cholera to trachoma to heart problems. Suffering from a debilitatingly painful hip, his doctors sent Sung to Beijing's leading hospital for treatment in 1941. There he was diagnosed with tuberculosis and cancer. After surgery, he remained in Beijing, settling in the Western Hills, also known as the Fragrant Mountains, to convalesce. In these last years of his life Sung realized that his peripatetic evangelism had not been enough. One night he dreamed that God warned him that he could not reach everyone by himself. He would need to train others to spread the Word. And so in the Western Hills of Beijing he established the Home of Grace, supported by a leading industrialist from Tianjin who had been converted through Song's preaching. His followers came from across China to study and train, some for short periods, others for long. They prayed, turned the wheel in Bible study, and discussed the needs of the church in China.

After Sung's death in 1944 those who had been with him in Beijing spread out across the country to continue his work. But over the ensuing years many ran afoul of the new government and its religious policies. Among Sung's students and strongest supporters were many from well-off industrialist families who sided with the Nationalist cause in the emerging civil war. For instance, Mrs. Dong, who launched the Fuzhou Home of Grace, was the wife of a high-ranking Nationalist government official. As a result, after 1949, they quickly came under close scrutiny as potential counterrevolutionaries. In addition, like many evangelical Protestants of the time, members of the Home of Grace distrusted the atheism espoused by the Communist Party. Their skepticism led to resistance of the Communist-backed TSPM and refusal to cooperate with the efforts of the government's Religious Affairs Bureau.

According to one Home of Grace longtime leader who, as a teenager, was with John Sung in Beijing:

> *By the early 1950s, after the Communists arrived, because of issues of purity, holiness, and faithfulness, we could not participate in the Communists' Three-Self Movement. For this reason—faith—we kept separate, and the Home of Grace was shut down. The significant leaders and workers were all arrested and imprisoned.*

In Fuzhou, Mrs. Dong's student, Mrs. He, died in prison in 1969 after being in and out of detention for fifteen years on charges of being a counterrevolutionary. Her student, Sister Jiang, was incarcerated in 1975 for six years on similar charges and for conducting unauthorized religious services.

Though the work of the Home of Grace has resumed in a number of places in China, including Changle, where a unique relationship existed with the TSPM in the 1980s and early 1990s, the scars of the earlier period barely mask the deep wounds of John Sung's followers. Skepticism of Home of Grace leaders toward the government and the TSPM is still palpable. According to one senior leader now in the United States, interviewed in 2000:

> *Now some of our older leaders have come out of China after many years of imprisonment. Others are out of prison, but still in China. Our numbers in China are not few. But there is no formal/official work. Because of Three-Self. Because of the Communist system there is no way to formally reopen the Home of Grace in China. There is no way to compromise with the Communists without losing our faith. So our brothers and sisters have dispersed across China to continue the work of spreading our methods of Bible study and prayer that were developed on Xiang Shan outside Beijing and to help churches love God and study and follow God's own word in the Bible.*

Rev. Liu Yangfen and the Cultural Revolution

With the outbreak of the Cultural Revolution in 1966, all public religious expressions, whether Protestant, Catholic, Buddhist, Daoist, or popular, were terminated, whether they were manifested in officially registered churches and temples or not. Many religious leaders, both clergy and lay, were targeted for persecution and reform. The story of Rev. Liu Yangfen, who plays a central role in the story of Fuzhounese Protestants in New York, serves as an example of the experiences of many Christians during this period. In 1946 Rev. Liu, a second-generation Christian, was sent by the

Methodist mission board in Fuzhou to Vanderbilt University, a Methodist school in Nashville, Tennessee, to study hospital administration. At the time, more than thirty mission hospitals in Fujian Province were intending to centralize their administration and coordinate their services. Liu was expected to head up the work. Returning to Fuzhou in 1949, exactly two weeks before the Communist forces "liberated" the city from the Nationalists, Liu soon turned from hospital administration to pursue his sense of calling to the ministry, eventually serving as the senior pastor of the Flower Lane Church in downtown Fuzhou until it was closed in 1966.

Liu came under constant criticism for his connection to the foreign missionaries and his studies abroad, not to mention his commitment to Protestant Christianity. One night a group of young people, Red Guards, ransacked the library at the Flower Lane Church, piling all the church's books as well as Liu's in the courtyard and setting them ablaze. Liu, donning a dunce cap, was forced to kneel in front of the fire until the hair on his head and face was singed off. Later he was sent to the mountains in northwest Fujian for labor "reeducation." There he worked with rural farmers, serving as their "barefoot" doctor. Only in 1979 was he "rehabilitated" and allowed to return to Fuzhou to reopen Flower Lane Church.

From 1979 to 1985 Liu worked tirelessly to reopen churches throughout the Fuzhou area, restarting the provincial seminary in Flower Lane Church and traveling widely in the area to assist churches in reclaiming buildings from the government and training new leaders for their congregations. In 1985, Liu left Fuzhou. His daughter, born in Nashville during his student days, had left Fuzhou via Hong Kong in the late 1970s and established citizenship in the United States. Liu followed her to New York, where in recent years he has been a central figure in the emergence of both Fuzhounese Protestant congregations. His spiritual biography has had a particularly sanctifying effect, which has proven to be a key to his ability to bridge the theological chasms that have been transplanted from Fuzhou to New York, particularly between Little Flock Christians and other Protestants.

Despite the intense persecution of religion during the Cultural Revolution, religious belief and expression did not cease; they simply went underground. During these years when public worship in churches was precluded, house churches grew rapidly. Protestants and Catholics gathered secretly in darkened living rooms for prayer and Bible study. Without access to clergy or formal institutions, local lay Christians quietly organized themselves to continue their ritual practices. Today many Chinese Christians look back on those years of suffering as a time of tremendous spiritual and numerical growth, as molten steel is forged in a crucible. Or, in Rev. Liu's words:

We were like roots of bamboo buried in the earth, not dead, but awaiting our time to spring back to life.

Post-1979 Revival

The Third Plenum of the Eleventh Communist Party Congress, held in December 1978, restored China's policy of freedom of religious belief after more than twelve years of suppression. This party congress, which also launched Deng Xiaoping's economic reform program, began the process of condemning "leftist errors" made during the Cultural Revolution, including that era's total repudiation of the Chinese Communist Party's "correct religious policy" (MacInnis 1989: 3). Restrictions on religious practice relaxed almost immediately, though the process was gradual as religious believers and government officials began to experiment with the new policies. By the end of 1979, thirteen Protestant churches had reopened in China. Four of them were in Fujian Province, including the first one in Xiamen in August.

In October 1979, Rev. Liu's Flower Lane Church became the first church to reopen in Fuzhou. With only one building open, all of Fuzhou's denominations worshipped there for a period of time, though many of them held separate services to preserve their distinctive theology and practice. Starting in the late 1970s, many who had been imprisoned or sent to rural areas for labor reeducation were released from prison and returned to their homes. Catholic bishop Zheng Changcheng of Fuzhou, an ardent Vatican loyalist, was released after twenty-nine years. Church properties confiscated and occupied for other uses were gradually returned to religious organizations, often with financial compensation for damages done or time occupied. In Fuzhou, as in the rest of China, Protestant denominations retained their particular ritual and organizational characteristics but ceased to formally identify themselves as such, falling instead under the institutional umbrella of the TSPM. The Fujian Provincial Protestant Seminary was reopened, first at Flower Lane Church and later on its original campus. Churches, both Protestant and Catholic, began to fill with parishioners beyond their seating capacities, spilling into outdoor courtyards and into neighboring streets.

After 1979 the state began the arduous process of reestablishing the religious and political infrastructure to administer the large network of religious organizations and activities that was beginning to emerge. A new national constitution, adopted in 1982, included Article 36 on religious freedom. Document 19, "the most definitive statement of religion and religious policy ever issued by the Chinese Communist Party" (MacInnis 1989: 2) was circulated to party and state cadres across the country and to the various levels of the Religious Affairs Bureau. These policy statements established the legal foundation for religious tolerance. The new religious policies seemed driven by a realization that with the launching of economic reform and opening, restrictions on religion of the earlier era could not continue. Attempts to completely and strictly control or eliminate religion would only drive it further underground.

Registration of Religious Organizations and Sites

Christianity grew rapidly during the 1980s and 1990s. Protestants, for instance, reported opening one new church every day in China over the period. In Fujian Province, by early 2001 there were 1,500 registered churches and another 2,500 official meeting points. But just as reforms made local economic and social events less manageable for the Chinese government, so too the rapid growth of religious groups made it more difficult to monitor and administer the religious scene, particularly its explosion of church, temple, and ancestral hall construction. Beginning in the late 1980s and culminating in 1994, the state implemented a series of policies requiring the registration and approval of all religious organizations and sites. In order to qualify for registration, religious groups, regardless of their faith tradition, were required to meet several conditions:

1. There must be a designated meeting site and name.
2. There must be believers who regularly participate.
3. There must be an administrative structure set up by the believers.
4. There must be a clearly designated religious worker in charge of the activities or appropriate staff as required by the religion.
5. There must be rules and regulations for management.
6. There must be a legal means of financial income.

In addition, the guidelines required three sets of material:

1. An application for establishing a religious activity site.
2. A certificate proving ownership of the site.
3. Support of the local government.

Perhaps most problematic is the requirement that Protestant and Catholic religious sites register through the TSPM or CCPA unless there is none in the locality, in which case they may register directly with the Religious Affairs Bureau or with the local police.

The implementation of this policy has been extremely controversial, both within China and abroad. Both Protestants and Catholics have significant numbers of members who on political and theological grounds refuse to cooperate with the state-sanctioned religious structures. Over the past twenty years, observers outside and inside China often use the terminology of "open church" and "underground church" to distinguish Protestants and Catholics who cooperate with the government and those who resist cooperation and control. In reality the dichotomy is not so clear. There is in fact a continuum of opinions and expressions. In addition, the implementation of state religious policy is not monolithic. Rather, it tends to be mediated by church-state relations in each locality.

The new registration system places additional pressure on Christians to comply with government policies and guidelines or risk falling outside the state's legal framework. But significant diversity exists among both the registered and unregistered groups:

- Not all "house churches" are "underground." Registered congregations may meet in church buildings or in house meetings. Registered house meetings are usually associated with a nearby church and are physically clustered around it. Their activities and leadership are determined by that "mother" church.
- Registered congregations may participate fully in the state-authorized religious structures such as the Protestant TSPM or the Catholic Patriotic Association or they may participate infrequently, only as required, or only as necessary to protect their own interests.

Diversity also exists among unregistered congregations, particularly in their relationship to the state religious and security apparatus:

- Some operate openly, with full knowledge and tacit approval of the local Religious Affairs Bureau or the Public Security Administration officials. They encounter interference only when issues of public safety or public nuisance arise, for instance when too many people attend activities or the activities become too noisy and neighbors complain.
- Some unregistered congregations operate more quietly, seeking to avoid state management and interference or engagement of any kind with the state apparatus.
- Some unregistered congregations operate in direct conflict with and open defiance of the state, resisting state mandates and conducting activities clandestinely to avoid arrest and detention.

While government officials argue that registration serves to protect the Chinese people from unscrupulous religious leaders and con men, many Christians see the regulations as a framework for cracking down on religious groups out of favor with the government.

> By enshrining the administrative mechanism of registration in the spate of religious laws passed since the late 1980s, the Chinese state has provided itself the legal means to suppress unregistered Protestant activities while simultaneously insisting to the world that "no-one in China is punished because of his or her religious belief"—only for breaking the law. (Dunch 2001: 196)

In an attempt to draw more local groups into the registration process, new regulations are being circulated which propose a change so that unregistered churches and meeting points can register directly with the Religious Affairs Bureau and avoid registration and control from the patriotic movements.

In essence, the regulations on registration of religious organizations and locations define heresy in political rather than doctrinal terms. Religious activities outside the registration system are most likely not orthodox in the eyes of the state. And so the registration system provides a powerful tool for the government as it continues its attempts to enforce a sense of order vis-à-vis potential chaos and promote its ideas of orthodoxy over heterodoxy.

Catholics, the Vatican, and the Chinese State

Relations between China's Catholics and the state have been particularly vitriolic in recent years. Contestation of authority to consecrate bishops and clergy is one example. The Chinese Catholic Patriotic Association continues to do so without approval from the Vatican. The Vatican in turn secretly designates and ordains bishops in China, some of whom travel quietly to Hong Kong for the ceremonies. The result in much of China is parallel Catholic structures. In Changle the number of underground Catholics, priests, and churches far surpasses those related to the Patriotic Association. Each group has its own bishop. And while members of the two sides may know one another, they do not cooperate. In fact, levels of animosity and distrust run high, particularly between the unregistered churches and the Patriotic Association churches.

In the 1990s the unregistered congregations have become more confrontational, challenging government restrictions on construction of new churches and on public displays of piety. In the Fuzhou area, and in many places across China, a great number of churches, both Protestant and Catholic, have been newly erected without government authorization. Many of these in the Changle area have been built relying heavily on remittances from members working in the United States. All have been built in plain view of local government authorities. In the rural areas around Changle, Catholics—sometimes thousands strong—conduct open-air worship and baptisms, often in the middle of the night, despite government prohibition.

As unregistered congregations across China have become more aggressive, the Chinese government has become more repressive. Catholic priests and bishops are frequently detained and sometimes tortured (Human Rights Watch 1997). Recent reports from Changle County (Langfitt 2000) confirm that nearly twenty "underground" Catholic churches, built without government permission, were demolished by the authorities in 1999 alone. While some reports suggest that this may be part of a larger government effort to curb the illegal construction of religious edifices, many Catholics see it as a direct expression of the state's efforts to repress Catholicism in China. Although the Vatican and the Chinese government have engaged recently in secret negotiations to normalize relations, there has been no agreement on the Vatican's desire to reestablish its hierarchical control over Chinese Catholic institutions (Madsen 2001).

Three Instances of Protestant Proliferation in the Greater Fuzhou Region

Fuzhou City and its surrounding towns and villages are home to a rich diversity of religious expression. Three instances of Protestant proliferation reflect both the dramatic effects of economic, political, and religious reforms since 1979 and also the effects of recent infusions of remittances from Fuzhounese immigrants in the United States. Three strands of Protestantism are portrayed in these instances: TSPM related, Little Flock, and the Home of Grace, all of which are heavily represented in New York's Fuzhounese churches. The following descriptions illuminate the origins of theological and political divisions that have emerged so strongly halfway around the world.

Kangzhuang Protestant (Little Flock) Church, founded in 1937, and Peace Protestant (Anglican) Church, established in 1918, are located in Tingjiang, about thirty-five miles east of Fuzhou on the northern bank of the Min River. The different histories, politics, and theologies of these two congregations in this emigrant area reflect how the current moment of religious expansion is highly conflictive, with pre–Cultural Revolution and even pre-1949 fault lines forcefully reemerging as if they were a permanent substrate of Christianity in China.

The Houyu Protestant (Little Flock) Church on the southern bank of the Min, is directly across the river from Tingjiang. A ferry runs between them and as a result the Houyu and Tingjiang Little Flock churches have regular interaction. The development of the Houyu church, also in an emigrant community, provides further insight into the powerful role played by remittances in Fuzhou's emerging religious landscape and the strong connections between Fuzhounese Christians in New York City and their home communities in China.

The Home of Grace, located south of Changle to the southeast of Fuzhou, is an unofficial training center and network of churches. It traces its history, to the Fuzhounese evangelist John Sung, and its recent experiences offer a fascinating study of the complexity of relationships between Protestant Christians and the Chinese state.

Tingjiang

Protestant mission work in the Fuzhou area and northern Fujian Province in the nineteenth and early twentieth centuries was divided among three groups—the Church Missionary Society (Anglican—*Shenggong Hui*), the American Board of Commissioners for Foreign Missions (ABCFM; Congregationalist and other Reformed traditions, which later merged to become the *Zhonghua Jidujiao Hui*), and the Methodist Episcopal Church (American—*Mei yi Mei Weili Gonghui*)—as part of a comity agreement between major missionary groups in China. Since their founding in Fuzhou in the 1840s, these three missions had established extensive networks of churches, schools, hospitals, and other social service agencies throughout the region. The Methodists focused to the west of Fuzhou, up the Min River to Minqing and Shaowu and south to Putian and Fuqing. The ABCFM worked to the southeast. The Anglicans focused on the Min River Valley to the east of Fuzhou and the coastal region to the north. This included the towns of Mawei, Minan, Tingjiang, Guantou, and Lianjiang County on the northern banks and, to a lesser extent, Changle County to the south.

The Tingjiang Peace Protestant Church, located on a small rise in the center of town, was founded in 1918 by the Anglican Diocese of Fuzhou. Anglican missionaries, as they extended their work down river from their base in Fuzhou City, reached Tingjiang by boat because there were no roads in the area. In the 1950s the Tingjiang Anglican Church became a member of the TSPM and, following the three-self principles, was required to manage independently of foreign support for the first time. The congregation continued to meet until the extreme religious persecution of the Cultural Revolution. Sister Chen, who died in 1998 at the age of 101, served as the church's evangelist for much of its history. Her daughter-in-law, also named Chen, followed her in this role. During the Cultural Revolution their home was ransacked more than ten times. The church was converted into a factory producing chopsticks and other eating implements, reopening for worship only in 1984.

On the western edge of Tingjiang stands the Kangzhuang Protestant Church, a beautiful new three-story sanctuary that seats nearly five hundred people next to a five-story education building and dormitory. Though officially registered with the government, this congregation draws a sharp distinction between itself and the Anglican Church and maintains a strong independence from the TSPM. Kangzhuang aligns itself with the Little Flock tradition described earlier in this chapter.

Kangzhuang Church traces its origins to Sister Lin Peijin, a third-generation Anglican, who was so inspired by an evangelistic crusade by Dr. John Sung in Fuzhou that she decided to combine her training as a midwife with work as an evangelist. In 1937 she moved to Tingjiang and opened a small health clinic. Congregational lore recalls how she served Tingjiang and the surrounding territories, often traveling up into the nearby mountains to deliver a child. And everywhere she went she preached the Gospel. Sister Lin began a Christian group at her health clinic. Evangelists and other lay people from Fuzhou's Little Flock, many of them women, came to help her. Together they formed a house church that met until the Cultural Revolution began in 1966. After 1966 they met clandestinely in homes. In 1970 Sister Lin was arrested for her activities and imprisoned for eleven years. She was released from prison after the reforms of 1979 and the congregation resumed meeting. House-church meetings in her home in the early 1980s regularly drew more than one hundred people. Still uncertain of the extent to which religious freedom would be honored by the state, the congregation secretly baptized believers in a pond at the back of the village.

As reforms continued on economic, political, and religious fronts, the local government returned the old Anglican church building to Tingjiang's Christians in 1984. Anglican and Little Flock members shared this building until 1994, when political and theological differences between the two groups boiled over. The flash point was Christmas. As biblical literalists, the Little Flock do not celebrate the festivals or holidays often associated with Christian tradition elsewhere, including Christmas and Easter, because they do not have specific biblical precedents. They consider these to be European cultural adaptations imposed on the core biblical message and ultimately distractions from serious piety. The Anglicans strongly disagreed and desired to celebrate Christmas as they had done in the past.

In a split oddly prescient of a split among Fuzhounese Protestants in New York several years later, the Little Flock group broke away from the Anglicans and sought permission from the local Religious Affairs Bureau to buy a new piece of land and build their own church. In an attempt to resolve this seemingly intractable conflict, the government agreed to allow them to build but would not allocate land for the construction. The Little Flock leadership cobbled together plots of privately owned farmland on the west side of town just off the newly constructed main highway from Fuzhou to Lianjiang.

Sister Lin dreamed of seeing the church finished before her death, and church members in Tingjiang and the large number of members abroad rallied to the cause. Church members built the sanctuary with their own labor on weekends and evenings. Even visitors returning home from New York put in a few days on the site. Some days as many as one hundred people worked together. Money poured in from former parishioners now in America, some directly, much of it through family members remaining in Tingjiang. Altogether $200,000 was raised. The building was finished in January 1996. Sister Lin died later that year at age eighty-six.

The Tingjiang Anglican Church also sought permission to build a new church, and construction was completed in November 1998 on the original Anglican church property. According to Evangelist Chen, daughter-in-law of the original evangelist, unlike the Little Flock church, most of the $60,000 for construction came from within China, not from overseas. "Each individual in the congregation contributed as they were able. Then I went to other public churches in the area for help." She utilized the network of churches associated with Three-Self Patriotic Movement. Each supporting congregation contributed the offerings from one week toward the cost of the new church building in Tingjiang. Reflecting the continuing existence of the old denominational identities in the area, Ms. Chen specifically targeted former Anglican churches for support. Many responded positively. At the opening ceremonies, the new sanctuary was filled with representatives from TSPM-related churches throughout the area, including eighteen ordained ministers, an extraordinary number in a region chronically short of ordained clergy.

DIFFERENCES IN RITUAL AND POLITY

Both churches continue active ministries despite Tingjiang's massive outmigration. At the Kangzhuang Church, worship begins before 7:30 Sunday morning. The first hour is filled with hymns, prayers said simultaneously, and finally communion. The second hour is reserved for preaching the word. The sanctuary is filled with nearly three hundred people this Sunday. Seventy-five percent of the congregants are women who fill the left-hand section of the church pews as well as the left half of the right section. All men, with the exception of two, sit on the far right. Nearly half the women cover their heads with a black netted hair covering, called a *mentou*, in conformity to Paul's urging in Corinthians. Those present are primarily older and younger, with few between twenty and forty years old, reflecting Tingjiang's recent pattern of outmigration. The sanctuary is unadorned. No cross is displayed, according to Little Flock tradition.

Communion, called *bai bing hui*, is considered to be central to Little Flock worship. This Sunday, as every Sunday, unleavened flat bread is passed among parishioners on silver plates, each person breaking off his or her own piece. Homemade grape wine is then circulated in a clear glass mug followed by a bowl of plastic spoons and an empty basket. Each person chooses a spoon, dips it in the cup, drinks the juice and returns the used spoon to the basket. Communion is served by men and women lay leaders. Little Flock congregations have no ordained clergy. Rather, leadership of the congregation is coordinated by an unpaid group of brothers and sisters with one brother often serving as the first among equals. The leadership team is mostly older. All have at least one relative in New York.

In addition to Sunday worship services and weekly Bible studies, prayer meetings, and a sizable youth/young adult group, the congregation serves as a resource center for work in the surrounding areas, a variation on the Little Flock principle of local church independence. Once a month, Little Flock members from other churches gather at Kangzhuang for meetings. Kangzhuang's lay leaders regularly travel to other places, including the Little Flock stronghold on Langqi Island, to lead services. Relationships with congregations of the southern banks of the Min River, like Houyu, are also strong.

Kangzhuang's worship and organization reflect general patterns within the Little Flock tradition. Other common characteristics include the practice of adult baptism by full body immersion. They reject denominationalism. Each church exists independently of other congregations. There is a strong antagonism toward or at least skepticism about the authenticity of the Three-Self Patriotic Movement's related churches and leaders. Little Flock churches tend to emphasize their correct path to salvation over and against others'. One Little Flock leader in Fuzhou said, "Some of our members go to the public churches to see their old friends. But we don't trust those churches to really preach the Gospel."

Worship attendance at the Anglican church averaged over one hundred people after the new building was finished, but has slipped to around seventy because of Tingjiang's massive outmigration. In total, thirty of the seventy-five families have left for America.

Comparing the theology and politics of her church to a Little Flock church, Evangelist Chen says,

Their worship is different. Women wear head coverings. They don't have a cross in the church. They think that if you have a cross it is an idol. Their communion is different from our Anglican communion. They don't need a minister to serve communion. A Brother is enough. They pray. They sing. They pray. Then they take communion. In the Anglican church we need a minister. We always have a minister—usually from

Fuzhou—come to serve communion the first Sunday of every month. Not even an evangelist can do it. It's very different.

After liberation all the churches worked together under the Three-Self. But the Christian Assemblies (Little Flock) are different. We love our country and love our church (aiguo, aijiao). They just love their church. According to the Bible there should be mutual respect and love. But they say if you come here with us you will be saved. If you go over there to the Anglican church you won't be saved.

Evangelist Chen expresses deep disappointment in the animosity and distrust between Little Flock and TSPM-related churches.

Tingjiang's Christian Assembly (Little Flock) doesn't recognize the Three-Self Patriotic Movement. And some in the Christian Assemblies are focused on undermining the public churches. They say, "Oh, there's no one going to church over there. They don't have any life or vitality. If you come here you will be saved. If you go there you won't." All the Christian Assemblies in Fuzhou are like this, criticizing the public churches. We've all suffered for our faith in China. How can they talk that way?

THE TINGJIANG—NEW YORK CONNECTION

While the Anglican congregation drew heavily on local TSPM-related support for its rebuilding project, the church is deeply embedded in the flow of immigrants—their ideas and resources—between China and the United States. Evangelist Chen herself emigrated to New York with her husband in 1999, leaving her family's church in the hands of a recent graduate of the Protestant seminary in Fuzhou. Ms. Chen's six children all preceded her to the United States, the first coming in 1984, and have opened restaurants in the New York area. She attends the Church of Grace, one of the two Fuzhounese Protestant congregations in New York's Chinatown, a choice clearly driven by theological and political factors.

We went over to the New York House Church on Market Street. We went once. But for them, House Church means Christian Assembly [Little Flock]. At first I thought it was just a house church, not related to the Christian Assembly. But it is clearly Christian Assembly. So I haven't gone back.

One Sunday at the Church of Grace in New York, Evangelist Chen withdrew from her bag an artist's rendering of a new church being built in Mawei—also of Anglican origins and just upriver from Tingjiang—beautifully reproduced in color on small wallet-sized cards with the church's address printed on the back.

The Mawei church is rebuilding. They have raised a good bit of money but are hoping to raise more. Altogether $250,000. I often went there to preach, sometimes twice a month. So when they found out we were coming to New York they asked us to help spread the word among people here about their project. They asked us to encourage people we meet to contribute money and send it to them. We can't take the money, but you can send it directly. Here's the name and address.

Upon arriving in the United States, Evangelist Chen and her husband immediately applied for green cards.

After we get our green cards I want to be able to go back and forth between New York and Tingjiang. My family is here. I haven't seen them in many years. But no one is there in Tingjiang. One by one the people are leaving to be with their families. So long as I am able to move about I will go back and forth to help with the church. When I can't move about anymore, then I will stay here in the United States with my children.

Little Flock in Houyu

A short ferry ride across the Min River, and clearly visible from Tingjiang, stands the imposing five-story Houyu Protestant Church, another Little Flock congregation, built against a steep hillside and rising above the farmland on the southern littoral of the Min River Valley. Like many towns and villages in the area, Houyu is an emigrant community having sent most of its working-age population to the United States. Houyu residents estimate that there are two thousand town members remaining and five thousand in America. Most of the migration occurred in the 1990s, creating tremendous social dislocation. The Houyu church represents yet another example of the remarkable contributions immigrants are making to the religious proliferation and diversification in the Fuzhou region.

FIGURE 8 Houyu Protestant Church.

The Houyu church traces its origins directly to missionary Margaret Barber, who visited the area with two Chinese evangelists in the late 1910s. There were no Christians in Houyu at the time. Mrs. Li Jiande's grandmother was the first convert.

My grandmother, she was possessed by a demon and made very sick till she almost died. It was very serious. My grandfather was a man of great education. He was a Chinese doctor. In that generation he was considered very smart. And my grandfather was able to do spirit possession. He had cured many people's illnesses. But he was not able to heal my grandmother.

There were three evangelists who came to Houyu. One of them was our very famous He Shou'en (M. E. Barber). From England. And two other Chinese. They came down the river to Houyu to evangelize. They sang hymns. They went all over walking the roads healing people and casting out demons. They came to our house and cast out my grandmother's demon. The three evangelists said tomorrow is Sunday. Jesus is risen from the dead. He can cast out demons and heal the sick. We will help you pray. If you believe, then tomorrow you will arise and walk. Really. Sunday they prayed. And Sunday she was healed. They stayed in her house for two or three days, maybe many days, teaching her how to pray, how to study the Bible, how to sing hymns, how to believe in Jesus. Ever since, the church in Houyu has been in my family's home.

This is the history of the Houyu church. Today there are many Christians there. From the beginning the church was in my family's home. Even during the Cultural Revolution during the most severe repression it was in my grandmother's house. She was persecuted terribly. There was no freedom. There was no way to have meetings during the day. Only at night. I remember this. I was still at home during the Cultural Revolution.

Li Jiande emigrated from Houyu in 1979 following her husband who had established residency in New York after more than twenty years as a sailor in Hong Kong. The house church meetings resumed in Li's family home in Houyu until they could not fit any more people. In 1989 the congregation contacted Li in New York. They had received permission from the local authorities to build a new church, but they needed financial support from their fellow townspeople in the United States. Says Li:

There was me. And there was another woman who has just gone back. We organized the brothers and sisters from Houyu. I was in charge of receiving the money and sending the money. She was in charge of making the contacts (lian-luo). We collected tens of thousands of dollars. Then there were many families in Houyu, the husband was here working, the wife was still at home in Houyu, sons in America, parents at home. They all contributed. Also many of the young people in China contributed their labor. We built the church ourselves. Now it wouldn't be possible. So many people have left in the 1990s. Now the church is just children and old people. The sanctuary seats five hundred people. When we first built it, it was full. But only one hundred attend regularly now. Houyu people in the U.S. are so plentiful. Very few are left at home. I don't know what the future will hold for our church.

The Home of Grace

The teachings of the evangelist John Sung continue to be propagated in the Fuzhou area and across China through networks of Christians associated with the Home of Grace. As described earlier, one Home of Grace training center reopened south of Changle in 1981, though without official sanction.

Its story of rapid expansion in the 1980s and 1990s and its abrupt closing by public security officials in 1998 reflect the tenuous existence of unregistered religious organizations that insist on operating outside the mainstream of religious orthodoxy and government authority.

Leaders of the Home of Grace suffered relentless persecution during the 1950s as a result of their connections to the Nationalist government and their reluctance to cooperate with the government authorized TSPM. Like other Christians, during the Cultural Revolution, their activities were completely suppressed. Big Sister Jiang, among the third generation of leaders at the Changle Home of Grace, was incarcerated in 1975 for conducting unauthorized religious activities.

After Jiang's release from prison in 1981 she returned to the Changle area to reopen the Home of Grace. As in its predecessor center in Beijing in the early 1940s, lay Christians, mostly women, would gather from churches across the Changle area and then return to work in the churches before going back for further study. The most ardent followers would commit to a two-year course. During the second year, people went out to work in the house churches and then returned to continue their training. Most of the work was conducted in Changle's rural areas, both in registered churches and in unregistered house meetings.

The work of the training center in Changle continued to grow steadily in the 1980s and early 1990s, drawing heavily on the volunteer leadership of dedicated women. For much of the time they were able to maintain an awkward yet sustainable relationship with government authorities, many of whom were willing to turn a blind eye to their activities. In this regard, religious and public security officials in Fujian Province and the Fuzhou area have been more lenient than those in interior areas of China. The large number of Christians who were immigrating to New York and returning remittances to the area also made local officials less willing to interfere.

Relationships between the Home of Grace and the local registered TSPM-related church became deeply intertwined as townsfolk often participated in the activities of both. The light hand of local religious authorities in applying government regulations allowed local Christians to support both without fear of retribution or pressure to take sides. In fact, relationships between the two groups were so open and positive that in 1984 one of the key younger fourth-generation leaders of the Home of Grace was appointed by the Changle TSPM to serve as pastor in charge of the local church, creating a unique opportunity for the programmatic and theological integration of an unregistered Christian training center with an official

TSPM-related church. In 1994, when the possibility emerged of rebuilding the church, Home of Grace members contributed significantly. Over the next several years a towering new sanctuary was built with two balconies. In the basement a social hall could seat five hundred. In the rear a dormitory was constructed with room for several hundred overnight guests. In the years that followed many Home of Grace activities were held in the church's facilities. Special revival meetings and Bible studies were held at Chinese New Year, Pentecost, and for worker training sessions. Participants would come from across the Changle area and beyond, staying in the church's dormitory and eating in the social hall for days or even a week at a time. At the height of its success, during a TSPM national conference held in Fuzhou on rural church development, official delegates traveled to the church and celebrated its accomplishments as a model to be replicated across the country.

Despite this unique opportunity, today the Home of Grace stands empty, its leaders disbanded and its evangelists scattered throughout the Changle region. The expansive new local church and its facilities are largely unused, except for a greatly diminished Sunday morning worship service. Conflicts of personality and power developed over time between two women leaders of the Home of Grace. Their separate power centers had exacerbated the situation. One had taken leadership of the local TSPM-related church in 1984 and overseen its rapid expansion and extensive rebuilding program. The other had successfully established an unregistered house church in her home in 1986 in the center of Changle City.

In April 1998 intense jealousies and a simmering power struggle between the two women erupted into open conflict, spreading across the Changle region as Christians took sides with one or the other. Complaints were lodged with the religious and government authorities. Activities were disrupted. The furor rose to such a pitch that the Public Security Administration was unable to ignore it and intervened to insure public safety.

In rural areas across China, including Changle, the ability to exorcise demons (*gan gui*) is seen as a sign of being blessed by the power of God's Holy Spirit. Healing and exorcism have been one of the primary means Chinese Christians have utilized to compete with the power of local Chinese religious spirit mediums and assert the superiority of Christianity. Within the Christian community the gift of exorcism reflects a leader's power, purity, and direct connection to God.

During the Chinese New Year festival in early 1998, a young woman from the town where the Home of Grace is located developed mental problems. Her father and older brother had recently been killed by a man fired from

the family's company. Her husband was in America, working. She was to-
tally bereft and needed support. The problems became most serious in
April, and the woman went to the Home of Grace seeking comfort and healing. The underlying tensions between the two women leaders came to the
fore as each attempted to exorcise the woman's demons. Each had her own
style and method. And each claimed superiority over the other. Charges of
heresy were made between the two women. Their followers lined up to support one and criticize the other. The conflict continued to escalate over several months, involving more and more people in public and private recrim-
inations, until finally on August 16 the Public Security Administration
raided the Home of Grace, shut down its work, and confiscated John Sung's
books, declaring Sung's teachings heterodox. The one young woman was removed from leadership of the local TSPM-related church.

Despite these problems, the work of the Home of Grace continues to
grow, and the two women continue to train evangelists and guide house
churches throughout the region. But in a sign of the complicated relationship between church and state, the two women operate under extremely different conditions and limitations. One continues to operate her house
church in Changle City, holding daily predawn Bible studies that draw between thirty and forty participants and Sunday worship services of over one
hundred. Local government and religious officials are fully aware of her unregistered house church and its role as a center for Home of Grace evangelists, but rarely interfere. At Christmas of 2000, however, when over eight
hundred worshipers arrived, overflowing the house and flooding the local
street, public security officials called her in and notified her that this could
not happen again for public safety reasons. The other woman has not only
been removed from her position at the church south of Changle, but has
also been banned from serving as an evangelist altogether. She ascribes this
banishment to the local religious authorities being jealous of her overwhelming successes. She persists in her ministry, however, working closely
with a younger group of evangelists who also travel throughout the Changle
region. She works hard to avoid detection by the Public Security Administration who regularly detain her for her activities.

According to sources familiar with the Home of Grace movement, by the
end of 2000 there were more than thirty churches supported by Home of
Grace–trained workers in the Changle area alone. In addition, work is
strong in nearby counties, south to Fuqing, north along the coast, and
throughout a Home of Grace network scattered across China. Moral and financial support continue from local Christians and Home of Grace leaders

and members throughout Southeast Asia, including Malaysia and Singapore, where the Home of Grace has a seminary, as well as from members who have immigrated to the United States. Says one of those based in New York:

> *All of our work has a connection to the churches—underground churches. We are the training center for the underground church. Every year we send coworkers to China to train workers, to visit churches, this kind of work. And people also come here to study.*
>
> *Even though the Home of Grace training center in Changle has been closed, there are a number of small Bible study groups still active in the countryside. We are supporting these groups. We send them Bible study books and songbooks. They are very hungry and thirsty for God's word and we do what we can to help them.*

Conclusion: Chinese Christianity and Heterodoxy

Christian leaders in the 1950s were confronted with a difficult choice. Many supported the goals of the Chinese Communist Party to restore China's national autonomy and renew China's national character through economic, political, and ideological reform. They also sought to forge an institutional space for Christianity within a new, formally atheistic, social order. Over the past fifty years, participants in the Protestant Three-Self Patriotic Movement and the Chinese Catholic Patriotic Association have struggled to maintain their religious integrity while negotiating a public space for freedom of belief within the formal structures of Chinese society. It has been a process involving significant compromises, conflicts with the state, and intense criticism from within the Christian community. It has had to overcome the huge setbacks of the Cultural Revolution which interrupted the process of accommodation and left deep wounds for many. But it has also been a process with some successes. Through creative effort these Christians have managed to carve out space for an acceptable form of Christian orthodoxy.

This chapter, in particular its concluding local histories, offers significant insights into the Protestant expressions that have emerged to fill that space and its margins as well as insights into the reasons why the Chinese government is still troubled by Christian churches and continues to go to such lengths to monitor and regulate religious expression. Many of China's

Christians simply have not bought into the established orthodoxy. They are reminiscent of so many earlier, troublesome, heterodox groups. They are lay led—most often by women, rural based, egalitarian in nature, and fundamentally millenarian, with a view of personal and collective salvation far removed from that espoused by the Chinese Communist Party. Many bear the deep wounds of the Cultural Revolution.

As economic reforms have restructured Chinese society over the past twenty years, the Chinese people, especially rural people, are facing economic disparity and uneven development well known in pre-Communist eras. Coal miners are striking for better working conditions. Rural farmers are rising up to resist exorbitant and unbearable taxes. Workers laid off from privatized state-run industries are protesting their loss of jobs, health benefits, and pensions. Tens of millions of internal migrants float from rural areas to cities in search of wage labor. In the midst of such potential chaos, the Chinese state is particularly concerned with maintaining social stability. In the religious sphere, it consistently acts in such a way as to confirm that it is wary of the revolutionary potential not only of popular religious movements such as Falun Gong, but also of rural Catholic and Protestant Christians.

Madsen (2001) has suggested that rural Catholicism in China today should be viewed as a form of Chinese popular folk religion with all its potential for heterodox belief and action. In particular he sees a strong connection between folk Catholicism and heterodox sects in Chinese popular Buddhism. As we have seen, these similarities include

- Millenarian visions of radical salvation
- Immediate and physical salvation
- Voluntary associations undermining dominant social structures
- Long-distance communication and action networks
- Radical leveling of class differences
- Egalitarian approaches to lay leadership, particularly women's leadership.

Drawing upon the local examples presented here, a case can be made to include much of China's rural Protestant Christianity in this framework. Here Catholics and Protestants can be seen to focus intently on the magical and the miraculous, on exorcisms, healing rituals, visions, and direct revelation. Their faith is largely antimaterialistic and antimodern. It is far removed from the orthodox expressions of Christianity supported and promoted

FIGURE 9 Guhuai Catholic Cathedral, Changle.

through the state-recognized religious associations. It is sustained, and sometimes enhanced, through infusions of immigrants' resources and support from beyond China's borders.

What role these Christians will play in the future development of the dynamic Chinese social and political situation is uncertain. These religious communities are inherently unstable and factionalized. The pressure placed on them by the state to conform is at times intense. But in the midst of the tremendous changes shaking China, these grassroots organizations continue to add members, build networks of support and communication within China, and develop links through their emigrant members to religious organizations and communities beyond the bounds of the Chinese state.

5

Chinatown's Religious Landscape
The Fuzhounese Presence

Chinatown's religious landscape today reflects the complex immigrant history of this urban New York neighborhood. Walking around one discovers old Jewish synagogues, both active and empty; Catholic churches built by Irish and Italian Catholic immigrants and now home to Cantonese, Fuzhounese, and Hispanic congregations; Protestant churches ranging from old mainline denominations like the Methodists, Episcopalians, and Presbyterians to Hong Kong and Taiwanese imports like Overseas Chinese Mission and Ling Liang Church. There are newly formed independent religious communities primarily comprised of undocumented workers from southeast China, operating in the local Fuzhou dialect; large Buddhist temples whose leaders are monks with advanced theological training and whose constituents are primarily older Cantonese immigrants or recent middle-class Hong Kong and Taiwanese immigrants; and numerous storefront Buddhist, Daoist, and Chinese popular religion temples oriented around home villages, whose festival celebrations, fortunetelling, and spirit possession reflect the vibrant and complex religious life of rural mainland Chinese from the areas around Fuzhou. The diversity of these religious communities reflects not only the neighborhood's immigrant history, but also its contemporary stratification.

By the end of 2002, fourteen congregations specifically served the Fuzhounese in Chinatown. Chapter 6 contains an analysis of the history of Fuzhounese Protestants in Chinatown by presenting a study of their two congregations, the Church of Grace and the New York House Church. After providing an overview of religion among the Chinese in Chinatown, the current chapter will focus on four additional groups representing the diversity of Fuzhounese traditions—the He Xian Jun Buddhist Temple, the Daoist Temple of Heavenly Thanksgiving, and Transfiguration and St.

Joseph's Catholic churches. The data collected during this study consistently show that these groups, which include large numbers of undocumented workers, play key roles in the migration and immigrant incorporation process. They serve as key locations for mobilizing the social capital necessary for survival in Chinatown's highly exploitative ethnic enclave while at the same time reflecting much of the stratification in the surrounding community. They function as nodes for building and accessing transnational networks that influence events and institutions in New York and at home in China. And they contribute to the construction of alternative identities that serve as counterpoints to the dominant structures and discourses of the ethnic enclave and U.S. society.

Only a few studies document Chinese religious expressions in the United States, and these focus primarily on Chinese Christians. Even fewer resources describe the religious reality of New York's Chinatown, with the exception of a limited number of church histories written for internal congregational purposes such as anniversary celebrations. Studies of Chinatown (i.e., Kuo 1977; Wong 1982, 1988; Kwong 1996 [1987]; Zhou 1992; Yu 1992; Lin 1998; Tchen 1999) mention religion only in passing or neglect it completely. No research had been conducted on Fuzhounese religious communities. Except where otherwise noted, I gathered the data for this study from firsthand ethnographic fieldwork including street-by-street mapping, participant observation, and personal interviews conducted between April 1997 and July 2002. I have reconstructed institutional histories from oral and primary sources.

I drew information about religious organizations in Chinatown initially from publicly available lists circulated in Christian and Buddhist networks, as well as the regular advertisement of religious services in the main Chinatown newspapers and Yellow Pages. A visual check of key streets quickly revealed inadequacies in the publicly available lists. Buddhist institutions in general were severely underrepresented. Most of the religious communities created by recent Fuzhounese immigrants—largely new and independent—simply were not on any of the maps, formal or informal, that had been drawn. Most of them had no legal organizational status in New York and were advertised by word of mouth through family, village, and faith networks.

A series of street-by-street observations I conducted in 1997, 1999, and again in 2002 captures more fully the historical and religious diversity of the approximately sixty-block area considered to be part of Chinatown today (see map in chapter 1). Beginning in the oldest section of Chinatown, bounded by Canal Street, Bowery, Baxter Street, and Worth Street—what most people think of as "Chinatown"—the surveys extended outward to the edges of today's Chinatown: south to the East River, east through the formerly Jewish Lower East Side, and north through what is still known as Little Italy but whose Italian presence is maintained primarily now in two blocks of tourist-oriented Italian restaurants and shops along Mulberry Street.

Of the eighty-four religious institutions identified in the study, fifty-nine are exclusively Chinese. In addition, three Catholic churches have multiple congregations in one parish, combining Chinese and Italian or Chinese and Hispanic. The twenty-two non-Chinese institutions include a wide range of congregations: Protestant (Hispanic, African American, European American), 10; Jewish, 4; Roman Catholic, 4; Greek Orthodox, 1; Ukrainian Orthodox, 1; Jehovah's Witness, 1; Japanese Buddhist, 1. The sixty-two institutions with Chinese members include Buddhist, 26; Protestant Christian, 23; Chinese Popular Religion, 8; Catholic, 3; Daoist, 2.

Fourteen congregations specifically serve the Fuzhounese population in Chinatown. Five are popular religious temples venerating local deities from the home village or region in China from which their adherents have come. Four congregations specifically identify themselves as Buddhist temples, though these may incorporate elements of Daoism or popular religion as well. Two independent Protestant Christian congregations have been established. One temple, the Temple of Heavenly Thanksgiving, identifies itself as Daoist, but includes Buddhist and Daoist deities on its altar as well as the sage Confucius. The two Catholic churches with Fuzhounese constituents are multiethnic parishes including older groups of Italians along with Cantonese-speaking Chinese from south China and Hong Kong and more recent Fuzhounese arrivals. In addition, dozens of small Protestant and Catholic house-church groups meet in adherents' homes, intentionally outside the larger institutions examined in this study. Excluding the two Catholic parishes, the other twelve Fuzhounese religious groups are independently established with no formal institutional association beyond their own local organization. Mirroring the Fuzhounese migration, these institutions are all recently established and as such are fairly fragile. Only the He Xian Jun Buddhist Temple (1987) and the Protestant Church of Grace (1988) were founded before 1990. All of the others were established during the past decade.

Chinese Religious Diversity in Chinatown: An Overview

The Chinese religious community in New York City reflects the diversity of the Chinese diaspora. New York's Chinese churches and temples have been formed by ethnic Chinese immigrants from Taiwan, Hong Kong, Macau, Singapore, Burma, Malaysia, Indonesia, Thailand, and Vietnam as well as mainland China. The mainlanders include the earliest immigrants from the Taishan area of southern Guangdong Province; scholars, businessmen, and professionals from China's major urban centers; post-1989 Tian An Men political asylum seekers; Fuzhounese from towns and villages of China's southeast coast; and a small recent wave of undocumented workers from Wenzhou, a coastal city twelve hours north of Fuzhou by bus.

Each group brings a different linguistic tradition, cultural background, economic resource, and religious experience. They speak Cantonese, Mandarin, Fuzhounese, the local Taiwanese *minnan* dialect, Wenzhounese, and English. They use these languages in different combinations, sometimes with separate religious services within the same institution, sometimes with simultaneous translation during the same services, and sometimes with a determined effort to stick to one over the others. The religious institutions also represent different historical waves of immigration out of China and into New York. Early Cantonese immigrants and their grown children now established as middle-class professionals and business owners congregate together in certain churches and temples. Hong Kong and Taiwanese who have come since the 1970s gather in others. Fuzhounese undocumented immigrant laborers form their own institutions. Second-generation Chinese may meet in the same building as their parents, but their English-language congregations are often distinct ritual and programmatic entities.

Chinese established their earliest religious altars in family and village association halls that began to emerge in the Five Points area of lower Manhattan, starting on Pell, Doyer, and lower Mott streets in the 1800s. The Methodist Five Points Mission, originally opened in 1848 to serve Irish immigrants, began its first work with Chinese in 1878, renting space at 14 Mott Street. Transfiguration Catholic Church, located at 29 Mott Street, began an outreach to Chinese in 1909. Two temples, referred to by non-Chinese as "joss houses," were constructed in the 1880s, the first an elaborate space on the third floor of 10 Chatham Square and later an even more magnificent hall at 16 Mott Street in the Consolidated Benevolent Association Building. The word "joss," meaning a Chinese idol or cult image, is not Chinese but derives from pidgin English based on the Portuguese or Latin "deus," meaning "god" or "deity." A joss house was then a Chinese temple or shrine. With the expansion of Chinatown in the late 1800s, not only did tourists begin flocking to its restaurants, tea merchants, and gift shops but also to its temples. The oldest extant Buddhist temple in Chinatown, the Eastern States Buddhist Association, opened in 1963 (Yu 1995; Chin 1995; Anbinder 2001).

Today churches and temples have expanded through a wide swath of the Lower East Side. In recent years, Chinese religious communities have also emerged in significant numbers as part of the economically diverse Asian community in Flushing, Queens, and in the working-class Chinese neighborhood of Sunset Park, Brooklyn. A few other Chinese congregations are scattered throughout the five boroughs, including Chinese Christian fellowships on most major college campuses. A recent explosion of Chinese meditation groups related to China's persecuted Falun Gong movement gathers in public parks and members' homes throughout the city.

Aside from counting numbers of religious organizations, measuring the religiosity of New York's Chinese population is a complex task. A telephone survey of 164 Chinese residents of Queens in 1997–1998 recorded the following responses to the question of religious affiliation: Protestantism, 13.4 percent; Catholicism, 6.7 percent; Buddhism, 21.3 percent; Other, 1.8 percent; No Religion, 56.7 percent. Respondents were selected at random from Chinese surnames in the Queens telephone directory (Min forthcoming).

While this is a laudable effort to identify the religious preferences of Chinese in New York City, the analytic framework of the survey forces respondents to fit their beliefs into an institutional framework that does not reflect the religious experience of most Chinese, and certainly not the religious practices of recent immigrants from Fuzhou. Many studies of Chinese religion stress the intertwining of Buddhism, Daoism, and Chinese popular religious beliefs at the local level and their integration with family and village customs and activities (Weller 1987; Sangren 1987; Shahar and Weller 1996). As exemplified by the Fuzhounese He Xian Jun Temple of Master Lu examined later in this chapter, most religious expression in mainland China's rural areas is popular in expression, not readily reduced into the formal categories of Buddhism or Daoism. Chinese popular religious expression, which includes funerals, weddings, veneration of ancestors, and festivals related to the Chinese lunar calendar, is vibrant and central to family and home village life. Such beliefs and practices do not disappear when immigrants arrive in New York. They continue in homes, stores, shops, restaurants, and temples. They may be modified to fit a new cultural environment, but they continue. Asking Chinese New Yorkers by telephone to place their religious beliefs within the framework of world religious systems such as Protestant Christianity, Catholicism, or Buddhism miscalculates the complexity and diversity of Chinese religious expression. In this regard it should come as no surprise that the majority of respondents claim no religious affiliation.

As we have already seen, since 1949 the Chinese government has also attempted to fit all public forms of religious expression into the world religion framework, drawing upon an imported European, heavily Marxist, intellectual tradition. All other popular religious expressions were declared to be feudal superstitions. The government's actions have not been an analytical project, however, but an organizational one. Temples and religious practitioners across China, despite the complexity of their religious expression, have been forced to register with one of the five major religious organizations in order to receive official sanction. So a temple combining Buddhist, Daoist, and popular religious elements, like Master Lu's, finds itself registered with the Buddhist Association in China and Master Lu himself as a Buddhist religious practitioner. This organizational framework is not effective in advancing understanding of much of China's rural religious expression. Nor is it an effective analytical framework for examining religious beliefs and practices among Chinese in New York.

An unpublished survey of New York's Chinese religious communities conducted as part of the Religion and Immigrant Incorporation in New York project at the New School University documents ninety-nine Christian churches and forty temples in the New York area. Among the Christian churches, 38 percent are in Manhattan, 41 percent are in Queens with a significant concentration in Flushing, and 11 percent are in Brooklyn. Included in these numbers are eight predominantly Taiwanese congregations in Queens. Not included are the numerous Chinese churches in New Jersey, upstate New York, and Long Island that are primarily populated by middle-class, often highly educated immigrants from Taiwan, Hong Kong, and the Chinese mainland. Among the temples, 20 percent of those surveyed are in Manhattan, 35 percent are in Queens, 8 percent are in Brooklyn, and 5 percent are in the Bronx. A number of the New York City Buddhist congregations have built temples, retreat centers, and monasteries in northern New Jersey and upstate New York where members go for dharma teaching, meditation retreats, and ritual ceremonies. Members may go individually, but the temples also regularly organize buses and group excursions (Huang and Zhou 2000).

Chinese religious life and practice in New York is clearly much broader and deeper than reflected in the statistics of Huang and Zhou's fine yet preliminary study. For instance, certain segments of the Chinese religious population, including independent and particularly non-Christian institutions, are less likely to appear on publicly available lists. Huang and Zhou's survey identifies forty temples in the New York City metropolitan area. In comparison, my current study has identified thirty-six temples (Buddhist, Daoist, and popular) in Manhattan's Chinatown alone. Unaffiliated institutions, regardless of size, are difficult to detect without street-by-street observation. This appears to be true for the newly created Fuzhounese religious institutions as well. While making the documentation process more time consuming and labor intensive, street-by-street observation may be a necessary tool in mapping contemporary religious communities, particularly those with significant numbers of recent immigrants.

Individual, family, and business-oriented religious expressions are also difficult to document in a survey of institutions. Drawing upon rural and urban Chinese popular religious practices, Chinese immigrants continue traditional activities. In many Chinese homes throughout the New York area, offerings are made to the kitchen god. In many Chinese restaurants, stores, and businesses, small altars may be found at which owners offer prayers. These religious practices, intimately intertwined with Chinese family and village culture, may not be as readily identifiable out of context in a U.S. environment.

Public processions and festivals also do not register on a map of religious institutions. Yet they play a distinct role in projecting an ethnic community's religious beliefs into the public domain. Chinatown's Chinese Protestants hold an annual evangelistic crusade in Sara Delano Roosevelt Park sponsored by the Christian umbrella organization Chinese Christian Herald Crusade. Fuzhounese Catholics at Transfiguration Church have initiated an annual August procession on the Lower East Side, honoring the Feast of the Assumption of Our Blessed Mother Mary. The celebration of the Buddha's birthday in late May/early June, which began circumambulating Manhattan's Chinatown, now travels east down Kissena Boulevard in Flushing, Queens. These events have not yet achieved the wide public recognition of their counterparts/predecessors like the St. Patrick's Day parade, the Puerto Rican Day parade, the Columbus Day parade, the India Day parade down Fifth Avenue, the Caribbean Day parade in Brooklyn, or even the annual Chinese New Year celebration. But through these nascent public displays and processionals, Chinese religious communities are seeking to project their presence into the public discourse and accentuate their claim to a place in the most multicultural, multiethnic, multireligious of global cities.

The Fuzhounese Religious Communities

Over the past fifteen years, Fuzhounese immigrants have established their own religious communities in New York's Chinatown, adding their unique flavor to the area's variegated and textured religious fabric. The Fuzhounese migration, spurred by economic restructuring in both China and the United States and facilitated by a vast and highly organized international human smuggling syndicate, has uprooted whole communities of people, dislocating them economically, culturally, and legally, placing them in a receiving country for which they are unprepared and which is unprepared to incorporate them. Amid this dislocation, Fuzhounese immigrants are constructing and maintaining religious communities as one means of building supportive networks and activities, including religious networks and practices, and as a mode for negotiating their place in this complex and volatile global process. The stories of Fuzhounese immigrants associated with the He Xian Jun Buddhist Temple, the Daoist Temple of Heavenly Thanksgiving, and Transfiguration and St. Joseph's Catholic churches, reconstructed in this chapter, as well as those of the Church of Grace and the New York House Church in chapter 6, reveal the complex roles these congregations play in the Fuzhounese migration process, in immigrant incorporation in the United States, and in building networks that link religious communities in lower Manhattan and the lower Min River Valley of Southeast China.

He Xian Jun Buddhist Temple

On Eldridge Street, which runs through the heart of Chinatown's new Fuzhounese community, stands a storefront-turned-village-temple. This October day, the ninth day of the ninth month of the Chinese lunar calendar, is a major feast day honoring the Chinese Buddhist bodhisattva, Guan Yin, goddess of mercy, and so the temple is being transformed into a festival hall. Tables and chairs fill every inch of the main room as well as a small courtyard farther back. A buffet line near the altar is stacked with a dozen different vegetarian courses. In the rear of the building, gas fires rage under commercial-sized woks in the crowded kitchen, where additional food is being prepared for the day's visitors. Today the main hall will be packed with women, mostly, taking their lunch breaks from the nearby garment shops and paying their respects to Guan Yin and Master Lu. More than two hundred people will make the pilgrimage during the course of the noon hour.

Master Lu, a short gruff man in his early sixties, established the small temple on Eldridge Street shortly after arriving illegally in 1985 from Fuqi Village east of Fuzhou. Fuqi Village lies on a hillside on the southern bank of the Min River. Out of four thousand villagers, nearly two thousand are now estimated to have made their way to or through New York. Fuqi's economy previously was built around farming and fishing. Today this emigrant community relies primarily on remittances from villagers working in the United States.

Master Lu is not uncharacteristic of local religious practitioners in both rural and urban China who incorporate a polytheistic blend of ritual and belief. For the ten years immediately preceding his migration to New York, Master Lu practiced his craft as a spirit medium in the towns and villages around his native Fuqi and on Langqi Island on the mouth of the Min River, home of his wife's family. What is particularly unique about Master Lu is that he has transferred the central location of his practice from rural Fuqi to urban New York. At the same time, he has built a direct connection to his hometown and maintained the local flavor of his work. Fuqi villagers visit him for advice in New York, just as they did back home. The deity, He Xian Jun, speaks to him in New York just as he did in China. Contributions from members support the temple in New York as well as the construction of a major temple complex in Fuqi.

The New York temple serves as something of a community center for the people of Fuqi and surrounding areas. Festivities are held on the first and fifteenth of every month (Chinese lunar calendar) as well as three times a year in honor of Guan Yin. The largest gathering occurs at the Chinese New Year, when many Fuzhounese working in restaurants across the country return to New York. Over seven hundred immigrants made the New Year's journey to Master Lu's temple in 2002.

The temple is named after He Xian Jun, a prominent Daoist deity in northern Fujian Province and the predominant local deity of Fuqi Village and surrounding areas. The association of a Daoist deity with an officially Buddhist temple reflects not only the integration of Buddhism, Daoism, and Chinese popular religious beliefs at the local level, but also the difficulty in using institutional religious frameworks to categorize the dynamic religious expressions of rural Chinese communities.

Master Lu has had an extremely intimate and personal relationship with the deity for over twenty-five years, a relationship that has not been lessened by the geographical distance between Fuqi Village in southeast China and Eldridge Street on the Lower East Side of Manhattan. In between festivals, Master Lu receives visitors. They come to ask the god's advice about everything from business ventures to children's names to potential success of petitions for political asylum. They come to pray for the health of sick relatives. They come to give thanks for safe passage across the ocean with snakeheads from China. He Xian Jun, who characteristically provides his adherents with dreams in response to their queries, is revered as a god of healing and resolving intractable problems. There is a steady stream of petitioners throughout the average day. Old friends drop in to say hello and show off a new grandson. Couples planning to be married come by to check the auspiciousness of their match or the date for their wedding. Sundays are busiest because many working Chinese have the day off. Master Lu intercedes on their behalf to inquire of He Xian Jun. The deity gives him a message or a vision to relay and interpret to the petitioners. At rare times, He Xian Jun actually possesses Master Lu's body in order to communicate, but mostly the responses come in the form of dreams or visual images.

I conducted the following interview with Master Lu in his New York temple one afternoon in September 1999. It traces the development of this poor rural villager from a childhood gathering firewood to support his family on the banks of the Min River to his position as a ritual master of a religious community that spans the globe. In addition to providing the rich imagery of his life's journey, the interview reveals Master Lu's intimate relationship with the deity He Xian Jun and the religious framework he has constructed to give meaning to his life experience, particularly his immigrant experience.

It was 1985. I found a snakehead in Tingjiang, across the river from Fuqi by boat. The price was $17,000 but I didn't give any money up front. Only after I got to America. If I didn't get here then I didn't have to pay. But when it was time to leave the country, I couldn't get out. When I got to Shanghai I couldn't get on the plane. I had a Chinese passport, but the smuggler hadn't gotten the right visa. I went home to Fuqi and waited. When I finally did leave China I traveled from Shanghai to Japan. From Japan to Canada. From Canada to Ecuador. Ecuador to

Mexico. From Mexico to Los Angeles. Los Angeles to New York. All on the plane except from Mexico to Los Angeles. In Mexico I climbed a mountain for an hour, then there was a small vehicle waiting for us to take us across the border. We all sat on that bus praying to He Xian Jun, "Protect us! Protect us!" I know some people who have been stopped at that customs checkpoint. One of my friends. So I was praying. In front of us they were searching a car. I was praying. But when we pulled up they just said, go through. We were so happy. There were five of us. One from Tingjiang, one from Min'an, two from Houyu, and me. We were all praying. We just zoomed right through.

How did you arrange housing and work?

Friends and relatives. Since 1975 I had been doing this kind of work [with He Xian Jun]. In 1975 He Xian Jun had already come to inhabit my body. We didn't dare to do this work at home. It was still during the Cultural Revolution and religion was being repressed very intensely. I went to other places to work. Neighboring villages. Langqi Island. In my relatives' and friends' homes. Then I would go away. Sometimes they could pay me. Sometimes they just gave me rice or oil. Or people would come secretively to my home, just as guests. People would ask me to come if someone was sick, or if there were problems in the family: fights, divorce, family problems. I would try to make peace. People would introduce me, one to one to another.

These people helped me come up with the money when I got to New York. We already had a lot of people from Fuqi in New York at the time. In 1981–1982 there were already some that were smuggled out through Macau or Shanghai. They would go to Macau to "visit relatives" and then just keep on going to New York. I worked in a restaurant for two years. Every month I paid $1,000 back to the people who had loaned it to me.

When did you first think about opening this temple?

Right when I got to America, He Xian Jun told me to open a temple. I told the god, since I borrowed other people's money, I'm embarrassed to just start a temple. After I've returned the money then I will do it. If I don't return the money people will say I'm lazy. But if I return the money I will be free to do anything. They can't say anything about it, regardless how little money I make. He Xian Jun told me in a dream to open this temple. And we had a conversation. He told me if you work in a restaurant it's too dirty. I can't get close to your body. The meat smells. Other smells. I was worried, though. I was illegal. I didn't get my green card until after the 1989 amnesty. If I worked in the back of a restaurant, the police probably would not catch me. But if I opened a temple. . . . What should I do? I asked the god. He said, "Don't worry. You won't get caught. No one will bother you." He told me where to open this temple, too. Originally it was a little farther up on Eldridge Street. He told me to move here to this building. I said no, because it wasn't a very good neighborhood at the time. He said it was OK, nothing would happen to me. So I moved the temple here in 1993.

I told He Xian Jun that since my family was poor if I could get to America I promise to build a temple for him in Fuqi. I made that promise before I came. If he would send me to America and I could make some money the first thing I would do is build a temple in Fuqi for him. I do my work. He does his.

How did you know you had this skill?

I didn't even know it myself. I just tried. If I got it right then I had the power. Like, is the baby going to be a boy or a girl? If I got it right, then I've got the power. Today you should go to such and such a place and do something. Did it work out? Yes? Then it works.

Does it really work?

Yes. If things didn't change, why would people trust me? Why would they contribute to building the temple back home in China?

The He Xian Jun Temple in New York plays a key role in the lives of immigrants from Fuqi and neighboring villages as they seek to make sense of their new and often hostile environment and negotiate their difficult existence in New York City. The temple, with Master Lu as the centerpiece, serves as a site for the exchange of information among its adherents regarding jobs, housing, health care, and coping mechanisms for dealing with any of the struggles of daily life. Another important and overlooked function of village-oriented temples such as this is as a source of credit. He Xian Jun Temple operates an informal revolving loan fund. "If people need help

FIGURE 10   He Xian Jun Temple, New York City.

paying off their snakehead they often come here. I don't have any money of my own to loan them. But if the temple has some money we loan it to them. They pay it back as they are able," Master Lu explained.

The temple and Master Lu also serve as an important link between New York and Fuqi. To honor his reciprocal pledge with He Xian Jun, Master Lu has orchestrated the construction of a beautiful temple complex on the hillside above Fuqi Village overlooking the Min River as it flows into the sea. With contributions of over one million dollars from adherents in New York, Master Lu has built a multileveled temple that dwarfs anything in the surrounding villages. Architectural drawings are prominently displayed inside the temple on Eldridge Street. A seven-story pagoda is the most recent addition and opened to great fanfare in September 2002, complete with rituals, parades, and speeches by local and provincial government authorities.

Land in China is at a premium, and religious organizations often are denied permission to build new religious edifices. But Master Lu is well known to the government authorities in Fuqi because of the remittances his temple channels back into the local community. He is also influential in Fuqi's overseas population in New York, where, in addition to his role in the temple, he serves as vice chairman of the Fuqi Village Association. As a result, the temple leadership in Fuqi has had remarkable success negotiating with village government authorities for what it needs. For instance, in return for being granted permission to build the temple on the steeply sloping hillside at the back of the village, Master Lu agreed to fund the construction of a new road through the village and connecting to the main thoroughfare that links Fuqi with neighboring villages and Changle to the south and Fuzhou to the west. The village would not have to take agricultural land out of production and would gain a significant new public road. The temple would get the land it needed for its new construction.

Master Lu returns to Fuqi Village at least once a year, usually in the spring. His brother has remained in Fuqi to manage the sprawling new temple complex. Master Lu's son is also there, living in the family's spacious new five-story home and waiting for his green card application to be processed. On his annual return visit to Fuqi, Master Lu conducts a month-long religious retreat for his followers. Hundreds of pilgrims from across the area visit Fuqi temple during this time. Monks from a large temple in Fuzhou City are hired to lead the rituals. The temple, like others throughout the region and across China, is playing a crucial role in revitalizing and reimagining Chinese religious life after a period of intense repression.

Master Lu also takes the occasions of his return visits to meet with local political and religious authorities. Despite living primarily in New York, he is recognized by the Changle Religious Affairs Bureau as a Buddhist monk and he retains membership on the Changle Buddhist Association Council. Back home in New York, Master Lu proudly displays videos of his visits, the many pilgrims who attend the festivals, and the beautiful new temple buildings. The videos regularly play on the temple's VCR and are loaned out to adherents around the tri-state area, another span in the bridge between Fuqi and New York linking religious communities.

Though he is a man of great renown in Fuqi Village and its environs, in New York City Master Lu's life is quite simple and circumscribed.

I spend my days here at the temple. When there are no visitors I fold paper devotional money and watch Chinese videos with my wife and family. I don't go out. I wouldn't know where to go. I don't speak any English. So even though I've had a green card for eleven years I've never applied to become a U.S. citizen. I'd fail the English test. I live in the temple, work in the temple. I've never even seen the Statue of Liberty.

The Temple of Heavenly Thanksgiving

Not far from the He Xian Jun Temple, in another storefront on the eastern end of Canal Street, the bright red sign over the door with yellow-orange Chinese characters reads:

Three   *Faiths*

Chang'an   *New York*

Temple of Heavenly Thanksgiving

It is a sweltering June day in 1997. Inside, the small store-turned-temple is decorated in austere fashion. A few chairs line the walls. A list of temple con-tributors and leaders is mounted prominently just inside the door. On the far wall is a glass-encased altar holding twenty small statues arranged on five ascending levels. A dragon is painted on the back wall of the altar encase-ment. Huang Di, the emperor, sits on the uppermost level. Confucius, Lao Zi (representing Daoism), and the Buddha sit side by side on the second level. A long table extends from the altar back toward the front door, its sur-faces covered with offerings of fresh fruit, ritual candles, and a few pots of burned incense.

A group of seven men and two women occupy the chairs lining the side walls of the temple. Mr. Li, one of the temple leaders, introduces the temple. "The members of the temple have all immigrated from the village of Chang'an or next door Dongqi Village." These two villages are located about thirty miles east of Fuzhou City on the north bank of the Min River, just east of Tingjiang and almost directly across the river from Fuqi Village. Most all of them have been smuggled into the United States over the past few years. When asked if many more Chang'an villagers were in New York, Mr. Li laughed and said, "Most of them are already in New York but more are com-ing all the time! It's mostly just grandparents and small children in Chang'an now. The young people—men and women—have come to New York, most of them illegally, to find work."

Sitting in the temple that very day was a young man, nineteen years old, casually yet neatly dressed and carrying a medium-sized duffel bag. He in-

FIGURE 11 Mahayana Buddhist Temple at Canal Street and Bowery.

deed had just arrived from Chang'an days before, smuggled into New York and now waiting patiently in the temple for a van that would pick him up and drive him to a city in the Midwest, where others from Chang'an and Dongqi Village had opened a Chinese restaurant and he was promised work.

> *I finally made it to America on my third try. I was arrested twice and sent back to China—once in Japan and once in Thailand. I finally came through the Middle East, eastern Europe, and then on a plane to New York with a fake visa. I just want to make money. There's nothing for me at home in Chang'an. So I came out. If I can make $200,000 then I'll go back to China.*

According to Mr. Li, the Heavenly Thanksgiving sect had been founded about ten years earlier in Dongqi Village. Mr. Huang, now the master of the Dongqi temple, had left China in 1957 for Hong Kong, where he earned a living as a sailor, eventually working as an engineer. On a visit to New York harbor in 1972 he jumped ship and remained in New York until 1986, when he was able to establish U.S. citizenship through the amnesty for undocumented immigrants. He returned to Dongqi in 1987. At that time a local village deity spoke to him and instructed him to form this new group. The group's key tenet was to build unity among religions and religious believers by integrating Confucianism, Buddhism, and Daoism into one ritual practice. Despite its fundamental belief in the unity of these religions, the first Heavenly Thanksgiving temple, built in Dongqi Village in 1987, was registered as a Daoist temple to fit Chinese government guidelines.

In 1993 a group of seven immigrants from Chang'an and Dongqi established a branch of the Dongqi temple in New York. Originally on Eldridge Street a short distance away, earlier that spring (1997) it moved to Canal Street. Since its founding, the temple has served as a gathering spot for immigrants from the two villages and as a place for worship and ritual on the key days of the Chinese lunar calendar. By 1997 most of the original group of seven owned restaurants in the New York area but rotated responsibility for the temple operations. And in each of their restaurants there was also a small altar for the gods of the temple.

In 1995, with funds raised from one hundred fellow villagers, several of the founders returned to Chang'an to build the third Temple of Heavenly Thanksgiving. With help from the original temple in Dongqi, construction began on a major temple complex hugging the hillside at the rear of Chang'an Village overlooking the Min River and the Pacific Ocean. Built on the site of an old Buddhist temple, this new structure rises steeply through five levels, each adorned with altars to the gods and configured in the same order as the miniaturized statues in the New York temple. From the highest landing the temple looks south over Chang'an Village, its newly constructed multistory homes built with remittances sent from the United States.

The religious community that is related to these three temples reflects many of the characteristics of other Fuzhounese religious groups. The Temple of Heavenly Thanksgiving in New York City clearly serves as a site in the immigrant journey for fellow believers. The leadership of the temple plays a role in the actual arrangements involved in the migration process. While serving as a ritual center, the temple is also equipped to assist immigrants in transit. On the main floor of the New York temple, behind the front room and altar, is a full kitchen. A set of stairs leads down to a basement level comprised of four smaller rooms filled with four to six beds each. These are used by fellow villagers passing through New York on their way to a network of restaurants spread from Virginia to Pennsylvania to Indiana and Michigan.

FIGURE 12 Sung Tak Buddhist Temple (1996), formerly Pike Street Synagogue (1904).

The temple serves as an important location for assisting the incorporation of new immigrants into the U.S. economy. Immigrants are connected to the network of restaurants and provided employment. This incorporation is limited, however, by the internal stratification of the temple network. Some members own the restaurants. Others work as undocumented laborers for well below minimum wage. Nevertheless, the social solidarity of the network provides off-the-books employment to the undocumented workers at wages far above what they could earn in China. At the same time, the workers' cheap labor enables the owners to reap a profit far above what they could earn if forced to employ U.S. citizens at the legal minimum wage or above. In this case, the Chinatown ethnic enclave and its effects are extended beyond New York by means of the village and temple network that encompasses work locations scattered throughout the United States.

The Temple of Heavenly Thanksgiving also demonstrates the ability of the emerging Fuzhounese religious networks to enable immigrants to contribute to and influence their home communities in China. While many immigrants interact with their sending community through remittances to build homes and support family members, participation in the Temple of Heavenly Thanksgiving allows members to contribute collectively to the larger social projects of their home village. Not only has significant money been invested in the construction of the home temple complex, but in 1999 the New York temple established a charitable foundation to engage in development and relief operations in the Chang'an and Dongqi areas as well as elsewhere in China.

Through my several visits to the temples in New York, Dongqi, and Chang'an, the difficulties of maintaining religious networks that span towns, cities, and nations often half a world away, particularly given the intense mobility of the migrant community, became clear to me. At times, the temples have been empty, the leadership gone elsewhere to work; at times, internal conflicts have erupted with control over the temples being contested. As with the other religious communities considered in this study, the story of the Temple of Heavenly Thanksgiving reveals the inherent fragility of these nascent Fuzhounese institutions. Their leadership is constantly mobile and so regularly reconstituted. They are unfamiliar with the United States and therefore limited in their ability to establish networks of support. Their attempts to bring together disparate elements of the immigrant community under broad organizational umbrellas often crumble.

Against the odds, however, like Master Lu's He Xian Jun Temple, the Temple of Heavenly Thanksgiving reflects the ability of local religious traditions, indigenous to the towns and villages of rural Fuzhou, to extend their reach and influence far and wide. In 1998 the Dongqi Village temple's spirit medium, long engaged in fortunetelling, prescribing healing herbal medications, and giving all manner of advice, immigrated with her husband to Indiana to open a take-out Chinese restaurant. Here she continued to serve as a spirit medium for the temple and its adherents. People with problems or questions, whether in China or in cities across the United States, would call her in Indiana. Petitioners with inadequate funds to call would leave their inquiries on slips of paper on the temple altars in China or the United States so that temple leaders could call in for them. On the first and the fifteenth day of the lunar month, the medium would go into a trance and be possessed by one of the gods of the temple. Confirming her efficacy, the temple master in Dongqi claimed he could feel the god leaving the village to go to America to inhabit her. In Indiana the spirit medium's husband posed the questions to the inhabiting god who would respond. The husband kept careful notes of the responses and afterward would return people's calls with the eagerly awaited answers.

By 1999 the handwritten notes were still being placed on the altar of the temple on Canal Street in New York. But the sign above the front door had been changed and the people in charge of the temple were different. After I made several inquiries, it became clear to me that one faction from the Chang'an Temple had replaced another. This new faction had a spirit medium as well, but a different person, located in Illinois, not Indiana.

Chinatown's Fuzhounese Catholics: Transfiguration and St. Joseph's Churches

The Fuzhounese Buddhist, Daoist, and popular religious temples and the two Protestant congregations in Chinatown have developed independently and without denominational precedent or institutional support. Manhattan Chinatown's two Fuzhounese Catholic congregations have followed a distinctly different developmental trajectory. At both Transfiguration Church and St. Joseph's Church, the new Fuzhounese Catholics have been incorporated into already existing parishes steeped in immigrant history.

Transfiguration Church

Transfiguration Church's work with Chinese spans nearly one hundred years. The congregation itself was founded in 1827 in lower Manhattan. Throughout its history, Transfiguration has been a parish of immigrants. Beginning with the Irish, followed by the Italians, the Cantonese, and now the Fuzhounese, Transfiguration has been home to wave after wave of New York's new residents. Its history mirrors their history on New York's Lower East Side and continues to do so today.

Father Felix Verela, an outspoken Cuban exile, was the parish's first priest (1827–1846) and guided the congregation through two great fires in New York, two cholera epidemics, and constant anti-Catholic and anti-immigrant social pressure. The great Irish Potato Famine of 1845–1847 set the tone for Transfiguration in the second half of the nineteenth century. By 1847 over one thousand Irish were arriving in New York every day. Transfiguration parish relocated in 1853 from Chambers Street to lower Mott Street, the heart of the new Irish community in the Five Points district and center of New York's most notorious slum, noted for its murders, muggings, prostitution, bars, and dilapidated housing. But by the late 1800s, the Irish began to move out of the Five Points area, being replaced by three new

FIGURE 13 Fuzhounese men serve as bearers during Assumption of Mary procession, Transfiguration Catholic Church.

immigrant groups—the Italians, the Jews, and the Chinese (Dolan 1975; Transfiguration Church 1977).

Transfiguration began to reach out to Chinese in 1909 with the arrival of Father Hilarius Montanar of the Paris Mission Society. Father Montanar had been working in Guangzhou, the area from which most of Chinatown's residents had come. During his tenure as priest he began English classes for the immigrants and served as an interpreter in public and private affairs. He returned to Paris in 1914, and Transfiguration's Chinese Mission closed between 1920 and 1940 for lack of Chinese-speaking clergy and because of the violent inter-Chinese conflicts of the period. Father Umberto Dalmasso, a Chinese-speaking Salesian priest, reopened the Chinese Mission in 1940. In 1949 the Diocese assigned responsibility for parish administration to the Maryknoll Fathers. Maryknoll, founded as the Catholic Foreign Missionary Society of America, was known for its extensive mission work in China, although that work was coming to a close with the Communist defeat of the Nationalists and the expulsion of foreign missionaries from China. The change in parish administration marked a significant commitment by New York's Catholic Diocese to focus on this new immigrant population.

Despite the presence of other Catholic parishes in the neighborhood, including St. James, St. Joseph's, and St. Joachim's, Transfiguration came to be known as the one serving the Chinese community, and its work expanded rapidly at a time when Chinatown's population was also seeing significant growth. In 1975, with Transfiguration's Chinese membership on the ascendancy and its Italian congregation in decline, the Maryknoll Fathers returned the parish to direct diocesan control. In 1976 Father Mark Cheung, himself a refugee from southern China, was appointed parish administrator, the first Chinese priest in the history of New York to be appointed to such a position. Transfiguration was now the most prominent Chinese parish in New York City.

Throughout its history, Transfiguration's Italian and Chinese congregations have maintained largely separate identities, separate masses, and separate programming. In the 1980s conflict heightened between the two groups and among the Chinese themselves. Succeeding Chinese priests were unable to resolve the conflicts, and by the early 1990s the parish and its school were racked by lawsuits and accusations of financial misconduct. In 1991 Cardinal O'Connor directly intervened and again appointed a Maryknoll priest with extensive administrative experience as parish administrator.

As the Fuzhounese population expanded in the late 1980s and early 1990s, Fuzhounese Catholics, many of them from the powerful underground Catholic church, found their way to Transfiguration. Most of Transfiguration's new constituents were rural Catholics, veterans of the conflict between China's underground Catholic church and the state-recognized Patriotic Church. They were and are still fiercely loyal to the pope and fiercely antagonistic toward the Patriotic Church movement. The religious practices of such people in China followed a pattern dedicated to maintaining the purity of Catholic tradition as it had been practiced prior to 1949, when the Chinese government severed its political connections to the Vatican and disallowed Chinese Catholic interaction with the Holy See. This meant, among other things, opposing Vatican II Catholicism along with any modernization tendencies suggested by the Patriotic Catholic Church. In addition, their experience of Catholicism was largely formed by clandestine organizational forms that emphasized rigid adherence to doctrine as well as personal piety and devotion over collective study, theological reflection, and community service.

Priests at Transfiguration regularly receive correspondence from the bishop of the Fuzhounese underground Catholic churches, written in Latin, requesting assistance for certain parishioners on their way to America. The letters document the parishioners' home church, baptisms, and membership as well as instances of persecution, and ask Transfiguration's priests to help them apply for political asylum based on religious persecution. The U.S. State Department has allowed many Catholic asylum seekers to cite China's population-planning policies, especially the one-child-per-family policy, forced abortions, or sterilizations, as grounds for claiming religious persecution. In such instances, documentation from China authenticated by a U.S. Catholic parish can provide substantial support for an asylum application. Not all claims of religious persecution are legitimate, and Transfiguration is careful to avoid being drawn too far into these cases. But enough cases are accepted by the State Department that many Fuzhounese are encouraged to make this claim when arriving in the United States, or later if apprehended. Snakeheads in some cases advise their clients that if caught they should cite religious persecution based on the one-child-per-family policy as an abrogation of their Catholic faith.

The staff leadership of Transfiguration has made a number of attempts to accommodate the Fuzhounese and incorporate them into the larger parish. First, in 1992, they added a Mandarin-language mass on Sunday morning at nine o'clock to cater specifically to the Fuzhounese and to complement the English mass at 10:15 A.M. and the Cantonese mass at 11:30 A.M. Confronted with the rapidly expanding Fuzhounese population, and without a priest who could conduct masses in Fuzhou dialect, Transfiguration introduced a Mandarin mass as the best alternative. The Fuzhounese responded positively to the use of Mandarin, which has emerged as a lingua franca among Chinatown's Chinese population, as a sign that Transfiguration would make room for them alongside the Cantonese and English-speaking congregations already present in the parish.

Also in 1992, Transfiguration launched the Ren Ai Society, a fellowship specifically for the Fuzhounese. Through this the church leadership has attempted to acculturate its Fuzhounese members to life in a modern Catholic parish. Bylaws were drawn up with a mission statement and organizational structure. Officers were elected. Members were encouraged to participate as liturgists, ushers, and choir members. Monthly meetings of the Ren Ai Society were held to mobilize members for retreats, spiritual formation, and service to the congregation. But attendance is sporadic and meetings chaotic. Only one officer has been willing to serve on the parish council (which is almost entirely Chinese of Cantonese descent). The newly formed Ren Ai Society youth group has no interaction with the church's other youth group made up of English-speaking Cantonese. Language is an admitted barrier. But so are class distinctions and Fuzhounese adherence to familiar patterns from home. Cantonese members see Fuzhounese congregants as largely uneducated and uncultured. Carrying the parish's financial burden and managing its organizational affairs, the Cantonese find it difficult to cross over class lines with these coarse immigrant laborers. Fuzhounese, for their part, feel marginalized and treated as second-class citizens within their own parish as the class divisions of the Chinese enclave are mirrored in Transfiguration's congregational structure and interpersonal relations.

Fuzhounese seem most comfortable replicating familiar customs and rituals brought from China. Each Sunday before the Mandarin mass, they gather in the sanctuary to pray and say the rosary. Annually before the Christmas midnight mass, more than one hundred come to pray together, using the Fuzhounese dialect. Each year after the special mass for Chinese New Year, Fuzhounese stay to make a special veneration to Mary, which they call *bai shengmu*, directly translated as "worship the Holy Mother."

The veneration of Mary is of great significance to the Fuzhounese Catholic immigrants and is the impetus for one of the major innovations at Transfiguration in recent years. At their request, Transfiguration has initiated an annual public procession in honor of the Feast of the Assumption of Mary into Heaven in mid-August. The procession, similar to clandestine processions in China, was proposed by parishioners from a village outside Changle where this had been practiced, albeit quietly in the evening or even just inside the walls of the church. Every year since 1996, Transfiguration members remove the large statue of Mary from the sanctuary and carry it through Chinatown, particularly in areas now inhabited by Fuzhounese.

Catholic tradition teaches that after her death, Mary was assumed into heaven, body and soul. This official church dogma was declared by Pope Pius XII on November 1, 1950, at the urging of lay Catholics throughout the church. The feast day is celebrated on August 15 of each year. (In China this is in close proximity to one of the major Buddhist celebrations for the goddess of mercy, Guan Yin.) As one parishioner said, "If we could have these processions in China where there is such persecution, why can't we have them here in America where there is freedom?" Transfiguration leaders have attempted to expand the procession to include the parish's Cantonese members and even other congregations, but it is still primarily Fuzhounese who lend support. In fact, Fuzhounese Catholics return to Chinatown from across the tri-state area to participate in this special act of devotion imported from their hometowns and villages around Fuzhou.

St. Joseph's Church

A second Fuzhounese Catholic congregation has formed at the nearby St. Joseph's Church as a result of a split within the Transfiguration Fuzhounese group. Tension between Fuzhounese immigrants related to the underground churches and those from the Patriotic Association in China had been present from the beginning of the Transfiguration Fuzhounese group. Conflict escalated in 1996. Maryknoll's national organization formally hosted approximately forty seminarians and young priests from the Chinese Catholic Patriotic Association under the auspices of the Program for Formation of Chinese Seminary Professors and Students sponsored by the U.S. Catholic Council of Bishops. Maryknoll had been encouraged to help Catholic priests wherever possible to leave China for further Catholic education and training, but the only ones who could legally depart were those associated with the Patriotic Association. In the United States, Maryknoll arranged for their support in dioceses across the country while they engaged in theological training.

With the full backing of the New York Catholic hierarchy, including Cardinal O'Connor, nine of the seminarians and young pastors studied at the New York Diocese's St. Joseph's Seminary in the Dunwoodie section of Yonkers. Later they came to Transfiguration to intern. Some of the Fuzhounese where highly critical because they felt that these seminarians and young priests, as members of the Patriotic Church, were not in obedience to the Holy Father and so should not be trained in their diocese or their church. The priests, they believed, had not been legally ordained and so should not be serving communion or presiding over other rites of the church. Some also questioned why only seminarians from the Patriotic Church were being trained and none from the underground church. A number of the older Chinese priests were adamant in believing that taking communion from these illicit priests was a sin. A group of Fuzhounese Catholics most ardently supportive of the underground Chinese church, encouraged by several Chinese priests, broke off from Transfiguration and moved several blocks away to St. Joseph's Church.

St. Joseph's was founded in 1904 by the Missionaries of St. Charles, a community of priests and brothers formed in Italy in 1887 to care for the vast numbers of Italian immigrants then flooding to the United States. Today the parish is still primarily Italian although the surrounding neighborhood is becoming predominantly Chinese. A small Chinese congregation, mostly Cantonese, has been in existence for just over twenty years. St. Joseph's runs a parochial school serving over 250 students in pre-kindergarten through eighth grade and has added a Sunday afternoon service at three o'clock to accommodate the new Fuzhounese congregants. A mainland Chinese priest from the underground Catholic church in Beijing has settled in St. Joseph's parish to work with the Fuzhounese after a term of nearly two years at Transfiguration.

In an interview in 1999, two key lay leaders of the breakaway group expressed fears for their safety even here in New York because of the presence of agents of the Chinese Communist government and its Religious Affairs Bureau. Nevertheless, they were continuing their work in support of China's persecuted but loyal underground Catholic church. At the time, a video of the destruction of unregistered Catholic churches in Changle (see chapter 4) was being circulated among St. Joseph's Fuzhounese members, and relief funds were solicited. Members also circulated a petition urging the Chinese government to cease the harassment and persecution of Catholics and the destruction of their institutions. Several members who had achieved status as U.S. citizens were considering returning to Changle and Fuzhou to present the petition to government and religious authorities in an attempt to bring pressure for religious freedom from overseas Chinese compatriots.

Conclusion

The stories of the four congregations considered here and the two congregations to be discussed in chapter 6 stand as testimonies to Fuzhounese immigrants' ingenuity and determination to create social forms for expressing religious and cultural beliefs in the face of oppressive economic conditions and largely undocumented immigration status. These religious communities are central networks for survival, both material and emotional. As religious sites they enable people to establish a boundary-crossing identity in a hostile environment where they have no local status—indeed, to articulate alternative identities that contest the hegemonic and oppressive U.S. economic, legal, and cultural environment. Immigrants thereby locate their experiences in larger structures of meaning in which their religious traditions play an anchoring role. As we shall see again with the Fuzhounese Protestant churches, this research also shows, however, the fragility of these networks and the difficulty of sustaining newly emerging institutions in competition with and at times subject to the flows and vagaries of the international labor market, not to mention problems in China and conflicts in the United States.

"Come unto Me All Ye That Labor and Are Heavy Laden"

Building Fuzhounese Protestant Churches in New York's Chinatown

"I baptize you in the name of the Father, and of the Son and of the Holy Spirit, Amen!" says Rev. Chen as he plunges a young woman under the water. She arises gasping, startled, crying from the experience. She steps out of the pool drenched and, braced by church members, staggers back to the dressing room, the water cascading from her soaked robes and hair onto the marble floor of the old bathhouse-turned-church on Allen Street, cleansed spiritually as generations have been cleansed physically in that space.

The church is jam packed, even more than usual. It is Easter Sunday, and family, friends, and the congregation fill every inch of space with their curiosity. The sanctuary is standing-room-only. The foyer, the upstairs social hall, the downstairs classrooms are all full. Closed-circuit televisions beam the service into each room. The crowds spill out the front doors and into the street.

Fifty mostly young Fuzhounese fill the front rows of the sanctuary at the Church of Grace waiting their turn for immersion into the faith. One by one they file into specially constructed dressing rooms beside the altar where they shed their street clothes and don long white robes. Assisted by members of the Board of Deacons, they step into the pool, socks and all. As one young convert explained her experience:

My parents are Buddhists. Deeply Buddhist. When I left for America they started burning incense for me and praying for me every morning. And not just to one god, but to many. When my brother made it successfully to Japan, my family gave several thousand yuan to the temple.

147

I first heard about Christianity from a friend here in New York. I visited the church and talked to the minister. I didn't really have much of an impression of Christianity in China. After all, my parents are Buddhist. But it seemed like a good place and good people and a very powerful god who answers prayers. So I decided to be baptized.

Beside the baptismal pool looms a bank of photographers and videographers with some of the most sophisticated camera equipment available in New York City. A floodlight constantly illuminates the scene. Flashbulbs erupt as each convert is immersed and raised again. In a process carefully orchestrated by church volunteers, within forty-five minutes each person will receive an official certificate of baptism, complete with name, date, location, pastor's signature, and color photograph commemorating and documenting the occasion. Some may use the documents to support applications for political asylum based on religious persecution. For most, they commemorate a dramatic transition—spiritual, physical, emotional—perhaps achieved, perhaps only longed for, that reconceptualizes their lives and their system of meaning-making.

FIGURE 14 Church of Grace.

Figure 15 New York House Church.

"Let's See How God Leads Us"

Fuzhounese have established two thriving Protestant churches in Chinatown that serve as both ritual and community centers for their immigrant
constituents. The Church of Grace, founded in 1988, and the New York
House Church, which split from it in 1998, are independent congregations
created with distinct Fuzhounese identities. Despite the recent schism, the
two Fuzhounese congregations are filling their worship spaces and rapidly
expanding programs and services for their immigrant constituents while
most Protestant congregations in Chinatown are small and struggling to
survive. Both churches use the Fuzhou dialect heavily in their services and
programs, a unique feature among Chinatown's Christian congregations
and one that stakes out a distinct place in the Chinese community.

Fuzhounese Protestants in New York—Background

On a rainy night on the last day of April 1992, five leaders from the Church of Grace, a small new Fuzhounese congregation, arrived at the New York City public land auction hoping to purchase a 1904 public bathhouse at 133 Allen Street that had been the city's last public baths when it closed in 1988 because of budget cuts. The evening before, braving torrential rain, they had gone to see the two-story property just above Delancy Street, at the extreme northern edge of New York's rapidly expanding Chinatown. The basement was flooded. The building showed signs of neglect and abuse, both from its nearly eighty-five years of serving poor immigrants living in the tenements of New York's Lower East Side as well as from being closed and abandoned for a number of years. Only one or two other prospective buyers came to inspect the lot.

It was not ideal, but the availability of church-sized buildings in Chinatown was severely limited, and church leaders pinned their hopes on this old bathhouse. The congregation had $50,000 in the bank and pledges for $50,000 more. The minimum bid had been set at $300,000. They hoped they would be able to raise the additional amount quickly if they won the auction, but they knew they could not pay much more for a building they would have to renovate extensively. The moment came. They made their bid at $300,000. They waited.

The dream of owning a church building of their own to serve the waves of immigrants from Fuzhou had been harbored and nurtured for many years. In 1978 a small group of Fuzhounese immigrant women began to gather for prayer and Bible study at Chinatown's Ling Liang Church. There Mrs. Dong, also originally from Fuzhou and wife of the minister, helped establish the Fujian Agape Fellowship (*Min Ai Tuanqi*). Ling Liang Church, part of a larger denominational network with roots in China and churches in Hong Kong and Taiwan, had been established in Chinatown in the 1970s by an earlier wave of Cantonese-speaking immigrants. The Fujian Agape Fellowship shared space with the main Ling Liang Church congregation, but largely remained separate. This separation was symbolized by the fellowship's exclusive use of the local Fuzhou dialect for its gatherings. As the only Fuzhou-dialect Christian group in Chinatown, by the mid-1980s its membership had grown steadily to several dozen, drawing from the gradually increasing flow of Fuzhounese immigrants.

Many of the earliest Fuzhounese immigrants came to New York via Hong Kong, where a sizable community of compatriots had gathered over the previous two decades. Mr. Chen Shufan, for instance, left Fuzhou in 1949 for fear of Communist reprisals after serving in the Nationalist government's navy. After spending eleven years as a naval officer in Taiwan, he relocated to Hong Kong hoping to reunite with his wife and children, whom he had left behind in Fuzhou. Others were able to arrange for short-term work permits in Hong Kong and Macau and never returned. Some stole across the China–Hong Kong border. Still others signed on as sailors in the coastal waters of south China and jumped ship in Hong Kong. Some later jumped ship a second time in New York.

In the 1960s and 1970s in Hong Kong, Mr. Chen and others were instrumental in establishing three independent Fuzhou-dialect Protestant churches, one on Hong Kong Island and two in Kowloon, to serve this distinct immigrant group which had difficulty with the local Cantonese dialect. Rev. Dong, then pastor of one of Hong Kong's Ling Liang churches, frequently preached in these churches. Before leaving for New York in the mid-1970s, he and his wife had become well known among Hong Kong's Fuzhou Christians. So it seemed natural to many New York immigrants to congregate in Rev. and Mrs. Dong's church and to start a Fuzhou-dialect-specific fellowship in the midst of an otherwise Cantonese-speaking Chinatown parish.

By the mid-1980s the Fujian Agape Fellowship had grown to several dozen members. All were recent immigrants. Even those who came via Hong Kong had originated in "Fuzhou." In reality, few were from Fuzhou City. Most were rural dwellers hailing from Fuzhou's surrounding towns and villages. Their families were farmers or fishers, and some were sailors who had left the area in earlier waves of outmigration. Others were shopkeepers, teachers, or local government officials. All shared a desire to improve their lives and the lives of their families. And all shared a certain ingenuity in manipulating local and international conditions to achieve their goals.

Few of them had legal status in the United States. Zhen Wei zhu had arranged an international air flight from Hong Kong to the Dominican Republic in 1980 which required an overnight stay in New York to change planes. His transit visa allowed him to leave Kennedy airport for the night. The next day he did not show up for the second leg of his journey to the Dominican Republic. Instead, he chose to remain anonymously and illegally in the United States. Others overstayed tourist visas. Their status as Hong Kong residents deflected the scrutiny U.S. immigration officials direct at the current arrivals straight from Fuzhou. A few came with the help of a fledgling human smuggling network. All worked in restaurants and garment shops in lower Manhattan. The garment shops were beginning to rebuild after the offshoring of the 1970s. Restaurants serving the growing tourist trade and American taste for Chinese cuisine continued to grow. Owners readily welcomed low-wage laborers to fuel this expansion.

Linguistic unity rooted in the Fuzhou dialect drew people together at Ling Liang Church, as did their common immigration experience and shared struggle to survive in the isolated and exploitative Chinatown ethnic enclave dominated by earlier Cantonese arrivals. From the beginning, the divisions of hometown, kin group, class, politics, and especially religious worldview and practice that would later drive them apart were present, buried just below the surface. Yet, so powerful was the need of these early immigrants for solidarity and support that it would be more than ten years after the establishment of an independent Fuzhounese church in 1988 that the tensions would erupt in full-scale conflict.

Misunderstandings and disagreements did emerge early on between the growing Fujian Agape Fellowship and the Cantonese-speaking members of the larger but stagnant Ling Liang Church. The struggling Cantonese congregation resisted incorporating the newly arrived and largely uneducated Fuzhounese immigrants into the congregational structure. Many Cantonese feared that with increasing Fuzhounese immigration, the expanding Fuzhounese group at Ling Liang Church would soon dominate. Within the Fuzhounese leadership itself, different visions of the future emerged in the context of this conflict. Some preferred that the Fujian Agape Fellowship remain a part of Ling Liang Church though maintaining a separate identity. Others imagined an independent Fuzhounese congregation when their membership increased sufficiently. Some favored independence but feared they could not sustain themselves financially or accumulate the resources needed to build and maintain a church in the United States. Ultimately the voices for independence had demographics on their side. The overall Fuzhounese population continued to expand in the mid and late 1980s, as did the number of Protestant brothers and sisters arriving from churches in Hong Kong, Macau, and back home in the Fuzhou area.

Rev. Liu Yangfen

One of those arriving in the mid-1980s was Rev. Liu Yangfen, whose experiences during the Cultural Revolution are described in chapter 4. This greatly beloved and highly controversial figure became a central character in the development of Fuzhounese Protestantism in New York and eventually in the split that shook the Church of Grace in 1998. In addition, since moving to New York, he has served as a focal point for building a complex religious network between New York and Protestant churches in the Fuzhou area.

Rev. Liu Yangfen arrived in New York from Fuzhou in 1985. Minister of Fuzhou's central Flower Lane Protestant Church in the 1950s, Liu was severely persecuted in the 1960s and early 1970s for his outspoken Christian faith and because a two-year master's degree earned at Vanderbilt University in the 1940s placed him in the targeted category of foreign collaborator and spy. For years he was assigned to labor reeducation in the impoverished mountain region of northwest Fujian Province. As we have seen, when, in the late 1970s, China's paramount leader, Deng Xiaoping, introduced his post-Mao economic reforms and moved to normalize social relations and institutions disrupted during the Cultural Revolution, the first church to reopen in Fuzhou was the Flower Lane Church. In 1979, Liu was politically "rehabilitated" and assigned as pastor in charge. As an elder statesman in the Christian community, he was revered by grassroots Christians for his resistance to the persecution of the Communist Party. Over the next six years he traveled throughout the urban and rural areas of Fuzhou, preaching in newly reopened churches, conducting baptisms, weddings, and funerals, serving communion, visiting house-church gatherings, and encouraging the reemergence of Chinese Christianity.

By the time Liu left Fuzhou for New York in 1985, his was a household name among Fuzhou's Christian community, both in the open churches and in the underground. His departure only aggrandized his legend. None of the new generation of ministers could compare favorably to his heroic profession of faith in the face of angry Red Guards and fanatical anti-Christian government bureaucrats. No one could forget his pioneering spirit in revitalizing Christian work in Fuzhou after the Cultural Revolution. Most claimed a personal connection to this larger-than-life figure: a family member baptized, a wedding attended, a relative who graduated from the same school. After his emigration his legend only continued to expand.

During the couple's study abroad in the 1940s, Rev. Liu's wife gave birth to a daughter. By virtue of her place of birth she could rightfully claim U.S. citizenship. In the 1970s Liu, a man of tremendous *guanxi* or connections despite his official ostracism by the government, succeeded in going through the back door to procure a visa for his daughter to travel to Hong Kong. There she declared her U.S. citizenship and migrated to upstate New York, where she and her husband opened a Chinese restaurant. In 1985 she petitioned for her father to join her. According to Liu, the decision to leave was not an easy one. "There was still much work to be done in Fuzhou. But I felt my time had come to an end. People were beginning to leave Fuzhou for New York and I thought I might be able to work with them there. I also thought I might still be able to assist the churches in China, but from the outside." Upon arrival in New York, the Fujian Agape Fellowship quickly sought Liu out and he began to travel once a month to New York City to preach. He also began to explore ways to assist the Protestant churches in Fuzhou.

A Church of Their Own

In 1988 the Fujian Agape Fellowship decided to establish an independent Fuzhou-dialect congregation in Chinatown. Beginning one Sunday morning in May, twenty members gathered for prayer and Bible study at the home of Chen Shufan on Orchard Street, a railroad style flat in an old five-story tenement building. They ate lunch together at a local restaurant. In the afternoon, several dozen Fuzhounese crowded into the large living room of Brother Lu Yangsheng on Monroe Street for worship. Rev. Liu preached that first Sunday with over thirty-five people in attendance. Mrs. Dong and Brother Jiang Kesong assisted with the liturgy.

By July the group relocated to a loft space at 22 Catherine Street that it shared with another church. The congregation rapidly expanded. Word spread through the growing Fuzhounese network. Most came from Manhattan as their work schedules permitted, still others came from upstate New York, Connecticut, and New Jersey. Seventy people attended the first Sunday services on Catherine Street. Said Chen Shufan: "We didn't know what would happen. Who would come? Would we have enough money to pay the rent and utilities? But we prayed and waited to see how God would lead. God has been very good to us."

Language and the Making of a Fuzhounese Identity

Key to the congregation's allure among recent immigrants was its identification with and commitment to the use of the Fuzhou dialect in its worship and programs. The model had been successful in building three Fuzhou-dialect-specific churches in Hong Kong and in the early days of the Fujian Agape Fellowship at Ling Liang Church. Now the congregation's leaders hoped that the Fuzhou dialect would prove as effective an organizing principle in the future expansion they imagined.

The unique Fuzhou dialect, known locally as *Fuzhou yu* or *Fuzhou hua* is spoken in the coastal regions near Fuzhou to the north and south of the Min River and in Fuzhou City itself. Linguistically it is close to the Min dialect prevalent in southern Fujian Province and in Taiwan. It is, however, unintelligible to speakers of Cantonese (southern China and Hong Kong) and Mandarin, the two predominant dialects in Chinatown. In China, Mandarin is called the "national language" (*guo yu*) or the common language (*putong hua*). It is based on the Chinese dialect spoken in northern China, including the area around the capital city Beijing. In the 1950s the Chinese government introduced Mandarin as the dialect of instruction in the nation's public schools and in national media. But for the vast majority of Chinese, especially the 75 percent of the population in rural areas, Mandarin is a second or third dialect learned after their own local one. At home, work, and play they speak their local dialect.

From its beginning, the congregation conducted worship services in Fuzhou dialect with simultaneous translation into Mandarin. Board meetings were conducted in Fuzhou dialect, and Fuzhounese was the dialect of most informal conversations. Among the older members it is often the only language they speak, though they may understand some spoken Mandarin. For the mostly rural immigrants from the Fuzhou area, the use of Fuzhou dialect proved a significant unifying factor in the midst of an ethnic enclave dominated by Cantonese and Mandarin speakers. The congregation's first three names after independence reflect its emerging sense of identity and its attempts to capitalize on its use of the Fuzhou dialect to project that identity into the wider Chinatown community:

1. *Fuzhou Dialect Fujian Agape Fellowship of New York*
2. *Fuzhou Dialect (and Mandarin) Crusade of New York*
3. *Chinese Christian Gospel Association, Fuzhou Dialect and Mandarin*

Eventually the congregation chose the broadest representation, opting to identify itself as Min (shorthand for Fujian Province) and dropping references to the Fuzhou dialect in its name: The New York Christian Church of Grace to the Fujianese. Within the congregation, however, the use of Fuzhou dialect is still predominant, and in the Chinatown community the church has established a distinct identity as the "Fuzhounese church."

Organizing a Congregation

By the time the Fujian Agape Fellowship struck out on its own in 1988, many of the earliest immigrants had been able to regularize their immigration status as a result of the 1986 Immigration Reform and Control Act. The provisions of this act provided a blanket amnesty to undocumented workers who could prove they had residency in the United States prior to 1982. Without legal status, the leaders of the Fujian Agape Fellowship had little hope of formally organizing their own congregation. But, reassured by their own legality, they moved to put in place an internal structure and formalize the status of the congregation in relationship to the structures of U.S. society. Over the next several years the congregation established a Board of Deacons and a number of small groups including a choir, youth group, women's fellowship, and student fellowship. In the fall of 1989 it established a building fund for the purchase or construction of a new church property. In May 1990 a building committee was established to actively explore possibilities for the congregation's future.

Externally, the congregation began the process of legal incorporation, seeking recognition under New York state law as a religious organization and petitioning the Internal Revenue Service for tax-exempt 501(c)3 status. To employ personnel, to avoid property tax, and to allow tax deductibility for members' donations, the congregation needed to regularize its status in relationship to the city, state, and federal governments. The process took nearly three years and provided many challenges to a congregation of recent arrivals, new citizens, and non-English speakers with little experience in negotiating the complex and sometimes mysterious American state bureaucracy. These steps would be essential for the congregation's success in its new environment.

In his introduction to *Gatherings in Diaspora* (Warner and Wittner 1998), sociologist Steven Warner suggests that a unique characteristic of religion in the United States is its tendency to evolve into a congregational structure. Even the religious practices of new immigrants, he argues, quickly transform into congregational forms:

> Because religion is so important to an immigrant group, and because the group's circumstances have been changed so drastically by migration, the religion must take on new forms to be capable of survival in the new land. . . . The most characteristic adaptation I expect to encounter among immigrant religious groups is the development of congregational forms. . . . The congregation is a local voluntary religious association, usually culturally homogeneous and often legally constituted as a nonprofit corporation controlled by its laity and administered by professional clergy. (Warner and Wittner 1998: 20–21)

The emergence of this congregational form should not be imagined as ex nihilo, out of nothing. For Fuzhounese Protestants and Catholics, congregations have been the organizational norm in China, not an adaptation to the U.S. environment. Even for Buddhist, Daoist, or Chinese popular religionists, much of the congregational form is required by the Chinese state, as we have seen in chapters 3 and 4. Immigrant religious communities do not develop congregational characteristics out of the air in the United States. Rather, immigrant congregations are disciplined by the regimes of U.S. law, civic and government structures, and bureaucracies. In order to achieve legitimacy and effective operation in the U.S. context, groups of immigrant religious practitioners must successfully negotiate an intricate maze of regulations and regulatory agencies. To purchase property or employ personnel they must be organized as a legal corporation that includes a Board of Trustees. Once property is purchased, construction or renovation must be approved by the local buildings department, an application that usually requires plans and authorization from an architect and engineer. Finding these professionals among a group of recent immigrants with little English facility may stretch a congregation's resources and networks. To legally occupy a building, a certificate of occupancy must be obtained specifying the types of activities and numbers of people allowed in a space. Inspections by fire and building departments attempt to ensure a group's adherence to fire and construction codes.

If the group wishes to employ personnel, the disciplining continues. Income taxes must be withheld and submitted to the Internal Revenue Service. Social Security taxes must be paid to the Social Security Administration. New York State unemployment and disability insurance must be calculated and disbursed, and W-2 or I-9 forms must be issued to employees. Functionally, a system of financial accounting and accountability meeting government standards must be established. For the Church of Grace, complying with these regulations has been and continues to be a difficult process, straining its human resources. At the same time, the experience has been an enforced civic orientation.

Finding Clerical Leadership

The desire to find a minister proved one of the driving motivations of the congregation's attempt to normalize its legal status vis-à-vis the U.S. state. Recruiting and retaining professionally trained and effective leadership is a problem confronted by many immigrant religious communities and is particularly nettlesome in Chinese Christian congregations. In the case of the Church of Grace, Rev. Liu was willing to help, but in 1988 he was already seventy-six years old. The strong lay leadership that had emerged chose instead to invite Elder Chen Shewo from Hong Kong. Chen, originally from Fuzhou and out of a Little Flock background, had served as the evangelist at Tsuen Wan Church, one of the Fuzhou-dialect congregations in Hong Kong. Many knew and respected him from their time together there. Chen and his wife eagerly accepted the invitation, and the congregation set about obtaining a U.S. work visa for him. First, however, they needed to establish legal status and recognition as a religious organization, a process that took three years.

In the interim, the Church of Grace's Board of Deacons maintained control of the congregation's administration, program, and ritual. The Reverend Liu continued to preach once a month. Responsibility for other Sundays rotated weekly among area ministers, a practice that has been retained throughout the history of the church, with some recent modification as the pastoral leadership has stabilized. Chen visited New York for several months on a tourist visa. In May 1991, uncertain of how Chen Shewo's case would be resolved, the congregation added a young evangelist, Mr. Zheng Yile, as minister in charge. But on all matters of congregational polity and practice, the board retained decision-making power. In December 1991, Chen finally received his work visa and arrived in New York to serve as senior minister.

The congregation's difficulty in bringing Elder Chen to its staff proved but a precursor to twelve years of frustration in recruiting and retaining pastors. Five senior pastors served the congregation for various lengths of time between 1991 and 2002. For more than two years, 1998–2000, the congregation had no senior pastor and relied on the services of junior evangelists.

In mainline Protestant traditions in China, the term *chuandao*, literally to "spread the principles or doctrines," refers to lay professional religious workers and is variously translated as evangelist, preacher, local preacher, catechist, or Bible woman. This status is clearly distinguished from the Chinese term *mushi*, literally "shepherd teacher," which is translated as pastor or reverend and refers to ordained Protestant clergy. In the Little Flock tradition, however, an egalitarian church polity does not recognize the status of ordained minister. Instead, all members are brothers and sisters (*dixiong jiemei*) of equal rights and responsibilities. For organizational purposes, one brother serves as the brother in charge, or first among equals, and is sometimes referred to as an elder (*zhanglao*). The Church of Grace has, over its history, combined both traditions, the mainline Protestant and the Little Flock. Elder Chen Shewo and Brother Wang De'en of the Little Flock tradition and Rev. Liu and most recently Rev. Chen Zhaoqing have all served as senior leaders of the congregation. For the purposes of this study, when referring to the senior leaders as a category, the term "senior pastor" is used to distinguish them from the evangelists on staff.

Despite the instability in senior pastoral leadership, attendance at the Church of Grace continued to increase. With determined and dedicated lay leadership centered in the Board of Deacons and the explosive growth of the Fuzhounese immigrant population after 1991, the congregation quickly outgrew its Catherine Street loft.

In April 1992, the Church of Grace successfully bid on and purchased the old public bathhouse on Allen Street at the New York City public land auction. Opened at the turn of the twentieth century to serve Jewish and Italian immigrants who lived in tenements without hot water or bathing facilities, it was the third municipal bathhouse in the city's history. Originally constructed as part of social reforms to improve the moral character and citizenship of immigrants by improving their health and sanitation practices, ninety years later it would be reborn among the latest group of immigrants as a spiritual center to improve their chances of eternal salvation. Under the leadership of Chen Shewo and the Board of Deacons chairperson Chen Yonghuang, funds were raised, renovation plans approved by the city, and construction begun. The Fuzhou-language churches in Hong Kong loaned $50,000 for the purchase and renovation—a reverse of the flow of

New York money to build churches in China. Church members in New York volunteered their time and money to complete the project.

Inside, the original bathhouse skylights were retained in the street-level sanctuary. The bathhouse had held forty-nine showers and two tubs for men on the ground floor and thirty-one showers and three tubs for women upstairs. In the renovations, the old marble slabs from the showers were relaid as the sanctuary floor. Overall, the interior was styled to reflect rural Protestant churches everywhere in China, simple and unadorned. The pews are hand hewn of plain wood, varnished and cushionless. In the front a central pulpit stands on a raised platform, surrounded by a communion rail. A few potted plants are arranged on either side. The stark white walls are left without ornamentation. A single piano was purchased for playing hymns, and a wooden offering box was installed in the foyer entrance.

All appeared on course for the August 1993 grand opening. But one month beforehand, Elder Chen Shewo abruptly announced his resignation. By the end of July he had relocated to Texas, only nineteen months after his much anticipated arrival. Chen's tenure at the Church of Grace had been stormy from the beginning. While a series of personal conflicts with the Board of Deacons and his wife's public unhappiness as a Cantonese among Fuzhounese created awkwardness in the congregation, the fundamental conflicts revolved around theology and power. Before accepting the congregation's offer to serve as Elder in Charge, Chen Shewo, a member of the Little Flock tradition, established one precondition. The Church of Grace must begin to follow Little Flock practices by offering communion every Sunday, not once a month as had been the church's practice. The Board of Deacons acquiesced. After his arrival in New York in late 1991, Elder Chen continued to press the Board to conform to Little Flock patterns. He insisted, for instance, that to be effective, all baptisms must be by immersion, fully submerging the new believer in water. He even argued that older members whose baptism was by sprinkling water on the head or anything less than full immersion should be rebaptized to ensure the ritual's efficacy.

Throughout Chen Shewo's service at the Church of Grace another conflict simmered between him and members of the Board of Deacons over the extent to which each would hold power in the congregation. Accustomed to exercising control over congregational affairs, the board had resisted Chen's desire for more power. Despite his position as senior minister, the board, for instance, retained control over who would preach. Chen only preached once a month. Preachers for other weeks were invited by the board, often without consultation with Chen. The strong board, comprised of founding

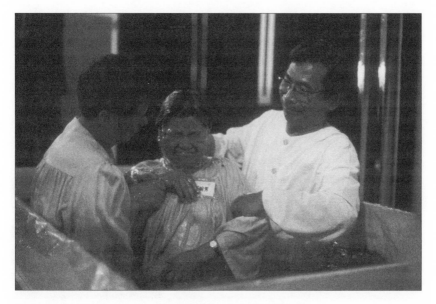

FIGURE 16 Baptism by immersion at the Church of Grace.

members of the congregation, chose to keep power in their hands. Chen Shewo, an older, strong leader accustomed to more deference, chose to retire to Texas to live with his son rather than work under those conditions.

In the crisis, Rev. Liu was asked to step in as senior minister on a provisional basis. The grand opening was pushed back several weeks, and on August 22 the Allen Street church building was filled with over two hundred people in attendance. Chen Shewo returned from Texas for the opening ceremony. Over the next four years the aging Liu served as senior pastor with the help of three younger evangelists.

One of these was Mr. Chen Yonghuang, from a town south of Changle, who came to the United States initially in 1980 from Hong Kong and received citizenship under the Immigration Reform and Control Act of 1986. Yonghuang served as chair of the Board of Deacons and the Board of Trustees from their inceptions, and during the renovation of the Allen Street building he went on unemployment benefits and served as construction manager. Rev. Liu encouraged him to attend a seminary, and in 1993 he relinquished leadership of the Board of Deacons in order to pursue his studies and begin work as the church's part-time evangelist.

FIGURE 17 Wedding at the Church of Grace, officiated by the Reverend Liu Yangfen, center rear.

A second evangelist, also from the Changle area, was Ms. Liu Baoying, who emigrated to New York in 1990. Baoying had been deeply involved in the Home of Grace in China. In New York she worked for several years in garment shops before being invited by Rev. Liu to serve as church evangelist in 1995. At the Church of Grace, Baoying worked primarily with the Womens Fellowship group and conducted home visits. She led a daily morning Bible study group based on the Home of Grace methodology developed by Dr. John Sung. Periodically she was invited to preach during the main Sunday worship service, an unusual occurrence in a church where, during its history, preachers and even worship leaders have been almost exclusively men. In 1997 Baoying started a house church meeting in her Brooklyn apartment, which in 1998 became the Church of Grace's Brooklyn branch. Baoying left New York in the fall of 1998, however, in the aftermath of the conflict in the Home of Grace in Changle. The Brooklyn branch continues under the guidance of the Church of Grace Board of Deacons and staff. In recent years, she has divided her time between New York City, where she leads several Bible study groups comprised primarily of women, and the Home of Grace training center in the southeastern United States. She travels frequently to Pennsylvania to support an emerging Home of Grace fellowship there and continues regular contact with Home of Grace networks in China, making periodic visits to support their work.

Mr. Chen Sheng, the third evangelist, is from a tiny village in southern Changle County and attended the Three-Self–sponsored Protestant Provincial Seminary in Fuzhou before serving for six years as evangelist in a rural church. In 1995 he left China to study at a small Chinese-language seminary in New Jersey. His sister, owner of a Chinese restaurant on Staten Island, sponsored him. He served an internship year at the Church of Grace in 1997–1998, remaining as an evangelist with particular responsibility for the church's growing youth and young adult program.

The Split

By 1997 the umbrella under which the disparate groups in the Church of Grace gathered began to fall apart. For years the common immigrant experience, the shared Fuzhou dialect, and more recently the unifying presence of the revered Rev. Liu had held together a congregation fundamentally divided along lines of hometown, class, and religious background. Tensions came to a head in the fall of 1997.

For several years, Rev. Liu had been seeking a successor. By 1997, at age eighty-five, his health was suffering under the stress of serving the growing Church of Grace congregation and the increasingly tense atmosphere surrounding the church's leadership. Surgery that summer left him unable to continue full time. In the fall of 1995, with Liu's encouragement, the Board of Deacons had invited Brother Wang De'en to visit for several months to explore the possibility of a longer-term call. Brother Wang was not Fuzhounese. A native of Jiangxi Province he had, however, visited Fuzhou, was acquainted with Rev. Liu, and like him had suffered severely in China for his religious beliefs. From a Little Flock background, Brother Wang had recently come out of China to live with his daughter in Vancouver, Canada.

Brother Wang served the Church of Grace from December 1995 to July 1996 before returning to Vancouver to attend to what he called "family business." His eight-month visit to the Church was uneventful, but after his departure two factions formed on the Board of Deacons regarding his future with the congregation. Some, particularly those with a Little Flock background, strongly supported his continuation. Others resisted.

According to a member of the Board of Deacons at the time:

There were two factions in the Board of Deacons. I really liked him. His preaching was very clear. But he was also very rigid. If he thought you were wrong, he told you so. So some people didn't like him. He was also Little Flock. Some people didn't feel that Little Flock and the Church of Grace were a very good match.

But he [Brother Wang] never said you've got to dress in a certain way or do things in a particular way. He always talked about how to be a good Christian, how to be saved, how to have a good relationship with God.

I thought he should come. Most people on the Board of Deacons did. Only a minority disagreed. They were afraid perhaps of the Little Flock aspect. But the majority agreed. So we wrote him a letter of invitation He said he would decide but he did not. "I still have a few things to take care of, I'll let you know," he said.

In preparation, some members of the church rented a neighboring apartment for him in early 1997. Among this group some were so excited about his possible return that they purchased cots so they could live in the apartment for special retreats and study with him. But Wang De'en did not respond to their invitation.

According to Wang De'en, interviewed in 2000:

I'm from the Little Flock background. The Church of Grace did not have a Little Flock way of doing things or background. While I was there I didn't get involved in their structure or management. I focused on preaching mainly and didn't get involved in anything else. I only stayed a little while. I wasn't a good fit for that congregation. So I left.

According to a member of the Board of Deacons:

We still don't know why he didn't come. Some people probably misunderstood and mistakenly believed that the Board didn't want him. But that isn't what we decided. Maybe some of the Christians down in the pews had some things to say, but not the Board. They may have said, "Oh, Little Flock is such and such," but this was a minority. Brother Wang himself decided not to come back.

In the fall of 1997 another issue of religious practice rose to the surface—whether to have communion weekly or monthly. In the Little Flock tradition, communion (*bai bing hui*) along with preaching of the Word is considered the central ritual practice. Throughout China, Little Flock worship services begin with a communion ritual including extensive hymn singing and collective prayer followed by a second hour or more of preaching. Ever since Elder Chen Shewo's tenure began in 1991, the Church of Grace had honored the Little Flock tradition of weekly communion. But after the congregation moved to Allen Street and worship attendance began to expand rapidly in the mid-1990s, a consensus began to develop among some key church leaders that the congregation should shift to monthly communion. Their rationale rested on the sense that weekly communion made the service too long. For Fuzhounese immigrants working grueling hours in restaurants, garment shops, and construction with at most one day off a week, a worship service extending beyond two hours constituted a hardship and an unreasonable expectation. They also felt that many people were coming late to worship to miss communion, showing up only for the preaching. Others felt that weekly communion had become mere ritual and habit, diminishing its significance. Still other church leaders, including Rev. Liu and those from the Little Flock tradition, adamantly resisted the change. At the peak of the crisis in the fall of 1997, discussions and debates ensued among the board on a nearly weekly basis.

Simultaneously, Brother Wang De'en did return to New York but not to the Church of Grace. Instead, with the encouragement of Rev. Liu, he launched a Bible study group at the home of a Christian in Queens. Many of his supporters from the Church of Grace, while continuing to attend there on Sundays, started going to Queens to participate in his study group during the week. Several long-term members and members of the Board of Deacons attended regularly—members who later formed the core leadership group of the New York House Church.

Then abruptly, the Board of Deacons decided to serve communion only once a month. Rev. Liu did not attend the meeting where this decision was made. He immediately announced that the board had clearly been aware of his preference and had acted otherwise; he assumed they no longer wanted him at the Church of Grace. Without further discussion he terminated his role there. Brother Wang's Queens Bible study group also withdrew from the Church of Grace and encouraged others to join them. In January 1998, with Rev. Liu in attendance and preaching, these Christians, largely of a Little Flock tradition, started the New York House Church in the living room of Brother Lu Yangsheng on Monroe Street. Ironically, this was the same living room occupied by the Fujian Agape Fellowship (now the Church of Grace) when it split from Ling Liang Church ten years earlier.

Points of Conflict: Communion, County, and Class

Theological differences, regionalism, and class stratification proved to be the fault lines in the Fuzhounese Protestant community. In interviews, members of both congregations consistently identify the communion controversy as the catalyst for the schism. The communion controversy, however, represented a more deeply perceived theological divide. For years the minority Little Flock group had operated under the Church of Grace umbrella. Two senior pastors, Chen Shewo and Wang De'en, were of Little Flock backgrounds. Rev. Liu never identified himself as Little Flock but consistently supported their positions. But within the congregation, power rested with the Board of Deacons, a group dominated by immigrants not of a Little Flock tradition and with key leaders deeply influenced by the Home of Grace. Additionally, none of the three evangelists hired under Liu's tenure came from a Little Flock background, but were influenced by the Home of Grace or the Three-Self Patriotic Movement. Members of the Little Flock tradition increasingly saw their concerns marginalized and their ritual traditions and congregational polity ignored or rejected. In this context, perhaps, it is not surprising that a group would split off in order to achieve more self-determination in its ritual form and institutional polity. Certainly the split had a clear precursor in the 1994 schism between Little Flock and TSPM-related Christians in Tingjiang. In New York, however, not the Christmas celebration but a communion controversy served as the match that lit the already laid kindling. Other incendiary points of tension and conflict included regional differences and underlying complex issues of class and power.

Kinship, surname, and village networks remain strong among Fuzhounese immigrants and are often the first networks mobilized for survival. At the Church of Grace, a sense of regional competition arose, particularly between people from the immigrant communities of Changle County and those along the banks of the Min, including Tingjiang, Lianjiang, Guantou on the north bank, Houyu and Xiangyu on the south bank, and Langqi Island. At the Church of Grace, many of those from outside Changle felt excluded from power. Popular discourse in the Fuzhounese

Christian community posits that the Church of Grace is comprised solely of people from Changle. Other representations suggest that the congregation is mostly made up of people from one town in southern Changle County.

In other words, discourse among the congregants suggests that after the conflict about communion, regionalism was the second most important cause of the split. A common characterization is often made that "all the people from Changle go to the Church of Grace. Folks from along the Min River all go to the New York House Church." Survey data collected at the two congregations in May 2000 confirm the general contours of these claims.

As the following table shows, a full 54 percent of Church of Grace participants cited an area in Changle County as their hometown. Only 30 percent named the areas of Lianjiang, Tingjiang, Langqi Island, or Mawei north of the Min River. In contrast, hometown identification of participants at the New York House Church is almost reversed: 56 percent cited areas north of the Min as their hometown, including Lianjiang, Tingjiang, Langqi Island, and Mawei; only 28 percent of participants claimed origins in Changle. Analysis of the data, however, shows that the split along regional or hometown lines is not as stark as portrayed in popular discourse. Although the data reflect a distinct correlation of region to church affiliation, the correlation is far from absolute.

Taking the suspicion of inherent regionalism to an extreme, an ardent though minority view within the Fuzhounese Protestant population holds

TABLE 6.1
Origins of Congregation Members

Hometown	Church of Grace		New York House Church	
	Total	Percentage of Total	Total	Percentage of Total
Changle	94	54.0	18	28.1
Lianjiang	20	11.5	24	37.5
Tingjiang	16	9.2	5	7.8
Langqi Island	12	6.9	4	6.3
Fuzhou	11	6.3	7	10.9
Mawei	4	2.3	3	4.7
Fuqing	1	0.6	3	4.7
Wenzhou	1	0.6	0	0
China—Other	11	6.3	0	0
New York	4	2.3	0	0

that the Church of Grace is controlled by a small group of people from one hometown. Receiving particular criticism has been a circle of family, friends, and acquaintances who came to be known for the way they asserted their power to influence congregational decisions. In reality, members from this hometown do play a role out of proportion to their numbers in the congregation. All four chairmen of the Board of Deacons were born and raised there. All three evangelists have had a strong connection to the area. Their young adult children also play prominent roles as leaders of the congregation, particularly in the powerful youth group, the choir, and the library/bookstore. The young adults themselves were born outside of the United States but because of language skills and educational experiences they serve as cultural brokers for their parents' generation and as a transitional group between them and the generation of Fuzhounese children now being born in the United States.

The core group of hometown friends knew each other well in China and play an influential role in the life of the New York congregation. Their friendship and sense of loyalty has only been solidified by the controversies faced by the Church of Grace in recent years. At Board of Deacons meetings they are the most vocal and their opinions largely prevail. Forceful in their vision for the congregation, they stick together during meetings and conflicts. They are also extremely dedicated and hard working. Many of the primary functions of the congregation would not happen without their involvement. Outside the church, they socialize and communicate on a regular basis. Religiously all have been associated, directly or through family members, with the Home of Grace in China.

Statistics regarding the relationship of hometown to choice of church perhaps say more about the differential geographic influence of indigenous theological movements in the Fuzhou area, particularly between the Little Flock, Home of Grace, and Three-Self Patriotic Movement (TSPM). In some towns, such as Tingjiang, both Little Flock and Three-Self churches exist, as described in chapter 4. Most members of the Tingjiang Little Flock church attend the New York House Church because of its familiar ritual practices and its reputation in the Fuzhou area as being the Fuzhounese congregation most receptive to Little Flock traditions and theology. But Tingjiang residents from the TSPM-related church like evangelist Chen and her husband (see chapter 4) do not feel ritually comfortable at the New York House Church and so attend the Church of Grace. In the Tingjiang case, a regional determination may be mitigated by religious tradition. Understanding variation in patterns of affiliation between the Church of Grace and the New York House Church seems to require a consideration of both religious tradition and regional origins.

Fuzhounese Protestants, Class, and Immigration History

Fundamental questions of class and power were an additional source of conflict among church members and within the Board of Deacons. While more difficult to analyze, differential status and access to power appear obvious when certain factors are considered. Among Fuzhounese immigrants at the Church of Grace, variables in internal stratification include legal status, occupation, level of education, residence before coming to the United States, language skills, and personal connections based on hometown. Fuzhounese immigrants at the Church of Grace and the New York House Church represent several of the compressed waves or generations in recent Chinese immigration history to the United States described in chapter 3.

The categorization of the relative conditions of immigrant generations and predicaments of the Fuzhounese community provides a framework for understanding the causes of the structural stratification of the larger Fuzhounese population and within the Fuzhounese Protestant churches of New York's Chinatown (see table 1.1, page 30). The attributes described among Fuzhounese immigrants as a whole are reproduced within the Protestant churches. Within the churches, differential access to power and authority often parallels the broader social and legal conditions of the membership.

A logical place to examine stratification within a congregation is in a comparison of the governance structure and the membership of the congregation. At the Church of Grace, an analysis of status markers, including legal status, occupation, educational level, residence prior to arrival in the United States, English and Cantonese language proficiency, and personal connections based on hometown, as reflected in the Board of Deacons, is revealing. At the end of 2000, nearly two years after the split, of the sixteen members of the board and the three religious workers, all but two were born in the Fuzhou environs, none in the United States. All but one have permanent legal status, including seven green cards, ten naturalized citizens, and one religious worker. Twelve of the nineteen (63 percent) were born in Changle County, including nine in one town alone. Of the others, two were born in Fuzhou City, and one each in Min An, Tingjiang, Langqi Island, Hong Kong, and Singapore.

Eleven of the nineteen (58 percent) lived elsewhere for a period of time before coming to the United States, nine in Hong Kong, one each in Macau and Singapore. As a result, nine of them speak some Cantonese. Nine also speak some English, though only six speak it well enough to conduct business or have in-depth conversations. Six of them speak the Fuzhou dialect and Mandarin exclusively. Occupationally, four are professionals (two accountants, one a real estate manager, and one a postal worker); three are in the restaurant industry (one as owner, two as chefs). Four work as seamstresses in garment shops (all women). Two are students, one a construction worker, one a housewife, and two are retired. Eight have completed some higher education, two with master's and three with bachelor's degrees. Seven are women and twelve are men, a reverse of the ratio of women to men among the total membership and worship attendance.

The aggregate membership of the Church of Grace Board of Deacons represents a privileged status in comparison to its own congregation's membership and in comparison to the core group of leaders of the New York House Church and its overall membership. The Board of Deacons at the Church of Grace is largely comprised of immigrants from waves one, two, and four outlined in table 1.1. Overall, membership of both congregations draws more heavily from wave three, revealing higher levels of undocumented status; of employment as laborers in restaurant, garment, and construction industries; of direct migration from rural areas around Fuzhou; and of language limitations. Nine of the nineteen Board of Deacons immigrated to the United States prior to 1990 (45 percent), a rate more than double the overall percentage for the two congregations. The Board of Deacons is also significantly older. Forty-five percent of its members are over fifty years old. In the Church of Grace general membership, only 19 percent are over fifty.

The Church of Grace: Its Location in the Fuzhounese Immigrant Experience

In the discourse of transnational processes and globalization theory, the Church of Grace and the New York House Church should be considered nodes of access to an intertwined web of social and economic relations that spreads from this New York entry point throughout the city, across the country, and eventually back to China. For many members of U.S. society, visiting New York's Chinatown feels like entering a foreign country. Yet even for those grown accustomed to the "foreignness" of Chinatown, the Fuzhounese sections of the enclave seem like still another reality. Entering these churches is strikingly reminiscent of walking into a church anywhere in rural China, more specifically the churches around Fuzhou. The language changes. The clothing changes. Personal kinship and village networks become revitalized. The food changes. The smells change. In a framework inspired by Victor Turner, the foyer of the Church of Grace is a liminal space for these Fuzhounese Christian immigrants, a place of transition between one reality and another, a place that removes them, even if temporarily, from their day-to-day reality and affords them a glimpse of something different (Turner 1969). Immigrants who, outside these churches, are foreigners in a very strange land are transformed into insiders. Outside they cannot speak the dominant U.S. language, English, or even the dominant Chinese dialects of Cantonese and Mandarin spoken in Chinatown. Inside, their language, Fuzhounese, is predominant. Outside they are seen by earlier Chinese immigrants as "country bumpkins" (*tubaozi*) and derided as uncultured and uncouth. Inside they celebrate a common cultural heritage of an exploring people.

In subtle ways, the Church of Grace and the New York House Church, like the He Xian Jun Temple and the Temple of Heavenly Thanksgiving described in chapter 5, provide sites for counterhegemonic discourse and network building that are central to immigrants' ability to create narratives and identities for survival on their immigrant sojourn in the United States. Outside, the immigrants are considered poor; inside they are considered as adventurous wage earners supporting a church in New York and a family and community at home in China. Outside they are itinerant workers moving from city to city, job to job; inside they find a central meeting place—a location for connection and reconnection with fellow Fuzhounese and with home. Outside they are isolated newcomers in a dominant U.S. culture; inside they are integrated into an extended Chinese communication network as news circulates among family and friends and recent arrivals from China. Outside they are members of highly stratified and hereditary family, surname, or village associations; inside they are equal members of a voluntary association that offers a dramatic leveling effect and an escape from cultural obligations. Outside they are exploited workers; inside they may be respected members and leaders of their church community. Outside they may be illegal immigrants, undocumented workers, invisible to the U.S. state or even targets of INS raids and crackdowns; inside they are children of God who through the death of Jesus have had their sins forgiven and through

FIGURE 18 Mr. Chen Shufan, Church of Grace deacon and founding member.

baptism have been admitted into the fellowship of true believers whose sole comfort lies not in worldly status, honors or possessions but in the freedom associated with obedience to God. Outside they are sinners, lawbreakers, one step away from imprisonment and deportation, the truncation of their dreams of freedom, liberation, and financial success; inside they are exhorted to remember that while a U.S. green card may be nice, only God's green card will get them into heaven.

This religious orientation and theological self-understanding distinguishes these churches from other Chinatown social institutions. It demarcates the religious institution from the village or surname association, from the union or political party. People participate and contribute not only because of the familiarity of friendship and village, but because of the church's ability to convey meaning and religious significance to immigrants whose lives are more regularly filled with disorientation and dislocation.

A Church Grows in Chinatown

Today the Church of Grace is experiencing explosive growth. By the summer of 2002, average attendance exceeded five hundred people for its main service—nearly doubling in two years—plus another fifty for a year-old English-language service. At 11:00 A.M., as the ninety-minute service begins, the sanctuary is packed with 350 people. In addition, sixty people sit on folding chairs in the foyer watching the service on closed-circuit television. The scene is replicated with seventy attendees upstairs in the church's social hall. In the basement, three Sunday School classes totaling nearly fifty children squeeze into tiny spaces.

The mailing list for the Church of Grace newsletter is well over two thousand, with addresses across the United States, including some Immigration and Naturalization detention centers. As discussed in chapter 1, the Fuzhounese population is highly transient and attendance at these churches reflects this fact. The pews may be consistently filled, but the participants change from week to week. On Christmas Day, one of the few days of the year that all Chinese workers are guaranteed to have off and a time when Fuzhounese employed across the United States return to New York City to visit friends and relatives, the Church of Grace's worship attendance soars, and noisy crowds spill out the front door into Allen Street.

Like the New York House Church, the Church of Grace serves as a Fuzhounese Christian community center on Sunday. Over bowls of noodles served after worship, the conversations roar. News of home from new arrivals. News of jobs and places to live. Discussions of recent events in China or in the U.S. media. A member of the Board of Deacons passes along a video tape from his home church in Min An which describes their building project and solicits funds from overseas compatriots. The president of the Women's Fellowship collects money from members for an emergency relief gift for a middle-aged garment shop seamstress whose husband just died of cancer in a Lower East Side hospital. She collects over $2,000 by the end of the day. A bulletin board lists job openings and beds for rent. Two nurses from the neighborhood health clinic encourage women to visit for checkups. The evangelists gather together first-time visitors for a discussion of basic principles of Christian faith and invite them to join the baptism and membership class that will be starting in a few weeks. A group of college students meets in a corner to discuss their upcoming exams. The Church of Grace lacks the focal point of the Reverend Liu at the New York House

Church, but the decentralized interactions are wide ranging and have their own style and order.

Continuing immigration has fueled this explosive growth. A survey of two hundred Church of Grace congregants conducted in May 2000 revealed certain striking trends in Fuzhounese immigration patterns (see table 6.2). Clearly, the trickle of Fuzhounese immigrants that came before 1990 was replaced by an ever increasing flood thereafter, with the most striking expansion in the last half of the decade. Fully 86.5 percent of those surveyed had arrived in the United States since 1990. Twenty-seven and a half percent arrived between 1990 and 1994; more than twice that number, or 57 percent, arrived between 1995 and early 2000. Only 10 percent arrived in the 1980s. While the lower number of respondents arriving in the 1980s may to some extent reflect the tendency of earlier immigrants to move out of Manhattan to live or establish businesses, the data reflect the overwhelming number of recent immigrants comprising the Church of Grace congregation.

A striking trend emerged in the 1990s regarding gender and immigration. Between 1990 and 1994 women comprised 42 percent of the Fuzhounese immigrants in the survey, men comprised 58 percent. But between 1995 and early 2000, the proportion of women immigrants rocketed to 68 percent of the total and men declined to 32 percent. Of all Fuzhounese women surveyed at the Church of Grace, 65 percent arrived between 1995 and 2000, compared to only 19 percent who arrived between 1990 and 1994. Overall, the data show the Church of Grace serving a rapidly expanding im-

TABLE 6.2

The Church of Grace Congregants' Arrival in the United States, by Year and Gender

Year	Men Arriving	Percentage of Total Men	Women Arriving	Percentage of Total Women	Total Number of Arrivals	Total Percentage
Prior to 1970	0	0	2	1.7	2	1.0
1970–1974	1	1.2	1	0.8	2	1.0
1975–1979	2	2.5	1	0.8	3	1.5
1980–1984	3	3.7	4	3.33	7	3.5
1985–1989	4	5.0	9	7.5	13	6.5
1990–1994	32	39.5	23	19.2	55	27.5
1995–2000	36	44.4	78	65.0	114	57.0
No Response	3	3.7	2	1.67	4	2.0

migrant membership after 1990, with a particular explosion of female parishioners after 1995.

The Sisters Fellowship

Women comprise two-thirds of the average worship attendance at the Church of Grace, approximately the same as at the Brooklyn branch and the New York House Church. This is similar to churches in China, though it does not reflect the larger Fuzhounese immigrant community, which has a male majority. Nor does it reflect the gender composition of the church's formal leadership structure, where both lay and clerical leaders are predominantly male. On the Board of Deacons, only seven of nineteen (37 percent) are women. Only one of the nine full-time religious workers employed by the Church of Grace in its history has been a woman. All four board chairmen have been men. Women tend to take leadership in more traditional service and teaching roles. For example, all of the children's Sunday School teachers are women, and women prepare most of the meals for the Sunday repast after church.

Women rarely take prominent leadership roles in the worship services, either as preachers, liturgists, or translators, though a few play more supportive roles as ushers or distributors of communion elements. The evangelist Ms. Liu Baoying provided an exception, offering a more public leadership role at the Church of Grace for a period of time. Another exception occurs four times a year during those months with five Sundays. On the fifth Sunday the sermon time during worship is left open for testimonies given spontaneously by congregation members. On these Sundays the speakers are almost all women—middle aged and older—who speak usually in Fuzhou dialect about their families, homes and home churches, the miracles and healings that brought them and their families to the Lord, and their supplications to the Lord Jesus to save them and all people from sin and death.

When questioned, most church leaders, male and female, claim that there is no fundamental difference in the status or roles of men and women at the Church of Grace. When asked why no women lead Sunday worship or why there are fewer women deacons, or why the current women deacons speak less frequently than the men in the meetings, leaders suggest that women are more bashful and less willing to be up-front leaders.

But the actions and ideas of women at the Church of Grace are far from stereotypical and hardly monolithic. Rather, their stories represent the complex set of negotiations in which Fuzhounese women engage as they navigate the relationship between gender, cultures, patriarchy, religion, and the changes brought about by migration. In response to questions about the role of women in the church and the relationship between women and men, a leader of the Sisters Fellowship and a church deacon reflects:

Do women and men have different roles or status at the Church of Grace?

> *No matter in the house, the family or the church, women should respect men because God first created men and men are created from God's image and glory. Women are helpers of men. So at church, and in the family, men should have more responsibility. But in reality some of them are not willing to take responsibility. So women must also assume significant responsibilities. For example, as the Bible says in Judges, there was a woman judge named Deborah.*

How about at home?

> *I think that in God's love, there should be no difference in the position of men and women in the family. They should love one another, with mutual respect.*

What do you think the Bible has to say about the proper role of men and women?

> *In the Bible, Paul says women should be quiet and listen. He doesn't allow the women to speak. But that was at that time. Now it is different. Some women have more Spirit and gifts than men. I see that in the Bible there are also women prophets. The work of both women and men is a gift from God.*

One place women are independently organized within the Church of Grace is in the Sisters Fellowship. The fellowship meets once a month for two hours on a Sunday afternoon. Bible study and devotions are the central focus of the gathering. The thirty to forty participants are predominantly middle-aged and older women, with the women maintaining a separate financial account and having their own treasurer. Collections are taken each month and are used to provide honorariums for speakers and emergency assistance to members who encounter personal and financial difficulties. In certain situations the Sisters Fellowship may orchestrate, behind the scenes, churchwide collections for women or families in need, personally canvasing members to solicit financial contributions. Sisters Fellowship meetings are conducted in Fuzhounese in order to include the oldest members who speak little or no Mandarin. The Sisters Fellowship serves as a central link for many of these elderly rural women, who held positions of respect and leadership in their home churches and communities but who now find themselves isolated by language and culture since their migration to New York.

Theological positions, while generally conservative to fundamentalist at the Church of Grace, are not well defined, publicly articulated, or rigidly enforced on many issues, including the role of women. Interviews in Fuzhou, though, particularly among Little Flock and house-church leaders, revealed at least one strain of local theology that explicitly defines women's role as subordinate. A leading figure in the Little Flock house-church movement in Fuzhou, for instance, argued that while most house churches were comprised almost exclusively of women, when a man was present, even just visiting, he should be placed in charge of the service. In fact, he argued, even women should be called Brothers because the Bible foretells that in heaven there will be no female, only male. So even people today who outwardly appear as female, inside they have men's spirits. Other house-church leaders, however, suggest that while men should hold more responsibility, these other views are quite extreme.

Given the prominent role of women in indigenous sects like the Little Flock and the Home of Grace in China, why are these patterns not continued in New York? Some women leaders in China suggest that their prominence is required because men are too busy to take leadership roles. So many men, they report, are away working, either in other parts of China or overseas, that women are forced to fill the leadership void. It is also clear that religious participation does not enhance social status in China, especially in many of the smaller church movements, providing a disincentive to male involvement. In New York, the opposite appears to be true. Men almost exclusively claim and actively participate in the key public leadership roles of the church—pastors, liturgists, board members, treasurers—despite their minority gender status. While women lead informal networks extending beyond the congregation, such as house prayer meetings and Bible studies, their formal roles in the church are far more circumscribed. Exceptional women, noted for their charisma, education, personal connections, or deep spirituality, continue to stand out, but they are disproportionally represented in the church's decision-making structures or ritual leadership. In a pattern familiar in other immigrant religious groups (George 1998), in the Church of Grace and the New York House Church the deeply rooted patterns of patriarchy and male privilege in Chinese culture are reasserting themselves when leadership confers status on men who, because of their migration, often are without significant status beyond the religious community.

With women's religious leadership roles in China and the de facto leadership women provide in most aspects of the Church of Grace and the New York House Church in New York City, we must assume that the conceptualization of women's roles in the congregation is a complex and contested one. In comparison to the more extremist view held by some house-church leaders in China, the formulation suggested by the Sisters Fellowship leader reflects a sophisticated negotiation between religious tradition, cultural norms, perceived biblical standards and congregational realities, a negotiation that embodies both the struggle of Chinese Christianity to confront the contemporary world where women's roles are changing and the struggle of the Church of Grace to adapt to the situation of its new immigrants.

TABLE 6.3
The Church of Grace: Age of Members

Age	Number of Men	Percentage of Men	Number of Women	Percentage of Women	Total Number	Total Percentage
1–9	2	2.5	3	2.5	5	2.5
10–19	9	11.1	15	12.5	24	11.9
20–29	19	23.5	28	23.33	47	23.4
30–39	24	29.6	26	21.67	50	24.9
40–49	13	16.0	23	19.2	36	17.9
50–59	5	6.2	12	10.0	17	8.5
60–69	3	3.7	6	5.0	9	4.5
70–79	1	1.2	5	4.2	6	3.0
80–89	1	1.2	2	1.6	3	1.5
No response	4	5.0	0	0	4	2.0

TABLE 6.4
New York House Church: Age of Members

Age	Number of Men	Percentage of Men	Number of Women	Percentage of Women	Total Number	Total Percentage
1–9	0	0	0	0	0	0
10–19	1	4.8	2	4.7	3	4.7
20–29	5	23.8	7	16.3	12	18.8
30–39	4	19.0	9	20.9	13	20.3
40–49	7	33.3	12	27.9	19	30.0
50–59	2	9.5	5	11.6	7	10.9
60–69	1	4.8	4	9.3	5	7.8
70–79	1	4.8	3	7.0	4	6.3
80–89	0	0	1	2.3	1	1.6
No response	0	0	0	0	0	0

The Youth Fellowship

The congregation at the Church of Grace is relatively young, particularly in relationship to the New York House Church. Survey responses show 63 percent of the congregation to be under forty years old and 81 percent under age fifty. In comparison, at the New York House Church only 44 percent are under forty years old.

The preponderance of young people is visibly evident in the Church of Grace congregation. Three children's Sunday School classes averaging forty to fifty kids run concurrently with the main worship service. The choir, with at least twenty members each Sunday, is virtually an extension of the youth group. Young people provide the simultaneous translation during worship, run the sound system, play the piano, staff the library and bookstore. Sunday afternoons and evenings the church building belongs almost exclusively to the youth fellowship, which spans older teenagers to young adults in their mid-thirties. After worship they have choir rehearsal, youth fellowship meetings, Bible study, informal dinners, and recreation, including setting up a ping-pong table in the main foyer.

The youth group is comprised of generations three and four as outlined earlier. They are both documented and undocumented, rural and urban, college oriented and work oriented. At the core of the group are college students or graduates, quite a few having grown up in Hong Kong, who easily cross from their parents' Chinese culture to the broader U.S. culture. Switching easily between languages, they clearly imagine themselves succeeding in the mainstream U.S. economy. This portion of the group serves as a bridge between the congregation and U.S. culture: they are well represented on the Board of Deacons; they lead the English-language children's Sunday School classes; they handle the congregation's financial accounting; they manage the computer database, library, and bookstore. Once a year the youth fellowship organizes a weekend trip for the entire congregation. Buses are rented, a retreat center is visited and booked, sight-seeing side trips are arranged, and money is collected. The youth handle all the arrangements, primarily because they are the ones in the congregation with the cultural skills to negotiate a foray of more than one hundred Fuzhounese immigrants beyond New York's Chinatown.

The youth fellowship's members also include undocumented restaurant, construction, and garment-shop workers who work grueling hours, speak no English, have little or no contact with mainstream U.S. society and little hope of advancement beyond the Chinatown ethnic enclave economy. They are transient and fragile, in and out of hospitals. The physical strain shows on their faces and in their bodies. They take no leadership roles and attend as they are able, rarely lingering for informal conversation and activities. Their lives are too full of pressure and anxiety.

With such a complex mix of participants, tensions sometimes run high within the fellowship and between the fellowship and the rest of the congregation. With its aggregate set of skills, the youth fellowship holds significant power in the congregation, making it perhaps the second most powerful group after the core of the Board of Deacons. The members are well organized with a full slate of officers elected annually by the youth fellowship. But this base of power also holds significant potential for creating tension and conflict. For instance, the youth group has advocated strongly for programs it supports and personnel assignments it views as helpful. It has also pushed the congregation to modernize its worship and structure more rapidly than older members and rural young members had wanted.

In one recent incident, the church staff proposed splitting the youth fellowship into two groups to address what they saw as competing programmatic and spiritual desires. Some of the young people from rural areas in

Fuzhou had advocated for more Bible study and prayer in the youth fellowship meetings. From their perspective, the group's inclination toward fun, games, food, and outside activities detracted from the main reason to have a church group, namely to know God better and develop a deeper spiritual life. As an interim step, church staff formed a separate youth Bible study and prayer group that met Sunday afternoons following the full youth fellowship gathering. Leaders of the youth group, drawn exclusively from the college-educated, urbanized immigrants, have until now resisted a permanent split of the fellowship, fearing it will ultimately diminish their cohesiveness and power within the congregation. A compromise solution currently in place has the full group meeting together, then splitting into three small groups: one for students, one for workers, and one for beginners. While serving as a successful compromise for the time being, this scheme also leaves open the possibility of furthering congregational stratification along lines of education, employment, and legal status.

The youth group's members are primarily of the 1.5 generation—born in China or Hong Kong and migrating to the United States with their parents. Some came on their own, first-generation immigrants in their own right, hoping to initiate a migration chain to include their immediate family members. A Fuzhounese second generation—children born in the United States to immigrant parents—is only now emerging. Its development is complicated by the large number of children whose parents are too busy working and lack an adequate family support network in the United States, and thus immediately send their children home to China to be raised by grandparents. In the pattern now emerging, most of these children are being brought back to the United States at age five or six to attend school. But leaving behind their surrogate parents in China, being reintroduced to parents in the United States whom they don't remember, and attending school in a language and culture with which they are not familiar is proving to be a very difficult transition for many of these children and their parents. The Church of Grace Sunday School classes for children ages ten and under are filled with these children. Some speak little English. Others who were raised in New York speak little Chinese. The ability of the church's volunteer teachers to cope with this complexity is severely limited. It is not yet clear what the future engagement of these children with the larger congregation will be, though now it appears to be terribly problematic.

Church of Grace: Social Concerns

In the fall of 1999, nearly two years after the split, a deacon at the Brooklyn branch proposed to the board of the Church of Grace the creation of the Church of Grace Social Service Corporation to cooperatively address the social needs of the congregation. In the proposal he suggested that if the congregation pooled its financial and personnel resources it could begin to confront the social crises facing the community. The Church of Grace Social Service Corporation could open its own company and factories. It could employ church members for fair wages working under decent conditions. It could even open a day-care center for children whose parents would otherwise be forced to send them back to China to be raised by grandparents.

Complete silence filled the room when the deacon finished presenting his fifteen-page handwritten proposal. Despite the significant social problems confronting the Church of Grace's constituent members, official public discourse rarely addresses human smuggling, sweatshops, grinding work conditions, high incidences of physical and mental illnesses, child labor, indentured servitude to Chinese snakeheads, long-term separation of family members in the United States and China, oppressive indebtedness, prostitution, or gambling. Although they are never addressed in sermons, such problems will make the pages of the church newsletter where they typically serve as background for testimonies of miraculous healing and exhortations to pray for comfort and relief. The church may serve as a focal point for an extensive informal network of mutual assistance and information sharing, but the congregation at that juncture provided no formal programs or services to address the community's social needs. In this context, the deacon's proposal was quite stunning.

One older deacon rose to his feet and said, "This is what I always dreamed we should be doing." But others questioned whether or not a church in the United States could legally engage in such activities. Some expressed the sentiment that this wasn't really a church's role. The majority felt that the congregation did not have the financial or human resources to make such an endeavor a reality, even though it may be appropriate.

Church leaders are clearly aware of the problems. Many of them came to the United States illegally and are only recently, if at all, removed from Chinatown's most difficult work environments. Yet, when presented with a thoughtful, if slightly grandiose proposal to address the needs around them, they quickly moved away from a call to activism and went on to other administrative business. Why?

Theological Orientation

The Church of Grace is theologically conservative, emphasizing faith not good works, and personal not collective salvation. Leaders wish to focus on the positive message of personal salvation and redemption revealed in the biblical stories of Jesus' life and the exhortations for "right" living in the letters of Paul. They focus on the power of the Holy Spirit and the love of God to comfort people in their distress. Says one older woman deacon when asked what Jesus means to her: "Jesus has taken my bitter life and given me rest and comfort in my sadness." Preachers urge congregants to recognize their sinful ways, to repent, to ask God for forgiveness, and to receive the gift of God's grace, embodied in the sacrificial death of Jesus.

Lack of Experience

Practically, most church leaders are novices at church management. Most have never been responsible for a complex social organization of any kind before, either in China or in the United States. Furthermore, Church of Grace leaders are uncertain of the proper role of a church in society, particularly U.S. society. In China the official religious domain is limited to personal devotion and congregational activities focused on piety, such as worship, prayer, and Bible study. Domains of power and social action are reserved for the state.

In the tightly controlled religious environment of contemporary China, only recently have local mainland Chinese churches begun to engage in socially oriented activities. These activities, which might include a Sunday afternoon free health clinic or a senior citizens tai-qi class, are carefully negotiated between local churches and the local Christian Council on the one hand, and the Religious Affairs Bureau and government officials on the other. Churches undertaking these activities are the Three-Self–related churches officially recognized by the Chinese Communist government and largely despised by many conservative Christians, who consider them to be modernized, secularized, manipulated by the Chinese state, and theologically impure (see chapter 4). Having grown up in this environment, most Church of Grace leaders have limited experience with enacting church programs that move beyond a concern for personal piety and therefore have been reluctant to break new ground in their seemingly fragile congregation.

Personal Distance

For many on the Board of Deacons, the crises of the larger community are no longer personally urgent. While many of them passed through illegal status and difficult working conditions, most have achieved some level of success, or at least stability. The failure to be moved to collective activism on behalf of their struggling Fuzhounese compatriots may in fact highlight the class stratification within the congregation between the board and the general membership.

The Church of Grace's engagement with social issues took a decided turn with the arrival in April 2000 of the Reverend Chen Zhaoqing as senior pastor. Born in Malaysia as a child of the Fuzhounese diaspora, Chen left his Malaysian Methodist upbringing and moved to the United States in the mid-1980s to work in campus ministry among Chinese students in Texas through the evangelical organization Ambassadors for Christ. After several disastrous hires and two years without a senior pastor at the Church of Grace, Chen has been enthusiastically received by most of the congregation. Some limited dissent has emerged, however, from members who despair that since his appointment he has been too busy "doing things" and not attentive enough to the spiritual needs of the congregation.

Indeed, since Chen's arrival the Church of Grace has moved toward an engagement with the social concerns of the Fuzhounese community as well as a closer integration into local, national, and international networks of Chinese evangelical Christians. An early Sunday English-language worship service—distinctly lacking in Fuzhou flavor—has been started, ostensibly for the congregation's 1.5 and second generations but attended primarily by recent immigrants wishing to hear and learn English. Weekly English as a Second Language classes have been launched. A cooperative program with Lutheran Family and Community Services provides activities for Fuzhounese minors detained by the U.S. Immigration and Naturalization Service and awaiting adjudication of their cases. A bulletin board for job postings and apartment listings has been revived after succumbing several years earlier to complaints that "a church should not be an employment agency." Representatives of a neighborhood women's health program set up a table in the lobby after church to sign up more than thirty women for consultations about services ranging from birth control and AIDS testing to nutrition and prenatal care.

These developments are not the radical comprehensive organizational response suggested and dismissed a few years earlier in the Board of Deacons meeting. They do reflect, however, an institutional approach shifting away from informal networking toward a compassion-based effort to ameliorate the clear personal needs of Fuzhounese immigrants. While still a piecemeal response, they do suggest a movement away from a separatist fundamentalism or evangelicalism with a narrow focus on nurturing personal piety, evangelizing Chinese people, and starting new congregations toward a civic evangelicalism combining public concerns with passionate evangelism (Tseng 2002).

New York House Church

I hope you'll write a history of the house-church movement in China. It's a history that needs to be told. They say there were 700,000 Protestants in all of China in 1949. But by the time the reform campaigns of the 1950s were finished and the Cultural Revolution had taken its toll, the persecution had winnowed the number down to the true core, about 70,000 true believers. They were in the underground house churches. The Communists despise the house churches. But they created them through the repression of Christians and the closing of churches in the 1950s, 1960s, and 1970s. The house churches have grown rapidly in the last twenty-five years. Now there are millions in the house churches, maybe tens of millions. The Three-Self leadership only recognizes 15 million. But our own survey, based on local government sources, counts as many as 120 million, mostly in house churches. If you could write that story it would be a great contribution. (Rev. Liu Yangfen)

When they split with the Church of Grace, the defectors named their new church "The New York House Church," staking a direct claim of connection to the house churches in China—to the fundamentalist, anti-Communist, largely underground lay Protestant Christian gatherings linked through a loose internal network. The core of the new congregation came from the Little Flock tradition and had been active in Little Flock–related congregations in China. The Little Flock movement developed in the Fuzhou area and in recent years has spread rapidly across China both openly and underground, sometimes in churches, mostly in homes. In their internal operations and external relations, New York House Church members moved deliberately to place their new congregation back within the confluence of this historical and religious stream after years of compromise at the Church of Grace.

Since its inception, the name "New York House Church" has indicated a physical location as well as a location in the religious and political landscape. After a year in the living room of Brother Lu Yangsheng on Monroe Street, the New York House Church moved into another home, this time the ground floor of a five-story walkup on Market Street, newly purchased and refurbished by Philip and Mary Lam. Philip, a leading real estate manager in Chinatown and vice chairman of one of the main Fujianese associations, has been a member of the Church of Grace Board of Deacons and Board of Trustees. Mary serves as a translator for the U.S. Immigration and Naturalization Service and U.S. Federal court system and teaches Sunday School at the Church of Grace. The couple, from Fuzhou via Hong Kong, have offered the ground floor of their home to the church for three years, free of charge. They chose to support both the New York House Church and the Church of Grace because, according to Mr. Lam,

> *Rev. Liu made a great contribution to the Church of Grace, helped us raise a lot of money to pay for the building and renovation. I'm sorry he left. But there are so many Fuzhounese in Chinatown now. They can't all fit in one church. Two probably won't be enough, either.*

Sunday morning worship begins between 9 and 9:30 at the New York House Church in a distinctly Little Flock style with prayers and hymn singing. About thirty people are present. The women sit mostly on the right side of the aisle, men mostly on the left, though this tradition is not strictly observed and in practice becomes more difficult to maintain as the floor-through hall fills to capacity later in the morning. A few women wear a black netted hair covering called a *mentou*, another marker adopted by the more ardent Little Flock followers. Only eight to ten of the sixty women present will wear them on an average Sunday. Members of the congregation are distinctly older than the Church of Grace or the Church of Grace's Brooklyn branch. Fifty-nine percent of the women are over forty years old, compared to 40 percent at the Church of Grace and the Brooklyn branch. Fifty-three percent of the men are over forty years old, compared to only 26 percent at the Church of Grace and a mere 20 percent at its Brooklyn branch church.

Shortly before eleven, the core group of sisters and brothers of the congregation begins the *bai bing hui*, or communion service. The Little Flock does not ordain ministers and its tradition discourages official leadership structures, believing instead in the equality of all members and relying on dedicated sisters and brothers to carry out the congregation's work. Today, communion servers are all lay people, also according to Little Flock tradition. Rev. Liu, seated in the front row, participates as an ordinary member. First, flat unleavened bread, most likely matzo, is crumbled in a plate and passed among the congregation. Members stand in their place when the plate is passed to them. Most people take a small flake and eat at their own discretion. Not everyone takes a piece; even some long-term members abstain. "In our tradition, if there is something between you and God that you haven't worked out, you shouldn't take communion. It could be bad for you," says one member in explanation. After the plate is returned to the altar, a clear glass mug of sweet grape-colored punch is circulated. Most core members drink directly from the cup. Others accept the offer of a plastic spoon to dip in the cup. Used spoons are collected, washed, and reused the next week. The ritual is an exact replica of *bai bing hui* in Tingjiang and other Little Flock churches in Fuzhou. By eleven o'clock the hall is packed and the preaching begins, usually in Fuzhou dialect, occasionally in Mandarin translated into Fuzhou dialect by one of the members.

Rev. Liu Goes to Work

When the worship service concludes well after noon with a few more hymns and prayers, the subdued congregation comes alive. A huge pot of Fuzhou noodle soup or Fuzhou rice soup is brought from the back room that serves as church kitchen and dormitory for one of the brothers. Hot steamed buns, plain and with meat filling, appear as well. The eighty to ninety people in the room crowd around, gather up their luncheon repast and settle back into small groups scattered around the room, drawing the individual chairs into circles for conversation.

It is at this point that Rev. Liu's work for the day really begins. For much of the morning ritual he participates as an equal among the brothers and sisters. For much of the afternoon he will be the center of activity, remaining in the hall late into the day talking with a long line of parishioners who, despite the pressures of work and family, take the time to approach this pillar of the Fuzhounese Protestant community, a symbol of religious virtue and a source of encouragement and assistance through the trials of their American journey.

Rev. Liu is well known in this community. People know that he is well connected and that he will help church members if he can. He knows doctors, people with places to stay, sometimes job possibilities, and also a good deal about the legal system and even a few trustworthy Christian lawyers. Or perhaps he knows of someone who will take an infant child back to grandparents in China for a reasonable fee. In the popular imagination, there is little that Rev. Liu cannot do. And so people take turns talking to him on Sunday afternoon, sharing with him their troubles and concerns and hopes. Says one woman deacon, "When brothers and sisters come with problems we try to help them out. Sometimes we know about jobs or housing. We do what we can." On Sunday afternoon and at times throughout the week, the New York House Church becomes a Fuzhounese Christian community center and Liu serves as the focal point of the network. When health issues have limited his Sunday participation, he actively continues his central role from home.

Newly arrived immigrants also seek out Rev. Liu and the New York House Church. Rev. Liu is well known in Fuzhou. Little Flock churches often tell their parishioners that upon arrival in New York they must visit him and the New York House Church. In some ways the church has become a stop on a Fuzhounese Christian underground railroad and Rev. Liu is the station master. New arrivals, both legal and undocumented, make their way to Market Street on Sundays. Their first task is to share news of home. How is their church? Their pastor? A well-known Brother or Sister? Has the church had any problems with the government? Then people discuss their current conditions and ask if there is anything Liu or the church can do to help them. Sometimes at first, help is just a prayer, words of encouragement and a sense that the people's problems have been heard and understood. They are not alone, which is important as one sinks into the travails of the ethnic enclave. Later, as opportunities arise, word may come of more material assistance.

On occasion, Rev. Liu has become actively involved in supporting recent immigrants' applications for political asylum based on claims of religious persecution. His assistance may take several different forms, among them providing letters of support for members' asylum applications, verifying church membership in New York and China, or locating a local sponsor to get immigrants out of INS detention. On occasion he has also accompanied members to their court appearances and testified on their behalf. He is well informed about church-state relations in Fuzhou. Even the most subtle conflict or controversy eventually reaches his ears. He also has more than half a century of personal experience of religion in China. An elderly, well-spoken (in English as well as Mandarin and Fuzhou dialect) ordained minister, he has proven an ideal expert witness for cases involving claims of religious persecution.

Rev. Liu says he accepts no payment for his help. Likewise, he never accepted a salary during his tenure at the Church of Grace. But Chinese Christian practice is for church members to generously support their pastors. Gifts of money are usually transferred discreetly in small red envelopes, the traditional Chinese *hong bao*. In addition, Liu lived for a number of years in the home of a parishioner before moving in with his son. At the New York House Church, grateful immigrant parishioners who insist on making a financial gift may be encouraged to channel their support to the New York House Church or to house churches and their leaders in China.

A third group of people who visit Rev. Liu on Sundays at the New York House Church or contact him at home are Chinese Christians who are planning to return to China on short-term mission visits to underground house churches. Throughout the year, small groups of two or more Chinese U.S. citizens travel as tourists to Fuzhou and other places in China, smuggling in Bibles, audiotapes of sermons, inspirational Christian messages, and a wide variety of written material. They quietly visit house churches and house-church leaders delivering these materials and illegal financial contributions from Christians in the United States. Some of them are individually motivated. Many represent Chinese Christian churches in the New York area that have taken up a particular concern for the growth of Christianity in China. Most are ardently anti-Communist, and these ideological beliefs feed directly into a desire to support the Chinese Protestant house churches, typically portrayed as severely persecuted in a country lacking religious freedom and seen as valiantly resisting the godlessness of the Chinese state.

Rev. Liu is a central figure for many of these short-term mission trips. His word and letter can open many Chinese doors. A rich repository of information about the history and contemporary reality of China's house churches, he is a valued resource to many a traveler. Liu himself produces tapes of sermons and purchases quantities of books and pamphlets with the support of New York House Church members. He sends the materials to

China, often with representatives of these short-term mission groups. Although he does not travel himself, his son is a regular visitor to the house churches, bringing greetings from his father and delivering not insignificant resources. Those returning from China call on Rev. Liu and the New York House Church to report on their activities and findings and to receive his blessing for a mission successfully accomplished.

Conversion in Chinatown

Twice a year, at Easter and again in the fall, the Church of Grace conducts baptismal ceremonies during Sunday morning worship. At the New York House Church baptisms are less frequent but occur at least once a year. As many as fifty people have been baptized on each occasion at the Church of Grace, and as many as twenty each time at the New York House Church. These baptisms are clearly ritual high points for the two congregations in which preaching of the Word and communion are normally the central elements of worship.

While the baptismal ritual at the Church of Grace is artfully orchestrated, the scene at the New York House Church is more chaotic and exuberant. A four-foot-high wooden frame has been built to form a precarious baptismal pool on the floor that serves as the sanctuary. A hose runs warm water from the sink in the back bathroom into the pool lined with heavy plastic sheets. The crowd is more raucous than at the Church of Grace: people talk while children play and cry all through the ceremony; a small crowd mills around the pool at all times. One of the congregation's core group administers the baptismal immersion, a major difference from the Church of Grace, where an ordained minister must be present. After the immersion a group of church leaders, including Rev. Liu, gather around the person to pray and offer a blessing. Each individual baptism is seemingly an event unto itself. The documentation process lacks the Church of Grace's precision clockwork, but each person is photographed individually and a group shot is taken at the conclusion of the service.

Conversion rates of Fuzhounese Protestants in New York are lower than might be anticipated in a population emigrating from a largely non-Christian country. Surveys show that 60 percent of those in attendance at the Church of Grace became Christians in China, with a slightly higher rate at the Brooklyn branch church (64.5 percent). Of the Church of Grace congregation, 26 percent were baptized after arrival in the United States (31 percent at the Brooklyn branch) and 12 percent made no response, suggesting they may still be uncommitted seekers. These figures contrast sharply with the New York House Church, where fully 86 percent of those responding to the survey became Christians in China and only 11 percent converted after arrival in the United States. Although the conversion rates of these three congregations in the United States, especially the Church of Grace and its Brooklyn branch, are not insignificant, clearly these Fuzhounese congregations draw upon a strong base of Protestants born into Chinese Christian families or who converted in China prior to migration.

TABLE 6.5
The Church of Grace Members: Location of Conversions

Gender	China	Percentage in China	United States	Percentage in United States	No Response	Percentage with No Response	Percentage in Other Location
Men	46	56.8	29	35.8	4	4.9	2.5
Women	75	62.5	24	20.0	21	17.5	0
Totals	121	60.2	53	26.4	25	12.4	1.0

TABLE 6.6
Brooklyn Branch of the Church of Grace Members: Location of Conversions

Gender	China	Percentage in China	United States	Percentage in United States	No Response	Percentage with No Response	Percentage in Other Location
Men	9	60.0	5	33.3	1	6.7	0
Women	22	66.7	10	30.3	1	3.0	0
Totals	31	64.5	15	31.3	2	4.2	0

TABLE 6.7
The New York House Church Members: Location of Conversions

Gender	China	Percentage in China	United States	Percentage in United States	No Response	Percentage with No Response	Percentage in Other Location
Men	18	85.7	3	14.3	0	0	0
Women	38	86.4	4	9.1	2	4.5	0
Totals	56	86.2	7	10.8	2	3.0	0

Understanding Differential Conversion

The differential rates of conversion between the Church of Grace and the New York House Church require further analysis. The congregations clearly differ in physical location, physical layout of their worship space, worship style, and theological orientation, factors which, when considered together, may provide insight into the differences. For people seeking out a new place to worship or to explore a new religious belief system, these factors may prove significant in their choice of congregation and ultimately translate into greater or lesser numbers of converts in each church.

For example, it is much easier to find the Church of Grace, which is located on Allen Street, a major thoroughfare of Chinatown. Its building is obviously a church and its signage is clearly visible, suggesting the openness of a public facility. The New York House Church, in contrast, is tucked away in a residential building on the much smaller Market Street. At first glance the presence of a church is not obvious, and its small signboard is not prominently displayed.

It is not possible to be a casual or anonymous visitor to the New York House Church. The door to the worship space is always closed during the service and one cannot look in without opening the door. The door opens into the middle of the room. The ninety or more seats are mostly filled. Once inside, the visitor stands midway between the front and rear of the room, exposed to half the congregants as she or he awkwardly seeks a seat in the crowded room. In comparison, the Church of Grace has two large doors that lead to an expansive entry foyer. From there the visitor or seeker can look through glass-paneled doors into the sanctuary or discreetly slip into a seat in one of the back pews.

The worship style and format of the Church of Grace is also more inviting to visitors. The service is significantly shorter than at the New York House Church. In addition, the Church of Grace distributes bulletins describing the order of worship, activities available for the congregation, and inspirational readings. During the worship service the liturgists formally welcome visitors, make community announcements, and invite seekers to join membership classes. The New York House Church worship service, which does not include these elements, proves much more difficult to penetrate for visitors unfamiliar with Little Flock traditions and rituals.

While both congregations espouse a conservative to fundamentalist theology, the New York House Church draws its members, core beliefs, and practices from the indigenous Chinese denomination, the Little Flock. This tradition, expressed primarily in its worship liturgy, communion sacrament, and preaching, is highly dogmatic and therefore less approachable for newcomers. Worship and theology are more eclectic and less dogmatic at the Church of Grace. While it is not possible to identify any single characteristic of these two churches as the causal determinant for their members' differential rates of conversion in the United States, the combination of factors provides insights into the interplay of obstacles that may deter newcomers and seekers from participating in one congregation rather than the other.

One of the Church of Grace evangelists categorizes conversions of Fuzhounese in New York into four categories. The first includes longtime members of churches in China who, because of extenuating circumstances, never received baptism. Clergy may not have been available to conduct the ritual, or in the case of underground churches no opportunity was available. The second category of converts includes those who attended church irregularly or were familiar with Christianity in China but never made the commitment to "believe in the Lord" until they arrived in the United States. The third category includes Fuzhounese who only heard about Christianity once they arrived in New York, and the fourth is comprised of people who are not Christians, do not believe in the fundamentals of Christian teaching, but are using the conversion process to bolster their claims for political asylum based on religious persecution. This, believes the evangelist, is not a small number, but a number that is very difficult to specify. "It is hard to be sure who is insincere. We ask them basic questions about their faith and provide basic teachings about the church. But ultimately it is between them and God."

The ritual emphasis placed on baptisms reflects their symbolic importance for these religious communities. They are, at their core, outward and visible signs of inner conversion, a transformation of these individuals in both body and spirit. And they are for many a personal yet public identification of their life journeys with a larger metanarrative, that of the Christian faith and of the United States, which many Chinese immigrants consider to be inextricably linked with Christianity. This is no small shift for Chinese who were born and raised in an environment infused with non-Christian religious practices, a culture deeply tied to popular religious traditions entwining the individual with family, lineage, and village, and a political discourse that has disparaged and at times harshly repressed all religious belief.

The baptism ritual also has tremendous importance for those congregants observing or administering this sacrament as they recall their own conversion and reflect on their own life journey. At the Church of Grace and the New York House Church, the baptism, the washing away of sins, the purification of body and soul, the acceptance of Jesus Christ as personal Lord and Savior, as guiding light and source of life, represents for many of these immigrants a claim to a new life narrative and a search for new frameworks of meaning for their radically changed reality.

Safe Harbor

For most Fuzhounese immigrants, the journey to America begins in the rural towns and villages to the north and south of the Min River. Whether by boat or plane, across the Pacific or through eastern Europe, with legal status or without, ten thousand miles later they arrive on the banks of another river, the Hudson, in an urban metropolis that is one of the most globalized cities in the world. Propelled by the desire to make a better life for themselves and their families and carried along by what is almost a riptide of powerful transnational flows of capital and migration, these immigrants are cast ashore on Manhattan's Lower East Side. But instead of a safe harbor, most Fuzhounese find the swirling vortex of a ravenous labor market and the rolling hydraulic of a densely constructed and unforgiving ethnic enclave where deportation is always a possibility.

For many Fuzhounese immigrants, the religious communities considered in this study are islands in the storm. They are a place to rest, to realign bearings, plan for the next step, find news from home, learn from other seafarers tips for navigating the treacherous waters, and give thanks to their deity for making it this far. Once immigrants are more established, the religious communities may serve as locations for throwing lifelines to others, for sending word home that they have survived, and for making concrete religious expressions of their gratitude for safe passage and good fortune.

The ethnographic data gathered in this study of religious Fuzhounese immigrants and their religious communities suggest five conclusions, which I will discuss further in the next sections:

1. Fuzhounese religious communities serve as a key location for mobilizing the social capital necessary for surviving in the ethnic enclave, particularly in the following ways:
    a. Reterritorializing previously existing social networks
    b. Exchange of information

      c. Exchange of financial resources

      d. Support for the legalization process.

2. Hierarchies of class may be replicated within the religious communities that reflect differential immigrant experiences and reinforce the stratification of the enclave.

3. Religious Fuzhounese immigrants have successfully constructed religious networks between home and host religious communities in Fuzhou and New York that significantly affect the migration process, the immigrant incorporation process in the United States, and the changing economic, political, social, and particularly the religious situation in Fuzhou.

4. Fuzhounese religious communities serve as sites for establishing alternative identities to the dominant hegemonic structures and discourses of the ethnic enclave and of U.S. society.

5. The immigration process engenders a search for meaning.

While these findings are discussed specifically in relationship to Fuzhounese religious communities, I would argue that they suggest a paradigm for understanding immigrant religious communities in the United States in general and also serve to enhance the contemporary study of immigrant incorporation into U.S. society.

Fuzhounese Religious Communities as a Key Location for Mobilizing Social Capital

In chapter 1, we questioned the claims of Portes and Zhou that the ethnic enclave provides a positive alternative to the primary and secondary economy for recent immigrants. In the enclave, they claim, practices of ethnic solidarity among coethnics enable new immigrants without financial capital to employ social capital—language, cultural affinities, common history, family and kinship networks, hometown and regional associations—to expand their earning capacity to the level of the secondary economy without leaving the enclave. Through a review of the ethnic enclave literature, this study has sought to critique that claim and to cast doubt on the premise that the enclave is a beneficial alternative to immigrant incorporation.

As Portes and Zhou suggest, ethnic solidarity clearly exists. But the concept must not be used to paint too rosy a picture. Within the ethnic enclave, imagined solidarity among Chinese is shattered by internal conflicts of class, region, gender, language group, political perspective, and religion. Kwong (1997a) has argued that the idea of ethnic solidarity is manufactured to reinforce the image of employers as benevolent patriarchs in the face of their exploitative labor practices. The concept of ethnic solidarity clearly needs to be considered within the larger context of immigrant realities and systemic disciplining of the labor force. Otherwise, the notion of ethnic solidarity may be glibly used without consideration of its complex role in the immigrant experience.

Likewise, social capital exists. While for most Fuzhounese social capital is not a long-term solution to their poverty, exploitation, and marginalized status in the U.S. economy, mobilization of social capital is still a key survival strategy for immigrants with no financial capital and no legal immigration status. While for most Fuzhounese the ethnic enclave is a trap, utilizing social capital enables them to survive in it. In this regard, the processes Fuzhounese utilize to mobilize social capital for survival should be carefully considered.

The cases examined here consistently reveal the important role of Chinatown's Fuzhounese religious communities as sites for mobilizing the social capital necessary for survival in the hostile and exploitative environment to which Fuzhounese immigrants are relegated. Social capital is mobilized in the following four ways.

Reterritorializing Previously Existing Social Networks

Through these religious communities, Fuzhounese immigrants reconnect to social networks based on kinship, surname, village associations, religious affiliation, or even specific theological principles and practices within a religious tradition. Newly arriving immigrants reconnect with family, friends, fellow villagers, members of the same home church or temple by visiting specific religious communities in New York. As noted previously, the Fuzhounese population of New York is extremely transient, moving from location to location, for instance from New York to Miami to Seattle to New York again, in pursuit of employment. Religious communities serve as points of reconnection in the midst of dislocation. Sunday services or monthly lunar celebrations are occasions for interaction of people with a shared history and set of beliefs. Religious rituals provide regular gatherings throughout the year, and year after year. For those working outside the New York area, return visits may be scheduled to coincide with religious holidays and festivals such as Christmas, Easter, the procession for the Assumption of Mary, the Chinese New Year, or the three annual celebrations of the goddess Guan Yin. In the case of the Church of Grace, newsletters keep parishioners in touch with the congregation.

Under the auspices of these religious communities, opportunities for creating new social networks also exist. Through activities and interaction, immigrants engage with others they may not have known previously but have come to know through the auspices of these Buddhist, Daoist, Catholic, or Protestant religious communities. Unlike many other social and cultural institutions, religion provides the basis for immediate and often profound acceptance within a community of people who previously may have been strangers.

Exchange of Information

Fuzhounese religious communities serve as a central location for the exchange of information needed for survival in the enclave. Over Sunday noontime bowls of Fuzhou noodles or at temple festivals, immigrants engage in a give-and-take of information regarding employment opportunities, available housing, transportation methods, and location of low-cost and reliable health care, either Chinese or Western. Beyond the main ritual settings, each congregation's religious professionals serve as key facilitators of this information exchange. Present at the religious facilities on a daily basis, these religious workers interact on a frequent basis with parishioners who drop in to solicit advice and share needs or successes.

Exchange of Financial Resources

In certain circumstances, Fuzhounese religious communities make available or facilitate the exchange of financial resources among immigrants. At times the religious institution itself may have a process for redistributing resources, for instance the He Xian Jun Buddhist Temple's revolving loan fund for repaying smuggling debts or the Church of Grace's Sisters Fellowship Compassionate Fund, which is used to assist members who are ill or unemployed or stricken by other misfortune. At times, the exchange of resources may occur on an individual-to-individual basis though still under the rubric of solidarity within the religious community. An example would be the $2,000 raised by parishioners at the Church of Grace for a woman whose husband had died.

Support for the Legalization Process

Fuzhounese religious communities may also serve as sites for organizing support of applications for legal immigration status. Immigrants exchange information and offer advice about the process. The efficacy of particular lawyers and paralegal firms is discussed. As in the case of Rev. Liu, clergy and other religious professionals may assist in the legalization process. In the Christian churches letters verifying membership may be prepared, baptism certificates provided, and documentation of religious conditions in China submitted, all of which may be of particular benefit for those seeking political asylum based on religious persecution.

With the exception of the Catholic congregations, which are distinguished by their location in long-established Catholic churches that are integrated into the Catholic hierarchy and social service networks, the other Fuzhounese religious communities largely lack formal social service programs. As independent organizations starting from an infrastructural void, these congregations have extensive informal networks for mutual assistance, but their organizational infrastructure has not evolved to include the organized services that have become the hallmarks of so many urban U.S. Christian churches and have so often drawn on government funding. Causes for this lack of a social service component range from theological resistance to lack of institutional experience, to reluctance to enter partnerships with U.S. government bodies.

Hierarchies of Class Replicated within the Religious Communities

Each of the religious communities is conceptualized, not broadly as Chinese, but specifically as Fuzhounese. Despite internal differences, Fuzhounese do imagine a commonality within their community. Perhaps the central organizing principle of this imagined community is the Fuzhounese local dialect. But the Fuzhounese immigrants are by no means monolithic, nor are the Fuzhounese immigrant religious communities. Despite often effective efforts to utilize Fuzhou regional identity and Fuzhou dialect as frameworks for mobilizing social capital and ethnic solidarity, in reality the Fuzhounese immigrant community is stratified along lines of financial capital, legal status, gender, language ability, home region, and circumstances of arrival. These hierarchies of class and status may be replicated within the religious communities, serving to reinforce the stratification in the surrounding enclave.

The case study of the Church of Grace offers a compelling example of the possibilities for replication of the enclave's stratification. The Board of Deacons represents an elite within the congregation, on the average evidencing significant advantages related to legal status, type of employment, language ability, educational level, and personal connections in comparison to the congregation as a whole. This stratification and its institutionalization in organizational form places the board members in a position to administer and benefit from the collective resources of the entire congregation whether that be the services of the staff, access to equipment, utilization of the property, or opportunities for self-enhancement.

The split between the Church of Grace and the New York House Church reflects the possibility that hierarchies within the enclave may not only be replicated but reinforced within the religious community. The purchase, renovation, and administration of the new Allen Street property was a collective effort of the congregation in 1992–1993. The sum of $300,000 was raised to purchase the property. An additional $300,000 was raised for the renovation of the dilapidated bathhouse into a multiactivity church facility. In addition, parishioners, especially members of the Board of Deacons, contributed thousands of hours of volunteer labor to the project.

The religious conflict and theological differences within the Church of Grace that escalated in 1997 were clearly intertwined with contentious issues of power and status, resulting in the minority leaving to establish the New York House Church. After years of operating within the Church of Grace under the umbrella of Fuzhounese solidarity and enduring what they considered a marginalization of their theology, religious ritual and individual participation in the decision-making process, this minority group moved out on its own. The conflict over communion was highly symbolic, but the process of decision making within the congregation was perhaps the most problematic as members of the central power circle forced through a decision over the minority's objections and in the absence of their main advocate, Rev. Liu.

The result was not only a schism of a theologically diverse congregation into two separate religious groups. The split entailed more materialistic ramifications as well. Those who left, clearly marginalized within the power stratification of the Board of Deacons, ended up worshipping in a borrowed living room for a year, followed by a rent-free lease on a floor-through of a Chinatown residence. Those who remained at the Church of Grace, by contrast, retained ownership over the Allen Street property—which, after renovations, was worth more than $600,000. All of the assets of the congregation, including the bank account, equipment, furnishings, and, significantly, the legal status of "religious organization" which had taken so many years to acquire and which provided such substantial benefits to its members, stayed with them. Conflict and struggle within the congregation resulted in a redistribution of power and resources that disenfranchised those who already had less status and power and aggrandized the position of those in positions of superiority.

Successful Construction of Religious Networks between Home and Host Religious Communities in Fuzhou and New York

Recent studies of Chinese transnationalism (Ong and Nonini 1997; Ong 1999), reviewed in chapter 2, focus primarily on middle-class and economic elites who have the financial resources and legal status to live and work in multiple locations. For them, transnational identity as part of an overseas Chinese diaspora is a byproduct of economic privilege. Within this framework, the human smuggling syndicates become the primary representatives of Fuzhounese transnationalism. The vast majority of Fuzhounese immigrants, including those smuggled into the United States, like those on the *Golden Venture*, are portrayed as objects of action by transnational flows and processes. The current study reveals Fuzhounese religious immigrants as determined, ingenious agents and actors in constructing transnational migration streams utilizing transnational flows to build networks of support and communication that mitigate against global schemes of exploitation and dehumanization. Many contemporary studies of transnationalism and diaspora tend to obscure the understanding of the structured inequalities of class and race confronting minorities in the U.S. national scene. In response, this book has helped to contextualize contemporary Fuzhounese immigration within the exploitative and highly stratified ethnic enclave.

Some Fuzhounese who arrived prior to the 1986 amnesty or who have successfully applied for U.S. political asylum under the 1989 or 1990 executive orders, may be able to participate in a more extensive set of transnational practices and identity building. They may have the legal status and financial stability to travel between New York and Fuzhou and engage in activities that span the two locations. Examples include the evangelist from the Tingjiang Three-Self–related Protestant church who hopes to live part time with her children in the United States and serve part time as a religious worker in her home congregation. Or Ms. Liu Baoying, whose religious beliefs and commitment to the work of the Home of Grace led her to consider establishing a house church in New York, all the while continuing relationships with the U.S. training center and traveling regularly to China to support Christian coworkers in the rural areas around Fuzhou.

For the majority of Fuzhounese disciplined by the economic regime of Chinatown and the citizenship criteria of the U.S. state, their transnationalism is much more nascent, grassroots, and fragile, an ocean-borne transnationalism of the working poor, not the jet-set transnationalism of the elite. It is a transnationalism of the common folk, not of highly organized institutional structures or well-to-do transnational migrants in the Chinese diaspora described by Ong and Nonini. Unlike the transnational entities so often discussed which transcend the state, most Fuzhounese immigrants mobilize small-scale transnational networks from a position deep within and vulnerable to state structures. As workers, many undocumented, they are disciplined by economy and state alike. Beginning with their international migration through the human smuggling networks, these immigrants seek to creatively overcome the restrictions of the state system, its borders and boundaries, and the local and global capitalist regime.

Religious communities are arguably the oldest transnational networks. Catholic, Buddhist, Muslim, and Protestant missionaries have traveled the world and built global linkages between local communities. To date, however, discussions of religious transnationalism have largely focused on the transnational institutions and global structures of world religions that transcend state boundaries (e.g., see Rudolph and Piscatori 1997). Transnational religious networks being established by Fuzhounese immigrants are more independent, multifaceted, decentralized, and opportunistic. Yet their influence spans the migration process between China and the United States, the immigrant incorporation process, and the changing economic, political, social, and religious situation in Fuzhou.

While clearly in early stages of formation, these networks are strong enough that events in one place affect the other. When the Home of Grace in Changle split and was closed down by the Chinese government, ramifications of the events were felt strongly in the Church of Grace in New York. In fact, a split occurred within the Church of Grace. Members took sides in the China controversy. Some stopped attending the New York congregation, suggesting that the core group on the Board of Deacons had favored one side over the other. In a parallel yet reverse process, when the split occurred between the Church of Grace and the New York House Church, word spread quickly among churches in Fuzhou. Local congregations and leaders, especially those of the Little Flock orientation, soon took sides and aligned themselves with one New York congregation or the other.

The Migration Process

In the cases of the Daoist Temple of Heavenly Thanksgiving and the New York House Church, the communities at times play a direct role in the migration process. The young man with his duffel bag clearly identified the Daoist temple as a way station along the international journey between rural Chang'an and the American Midwest. Leaders of the New York House Church lend advice, money, and even access to immigration authorities to parishioners seeking to emigrate from Fuzhou to New York. The leaders of the Home of Grace training center in the United States seek to bring not only other persecuted leaders permanently out of China but also local leaders who come for short-term training before returning to work in China.

The Immigrant Incorporation Process

Transnational networks link churches and temples in Fuzhou with counterparts in New York. These transnational networks are utilized by religious immigrants and religious communities to ease the incorporation process in New York. In Fuzhou, the New York congregations are well known. Fuzhou's religious leaders regularly advise parishioners to seek out their New York counterparts for assistance, ranging from jobs and housing to loans for repayment of smuggling debts and legal advice.

Influence in Fuzhou

In recent years, the transnational religious networks have significantly increased immigrants' influence in the Fuzhou area. Perhaps the most visible signs are the large new religious structures that dot the Fuzhou countryside—ancestral halls, churches, and temples built with immigrant remittances. Underlying these material symbols is a revitalization of local ritual practices enabled by a relaxing of local government restrictions and fueled by significant international support from overseas Fuzhounese. Money is flowing in, as are people and other material resources. Despite the outmigration of significant numbers of rural constituents, religious programming in the area continues to expand, thanks to remittances.

The expansive nature of these activities enabled by transnational networks between New York and Fuzhou can be registered in the worried responses of the Chinese state. In 1994 the government instituted a requirement that all religious sites must be registered with the Religious Affairs Bureau. In many respects this reflects the proliferation of unauthorized religious sites and buildings. The government-directed destruction of twenty Catholic churches in the Changle area alone reveals the self-confidence with which local Catholics have approached local church-state relations and the vehemence with which government authorities have responded. The arrest and harassment of underground Protestant and Catholic church leaders reflects the government's discomfort with the influence of their growing networks and, in particular, the involvement of those outside China in Fuzhounese religious matters.

This book clearly demonstrates the significance of transnational religious networks established by Fuzhounese immigrants. Through these networks they seek to transcend regulated national boundaries and construct broader notions of citizenship and participation. They utilize their emerging transnational religious networks to articulate an alternative existence and identity in the face of the homogenizing influences of global capitalism and the U.S. labor market. Their participation in the life of their home communities, encouraged, facilitated, and rewarded through religious networks, assists in creating and enhancing a transnational identity that may in fact serve as an alternative to immigrant incorporation in the host society.

Fuzhounese Religious Communities as Sites for Establishing Alternative Identities

For undocumented workers denied the rights of citizenship and excluded not only from the mainstream of U.S. economy and culture but also the centers/structures of power within the ethnic enclave, Fuzhounese religious communities serve as sites for establishing alternative identities to the dominant hegemonic structures and discourses.

In her book *Contesting Citizenship in Urban China* (1999), Dorothy Solinger examines the case of tens of millions of rural Chinese who have illegally migrated to China's urban centers to participate in the exploding market system despite lacking proper household registration (*hu kou*) to live fully as urban citizens. The market, she argues, while enabling some to get rich, cannot supply robust or permanent solutions to the problem of citizenship for these transients. And so, she suggests, migrants act on their own to form protocitizens of themselves against the designs of the state. Oddly enough, many rural Fuzhounese have chosen to emigrate to the United States because of the unlikely prospect of regularizing their rural *hu kou* in urban China. In an odd parallel, many Fuzhounese in New York find themselves in a situation similar to China's internal migrants, unable to establish full citizenship rights in their new context. Despite actively participating in the U.S. economic regime, including paying taxes, the most basic rights of U.S. citizens are denied them: legal status, labor protection, health care, the social safety net, not to mention the right to vote.

Immigrants to the United States, particularly undocumented immigrants, are too often portrayed as unwanted foreigners, burdens on the welfare, health care, and education systems, sources of crime and poverty, and threats to the nation's well-being. Can Fuzhounese be undocumented and yet responsible and moral members of a church or temple? Through participation in the religious community's varied activities—religious, social, and institutional—immigrants suggest that multiple identities exist and enact an alternative construction of their role in U.S. society.

In addition, the religious community serves as a liminal space, a transitional place, a place in between, touching both New York and China. It recreates physical surroundings, kinship and village networks, rituals, language, and food that recall life in China. It reconnects to cultural and religious traditions back home. Yet it is in the midst of America. Religious communities allow Fuzhounese immigrants to imagine themselves differently in the midst of a hegemonic discourse that describes them in unflattering and dehumanizing terms.

On Guan Yin's birthday, hundreds of recent immigrants from Fuqi Village leave their workplaces for lunch and make their way to Master Lu's temple on Eldridge Street. Exiting the temporal framework of American capitalism, where the sweatshop clock keeps track of the grinding hours and number of garment pieces produced, the journey to Master Lu's temple transports these urban workers into an alternative notion of time and place. In the temple, their lives are dominated not by the rhythms of the sewing machine and steam press, nor by fourteen-hour days and six-day work weeks, American holidays, customs, and the dense interactions of New York City. Inside the temple, the familiar rituals connect them to the rhythms and pulses of home, to the Chinese lunar calendar, and to their rural roots. Reevoked in these rituals are homebound ways of conceptualizing health, morality, and fortune. The rituals also reconstitute and reterritorialize frameworks of self-understanding affirmed by the presence of old friends, fellow villagers, and talk of home. For a moment, the temple's festival serves to resist the dominant hegemony of time and place and provides congregants an opportunity to reconceptualize their lives and work, their past, present, and future.

The Immigration Process Engenders a Search for Meaning

"I wasn't sure if I should go to New York," said Chen Shufan, reflecting on his decision to immigrate twenty years earlier.

> One young lady in the church said to me, "If God wants you to go, you will get there. If God does not, you'll remain in Hong Kong. But if you go to New York you will start a Fuzhounese church." So I decided to go. It was really miraculous. God spoke to me through that young woman and I knew once I got safely to New York that we would start a Fuzhounese church. And we did. (Chen Shufan)

> I just wanted to make money. My family was poor. I knew I could make money in America. But I said to the god, "If you let me get there safely, I will build a temple for you back in China." I worked in a restaurant for a while, but the god said, "No, the smell of meat is too powerful. I can't come to you when you smell like that. Stop and open a temple in New York first." So I did. He does his work. I do mine. Now we have a temple for him back home, too. (Master Lu)

> It wasn't an easy decision. But I was getting older. My wife had died. And my family had already left. When my visa came through I decided to go. But I hoped that when I got to America I would be able to minister to the Fuzhounese people there. (Rev. Liu Yangfen)

This book has consistently shown the significant role of the Fuzhounese religious communities in assisting immigrants in coping with the exploitative ethnic enclave and in building transnational networks that resist the dehumanizing effects of the global capitalist system. But a functionalist analysis of religion in the Fuzhounese community is inadequate to capture the full significance of what religion means in the life of Fuzhounese immigrants.

It has been suggested that the immigration process is fundamentally a search for meaning—an exploration of the relationship between the immigrant and the universe. Why am I here? Where do I fit in? Why is this happening to me? What does it mean? The suffering. The hope. The backbreaking toil. The movement of people from Fuzhou to New York is driven by circumstance and opportunity. The migration is motivated by circumstances in Fuzhou: political uncertainty in China, lack of job opportunities, and competition with neighbors. It is facilitated by global flows and a multi-billion-dollar human-smuggling industry, and a rapacious U.S. market for cheap exploitable labor. Yet immigrants interviewed for this study, like those quoted above, consistently describe their experience in religious terms. For them the immigration experience engenders a search for meaning, an attempt to understand themselves and others like them within the purposes of the cosmos.

In the story that opens the Introduction, Li Lin sits in the bow of his smuggling vessel singing the hymns of his childhood: "In the cross, in the cross..." His song is an effort to reach back, to return to his youth, his home, his mother, his childhood faith, his homeland. It is a claim to not being alone. In the cross, to be with Jesus, for Jesus to be with him, even in suffering. His song is also a song of desire, the desire that his journey have meaning, have a purpose, fit into some larger conceptualization of the universe. His song gives voice to the emotions not only of his transnational journey, but of a transtemporal journey between what has been, what is, and what will be. It is a song that seeks to return meaning to life, to make sense of transition, dislocation, and uncertainty.

When members of the Daoist Temple of Heavenly Thanksgiving place their prayer requests on the altar in New York, they invoke their connection to systems of meaning and power directly related to their life at home in China. They trust that the deity of the home temple will travel across the ocean, just as they have, migrating to America to respond to their request to cast light on their hopes and dreams. Furthermore, they believe that this deity will continue to speak through a transplanted spirit medium who seeks to bridge the space between human and divine despite conducting her work half a world away in a storefront temple or a Chinese take-out restaurant. And they pray that their system, which has enabled them to interpret the past and predict the future, to connect with what has been and glimpse their destiny, will be sustained while being stretched beyond anything they had ever imagined.

When I left Fuzhou for Taiwan in 1949 I had no idea I would some day help to establish a Fuzhounese church in Hong Kong. When I thought about migrating to New York I never imagined that I would help start Fuzhounese churches in America. I'm an old man now and I'm very proud of what this old, poor, simple Christian has done. But the other night I had a dream. I dreamed that I returned to Fuzhou after all these years. I returned to Fuzhou to start a church. Imagine that. Fuzhou. Hong Kong. New York. Fuzhou. A full circle. My life would make a full circle. I've already started talking to some of my friends to see if this could be possible. I know the churches in Fuzhou are already growing. But this church would be special. It would be made up of people who had left Fuzhou for New York and come back to stay. Or of people who go back and forth. That would be truly amazing. (Chen Shufan)

The massive outmigration from the towns and villages surrounding Fuzhou is but the most recent chapter in the story of Fuzhounese reaching beyond their shores as a way of improving life for themselves and their families. The influx of Fuzhounese to New York's Lower East Side is but the latest chapter in the story of immigrants to the United States seeking to exchange their labor, at great personal cost, for the possibility of dreaming new dreams. The increasing complexity of the global capitalist system, the deepening exploitation, not only by the U.S. economy but by Chinese coethnics in the enclave economy, and the willingness of the U.S. government to ignore the dilatory effects of the Fuzhounese's marginalized legal status significantly complicate the experience of these contemporary immigrants.

In light of these obstacles, the rapid Fuzhounese advances in establishing social institutions such as religious communities are striking. The extent to which they have mobilized transnational religious networks is remarkable. Fuzhounese immigrant religious communities in Chinatown are poised to play a unique role in immigrant incorporation. As more and more Fuzhounese regularize their legal status and stabilize their economic conditions, these institutions and networks can only continue to grow in complexity and depth. Their development over time will require ongoing attention and study, both of the effects on the Fuzhounese immigrant experience in New York and of the implications for religion and society in China.

Bibliography

Abu-Lughod, Janet
  1989 Before European Hegemony: The World System A.D. 1250–1350. New York: Oxford University Press.

Anbinder, Tylor
  2001 Five Points. New York: Free Press.

Asad, Talal
  1993 Genealogies of Religion: Discipline and Reasons of Power in Christianity and Islam. Baltimore, MD: Johns Hopkins University Press.

Basch, Linda, and Nina Glick-Schiller, and Cristina Szanton Blanc, eds.
  1994 Nations Unbound: Transnational Projects, Postcolonial Predicaments, and Deterritorialized Nation-States. Langhorne, PA: Gordon and Breach.

Brown, Karen McCarthy
  1991 Mama Lola: A Vodou Priestess in Brooklyn. Berkeley: University of California Press.

Card, David
  1990 The Impact of the Mariel Boatlift on the Miami Labor Market. Industrial and Labor Relations Review 43: 245–258.

Carnes, Tony, and Anna Karpathakis
  2001 New York Glory: Religions in the City. New York: New York University Press.

Castells, Manuel
  1996 The Rise of the Network Society. Cambridge, MA: Blackwell.
  1997 The Power of Identity. Malden, MA: Blackwell.
  1998 End of Millennium. Malden, MA: Blackwell.

Cayton, Horace R., and Anne O. Lively
  1955 The Chinese in the United States and the Chinese Christian Churches. New York: National Council of Churches of Christ in the USA.

Chen, Hsiang-Shui

    1992 Chinatown No More: Taiwan Immigrants in Contemporary New York. Ithaca, NY: Cornell University Press.

Ch'en, Ta

    1940 Emigrant Communities in South China: A Study of Overseas Migration and Its Influence on Standards of Living and Social Change. New York: Secretariat, Institute of Pacific Relations.

Chin, Charlie

    1995 Chinatown. *In* The Encyclopedia of New York City, ed. Kenneth T. Jackson, 215–216. New Haven: Yale University Press.

Chin, Ko-lin

    1999 Smuggled Chinese: Clandestine Immigration to the United States. Philadelphia: Temple University Press.

Clark, Hugh R.

    1990 Settlement, Trade and Economy in Fukien to the Thirteenth Century. *In* Development and Decline of Fukien Province in the 17th and 18th Centuries, ed. E. B. Vermeer. Leiden, The Netherlands: E. J. Brill.

Cohen, Myron

    1992 Religion and State in Chinese Society. *In* Asia, Case Studies in the Social Sciences: A Guide for Teaching. Armonk, NY: M. E. Sharpe.

Dean, Kenneth

    1989 Revival of Religious Practices in Fujian: A Case Study. *In* The Turning of the Tide: Religion in China Today, ed. Julian F. Pas, 51–78. Hong Kong: Oxford University Press.

    1993 Taoist Ritual and Popular Cults of Southeast China. Princeton, NJ: Princeton University Press.

    1997 Ritual and Space: Civil Society or Popular Religion? *In* Civil Society in China, ed. Timothy Brook and B. Michael Frolic. Armonk, NY: M. E. Sharpe.

    1998 Lord of the Three in One: The Spread of a Cult in Southeast China. Princeton, NJ: Princeton University Press.

Dillon, Michael

    1999 China's Muslim Hui Community: Migration, Settlement and Sects. Richmond, UK: Curzon Press.

Dolan, Jay P.

    1975 The Immigrant Church: New York's Irish and German Catholics, 1815–1865. Baltimore: Johns Hopkins University Press.

Dunch, Ryan Fisk
   1996 Piety, Patriotism, Progress: Chinese Protestants in Fuzhou Society and the Making of a Modern China, 1857–1927. Ph.D. dissertation, Yale University.
   2001 Protestant Christianity in China Today: Fragile, Fragmented, Flourishing. *In* China and Christianity: Burdened Past, Hopeful Future, ed. Stephen Uhalley, Jr., and Xiaoxin Wu. Armonk, NY: M. E. Sharpe.

Ebaugh, Helen Rose, and Janet Saltzman Chafetz, eds.
   2000 Religion and the New Immigrants: Continuities and Adaptations in Immigrant Congregations. Walnut Creek, CA: Altamira Press.
   2002 Religion across Borders. Walnut Creek, CA: Altamira Press.

Esherick, Joseph W.
   1987 The Origins of the Boxer Uprising. Berkeley: University of California Press.

Fairbank, John King
   1986 The Great Chinese Revolution: 1800–1985. New York: Harper and Row.

Feuerwerker, Albert
   1975 Rebellion in Nineteenth-Century China. Ann Arbor, MI: Center for Chinese Studies.

Foner, Nancy
   2000 From Ellis Island to JFK: New York's Two Great Waves of Immigration. New Haven, CT: Yale University Press.
   2001 New Immigrants in New York. New York: Columbia University Press.

Frank, Andre Gundar
   1998 Reorient: Global Economy in the Asian Age. Berkeley: University of California Press.

Gardella, Robert
   1994 Harvesting Mountains: Fujian and the China Tea Trade, 1757–1937. Berkeley: University of California Press.

George, Sheba
   1998 Caroling with the Keralites: The Negotiation of Gendered Space in an Indian Immigrant Church. *In* Gatherings in Diaspora: Religious Communities and the New Immigration, ed. Stephen Warner and Judith G. Wittner. Philadelphia: Temple University Press.

Gilbertson, Greta
   1993 Women's Labor and Enclave Employment: The Case of Dominican and Colombian Women in New York City. International Migration Review 29: 657–670.

Gilbertson, Greta, and Douglas Gurak
  1993 Broadening the Enclave Debate: The Labor Market Experiences of Dominican and Colombian Men in New York City. Sociological Forum 8: 205–220.

Gladney, Dru C.
  1998 Ethnic Identity in China: The Making of a Muslim Minority Nationality. New York: Harcourt Brace.

Glick-Schiller, Nina, Linda Basch, and Cristina Blanc-Szanton, eds.
  1992 Towards a Transnational Perspective on Migration. New York: New York Academy of Sciences.

Guest, Kenneth J., and Peter Kwong
  2000 Ethnic Enclaves and Cultural Diversity. *In* Cultural Diversity in the U.S.: A Critical Reader, ed. Ida Susser and Thomas C. Patterson, 250–266. Oxford: Blackwell.

Guo, Jiande
  1997 A Brief History of the Christian Assemblies in Fuzhou. Unpublished manuscript.

Harvey, David
  1990 The Condition of Postmodernity. Cambridge, MA: Blackwell.

Hicks, George, ed.
  1993 Overseas Chinese Remittances from Southeast Asia, 1910–1940. Singapore: Select Books.

Hood, Marlowe
  1997 Sourcing the Problem: Why Fuzhou? *In* Human Smuggling: Chinese Migrant Trafficking and the Challenge to America's Immigrant Tradition, ed. Paul J. Smith, 76–92. Washington, D.C.: Center for Strategic and International Studies.

Hsu, Madeline Yuan-yin
  2000 Dreaming of Gold, Dreaming of Home: Transnationalism and Migration between the United States and South China, 1882–1943. Stanford, CA: Stanford University Press.

Huang, Weishan, and Ping Zhou
  2000 Survey of New York's Chinese Religious Communities. Unpublished manuscript, Religion and Immigrant Incorporation Project, International Center for Migration, Ethnicity and Citizenship, New School University.

Human Rights Watch
  1997 China: State Control of Religion. New York: Human Rights Watch/Asia.

Jordan, David K., and Daniel L. Overmyer
    1986 The Flying Phoenix: Aspects of Chinese Sectarianism in Taiwan. Princeton, NJ: Princeton University Press.

Kinnear, Angus I.
    1973 Against the Tide: The Story of Watchman Nee. Eastbourne, UK: Victory Press.

Kuo, Chia-ling
    1977 Social and Political Change in New York's Chinatown: The Role of Voluntary Associations. New York: Praeger.

Kwong, Peter
    1996 [1987] The New Chinatown. New York: Hill and Wang.
    1997a Forbidden Workers: Illegal Chinese Immigrants and Chinese Labor. New York: New Press.
    1997b The Overseas Chinese Miracle. Asian American Policy Review 7.
    2001 [1979] Chinatown, New York: Labor and Politics, 1930–1950. New York: Monthly Review Press.

Lacy, Walter N.
    1948 A Hundred Years of China Methodism. Nashville: Abingdon-Cokesbury Press.

Langfitt, Frank
    2000 Faith, Power Collide in a Changing China. Baltimore Sun, August 27.

Levitt, Peggy
    2001 The Transnational Villagers. Berkeley: University of California Press.

Lieberthal, Kenneth
    1995 Governing China: From Revolution through Reform. New York: Norton.

Lin, Guoping
    1993 Fujian Popular Beliefs. Fuzhou, China: Fujian People's Press.

Lin, Jan
    1998 Reconstructing Chinatown: Ethnic Enclave, Global Change. Minneapolis: University of Minnesota Press.

Lyall, Leslie T.
    1964 [1954] John Sung: Flame for God in the Far East. Chicago: Moody Press.

Lyons, Thomas P.
    1992 China's War on Poverty: A Case Study of Fujian Province 1985–1990. Hong Kong: Chinese University of Hong Kong.

1993 Poverty and Growth in a South China County: Anxi, Fujian, 1949–1992. Ithaca, NY: Cornell University Press.

1995 The Economic Geography of Fujian: A Sourcebook. Ithaca, NY: East Asia Program, Cornell University.

MacInnis, Donald, ed.

1972 Religious Policy and Practice in Communist China: A Documentary History. New York: Macmillan.

1989 Religion in China Today: Policy and Practice. Maryknoll, NY: Orbis.

Madsen, Richard

1998 China's Catholics: Tragedy and Hope in an Emerging Society. Berkeley: University of California Press.

2001 Beyond Orthodoxy: Catholicism as Chinese Folk Religion. *In* China and Christianity: Burdened Past, Hopeful Future, ed. Stephen Uhalley, Jr., and Xiaoxin Wu. Armonk, NY: M. E. Sharpe.

Mahler, Sarah

1998 Theoretical and Empirical Contributions toward a Research Agenda for Transnationalism. *In* Transnationalism from Below: Comparative Urban and Community Research, vol. 6, ed. M. P. Smith and Luis Guarnizo. New Brunswick, NJ: Transaction.

McAlister, Elizabeth

1998 The Madonna of 115th Street Revisited: Vodou and Haitian Catholicism in the Age of Transnationalism. *In* Gatherings in Diaspora: Religious Communities and the New Immigration, ed. Stephen Warner and Judith G. Wittner. Philadelphia: Temple University Press.

Min, Pyong Gap

Forthcoming. 1997–98 Survey of Chinese, Indian and Korean Immigrants in Queens. *In* Attachment and Solidarity: A Comparison of Asian Communities in New York. New York: Columbia University Press.

Mydans, Seth

1998 Resentment Still Aimed at Chinese in Indonesia. New York Times, September 6.

Naquin, Susan

1976 Millenarian Rebellion in China: The Eight Trigrams Uprising of 1813. New Haven, CT: Yale University Press.

Ong, Aihwa

1991 The Gender and Labor Politics of Postmodernity. Annual Review of Anthropology 20: 279–311.

1999 Flexible Citizenship: The Cultural Logistics of Transnationality. Durham, NC: Duke University Press.

Ong, Aihwa, and Donald Nonini, eds.
1997 Ungrounded Empires: The Cultural Politics of Modern Chinese Transnationalism. New York: Routledge.

Overmyer, Daniel L.
1976 Folk Buddhist Religion. Cambridge, MA: Harvard University Press.

Palinkas, Lawrence A.
1989 Rhetoric and Religious Experience: The Discourse of Immigrant Chinese Churches. Fairfax, VA: George Mason University Press.

Pan, Lynn
1990 Sons of the Yellow Emperor: A History of the Chinese Diaspora. Boston: Little, Brown.

Pas, Julian F., ed.
1989 The Turning of the Tide: Religion in China Today. Hong Kong: Oxford University Press.

Portes, Alejandro
1981 Modes of Structural Incorporation and Present Theories of Immigration. *In* Global Trends in Migration, ed. Mary M. Kritz, Charles B. Keely, and Sylvano M. Tomasi, 279–297. Staten Island, NY: CMS Press.

Portes, Alejandro, and Robert L. Bach
1985 Latin Journey: Cuban and Mexican Immigrants in the U.S. Berkeley: University of California Press.

Portes, Alejandro, Luis Guarnizo, and Patricia Landolt
1999 Introduction: Pitfalls and Promise of an Emergent Research Field. *In* Ethnic and Racial Studies 22(2): 217–238.

Portes, Alejandro, and Ruben B. Rumbaut
1996 Immigrant America: A Portrait. Berkeley: University of California Press.

Portes, Alejandro, and Alex Stepick
1993 City on the Edge: The Transformation of Miami. Berkeley: University of California Press.

Purcell, Victor
1965 [1951] The Chinese in Southeast Asia. London: Oxford University Press.

Rawski, Evelyn S.
1972 Agricultural Change and the Peasant Economy of South China. Cambridge, MA: Harvard University Press.

Rosenthal, Elizabeth
  2000 Chinese Town's Main Export: Its Young Men. New York Times, June 26.

Rouse, Roger
  1991 Mexican Migration and the Social Space of Postmodernism. Diaspora 1: 8–24.

Rudolph, Susanne Hoeber, and James Piscatori
  1997 Transnational Religion and Fading States. Boulder, CO: Westview Press.

Sanders, J. M., and Victor Nee
  1987 Limits of Ethnic Solidarity in the Enclave Economy. American Sociological Review 52:745–773.

Sangren, Steven P.
  1987 History and Magical Power in a Chinese Community. Stanford, CA: Stanford University Press.

Sassen, Saskia
  1988 The Mobility of Labor and Capital: A Study in International Investment and Labor Flow. New York: Cambridge University Press.
  1991 The Global City: New York, London, Tokyo. Princeton, NJ: Princeton University Press.
  2000 [1994] Cities in a World Economy. Thousand Oaks, CA: Pine Forge Press.

Sassen-Koob, Saskia
  1983 Labor Migration and the New International Division of Labor. *In* Women, Men and the International Division of Labor, ed. J. Nash and M. P. Fernandez-Kelly, 175–204. Albany: State University of New York Press.

Schechter, Danny
  2000 Falun Gong's Challenge to China: Spiritual Practice or "Evil Cult"? New York: Akashic Books.

Seagrave, Sterling
  1995 Lords of the Rim: The Invisible Empire of the Overseas Chinese. New York: G. P. Putnam's Sons.

Shahar, Meir, and Robert P. Weller, eds.
  1996 Unruly Gods: Divinity and Society in China. Honolulu: University of Hawaii Press.

Skinner, G. William
  1957 Chinese Society in Thailand. Ithaca, NY: Cornell University Press.

Smith, M. P., and Luis Guarnizo, eds.
    1998 Transnationalism from Below: Comparative Urban and Community Research, vol. 6. New Brunswick, NJ: Transaction.

Smith, Paul J., ed.
    1997 Human Smuggling: Chinese Migrant Trafficking and the Challenge to America's Immigration Tradition. Washington, D.C.: Center for Strategic and International Studies.

Solinger, Dorothy J.
    1999 Contesting Citizenship in Urban China: Peasant Migrants, the State, and the Logic of the Market. Berkeley: University of California Press.

Spence, Jonathan
    1990 The Search for Modern China. New York: Norton.
    1996 God's Chinese Son: The Taiping Heavenly Kingdom of Hong Xiu Quan. New York: Norton.

Tchen, John Kuo Wei
    1999 New York before Chinatown: Orientalism and the Shaping of American Culture, 1776–1882. Baltimore: Johns Hopkins University Press.

Thompson, Laurence
    1996 Chinese Religion: An Introduction. New York: Wadsworth.

Transfiguration Church
    1977 Transfiguration Church: A Church of Immigrants, 1827–1977. New York: Park.

Tseng, Timothy
    1999 Chinese Protestant Nationalism in the United States, 1880–1927. In New Spiritual Homes: Religion and Asian Americans, ed. David K. Yoo. Honolulu: University of Hawaii Press.
    2002 Unbinding Their Souls: Chinese Protestant Women in Twentieth-Century America. In Women and Twentieth-Century Protestantism, ed. Margaret Lanberts Bendroth and Virginia Lieson Brereton. Chicago: University of Illinois Press.

Turner, Victor W.
    1969 The Ritual Process: Structure and Anti-Structure. Chicago: Aldine.

Vermeer, E. B., ed.
    1990 Development and Decline of Fukien Province in the 17th and 18th Centuries. Leiden, The Netherlands, and New York: Brill.

Waldinger, Roger
    1989 Through the Eye of the Needle: Immigrants and Enterprise in New York's
    Garment Trades. New York: New York University Press.

Wang, Gungwu
    1991 China and the Chinese Overseas. Singapore: Times Academic Press.
    1998 The Nanhai Trade: The Early History of Chinese Trade in the South
    China Sea. Singapore: Times Academic Press.

Warner, R. Stephen, and Judith G. Wittner
    1998 Gatherings in Diaspora: Religious Communities and the New Immigra-
    tion. Philadelphia: Temple University Press.

Watson, James L.
    1975 Emigration and the Chinese Lineage: The Mans in Hong Kong and Lon-
    don. Berkeley: University of California Press.

Weller, Robert P.
    1987 Unities and Diversities in Chinese Religion. Seattle: University of Wash-
    ington Press.

Wickeri, Philip
    1988 Seeking the Common Ground: Protestant Christianity, the Three-Self
    Movement, and China's United Front. Maryknoll, NY: Orbis Books.

Wilson, Kenneth L., and Alejandro Portes
    1980 Immigrant Enclaves: An Analysis of the Labor Market Experiences of
    Cubans in Miami. American Journal of Sociology 86: 295–319.

Wong, Bernard
    1982 Chinatown: Economic Adaptation and Ethnic Identity of the Chinese.
    New York: Holt, Rinehart and Winston.
    1988 Patronage, Brokerage, Entrepreneurship and the Chinese Community of
    New York. New York: AMS Press.

Woo, Wesley
    1991 Chinese Protestants in the Bay Area. In Entry Denied: Exclusion and the
    Chinese Community in America, 1882–1943, ed. Sucheng Chan. Philadel-
    phia: Temple University Press.

Woon, Yuen-fong
    1984 Social Organization in South China, 1911–1949. Ann Arbor, MI: Center
    for Chinese Studies.

Yang, C. K.
    1967 Religion in Chinese Society. Berkeley: University of California Press.

Yang, Fenggang
  1999 Chinese Christians in America: Conversion, Assimilation, and Adhesive Identities. University Park: Pennsylvania State University Press.

Yang, Mayfair
  2000 Putting Global Capitalism in Its Place: Economic Hybridity, Bataille, and Ritual Expenditure. Current Anthropology 41(4): 477–495.

Yoo, David K. ed.
  1999 New Spiritual Homes: Religion and Asian Americans. Honolulu: University of Hawaii Press.

Yu, Renqiu
  1992 To Save China, To Save Ourselves: The Chinese Hand Laundry Association of New York. Philadelphia: Temple University Press.
  1995 Chinese. *In* The Encyclopedia of New York City, ed. Kenneth T. Jackson, 216–218. New Haven: Yale University Press.

Yung, Judy
  1995 Unbound Feet: A Social History of Chinese Women in San Francisco. Berkeley: University of California Press.

Zhou, Kate
  1996 How the Farmers Changed China: Power of the People. Boulder, CO: Westview Press.

Zhou, Min
  1992 Chinatown: The Socioeconomic Potential of an Urban Enclave. Philadelphia: Temple University Press.

Zhou, Min, and John R. Logan
  1989 Returns on Human Capital in Ethnic Enclaves: New York City's Chinatown. American Sociological Review 54: 809–820.

Zurcher, Erik
  1990 The Jesuit Mission in Fukien in Late Ming Times: Levels of Response. *In* Development and Decline of Fukien Province in the 17th and 18th Centuries, ed. E. B. Vermeer. Leiden, The Netherlands: E. J. Brill.

Index

Aleni, Giulio, 87

American Board of Commissioners for Foreign Missions (ABCFM), 53, 54, 106

Anglicans (Episcopalians): Anglican Church Missionary Society (Britain), 53, 54, 106; in Fuzhou, 90–92; in New York, 120; in Tingjiang, 105–111; Trinity College, Fuzhou, 92

Asylum: claims, 31, 67; and religion, 144, 148, 188, 193

Ballord, M. L. S., 92

Barber, Margaret E., 92, 93, 112

Boxer Uprising, 82

Buddhism: in China, 71, 79, 157; Chinese Buddhist Association, 125, 133; in Fuzhou, 73, 74, 76, 147; in New York, 120, 121, 122, 127–133, 198

Cantonese: history in Chinatown, 3, 22–26; language, 30, 31, 122, 152; Taishan immigrants, 4, 62, 63

Catholics: in Changle, 78, 104, 119, 204; in China, 71, 80, 86, 104; church construction and demolition in China, 104; in New York, 120, 122, 139–146, 198, 199; "underground" churches, 6, 103, 204. See also St. Joseph's Roman Catholic Church; Transfiguration Roman Catholic Church

Chang'an: village, 5, 6, 27; Daoist temple, 134, 136, 138, 203

Changle, 16, 20, 47, 48, 50, 59, 60, 133; Catholics, 78, 104, 119; and Church of Grace, 161–163, 166–169; Home of Grace, 95, 113–117, 202; religion, 72, 86, 98

Chatham Square, 26

Chen, Huibing, 33–34

Chen, Qiang, 28, 32, 43

Chen, Ru, 19–21, 32

Chen, Sheng, 163

Chen, Shewo, 158–161, 165, 166

Chen, Shufan, 151, 154, 172, 206, 208

Ch'en Ta, 62

Chen, Yonghuang, 159, 161

Chen, Zhaoqing 159

Chinatown: bachelor society, 23, 25; contemporary conditions, 26; development in U.S., 24; housing, 34–35; languages, 123; map of, 14, 121–122; New York's, history of, 22–26; previous studies, 7, 121–122; religious landscape, 10, 120–146

Chinese Catholic Patriotic Association: formation, 89; registration with, 102; and Chinese state, 117–119

Chinese Exclusion Act, 24, 63; repeal, 25

Christian Assemblies. See Little Flock

Church of Christ in China, 90, 91

Church of Grace to the Fujianese: 5, 11, 19, 29, 120, 122, 127, 147–194, 198, 200, 202; age members, 178, 186–187; baptism, 147–148, 161, 190, 194; bathhouse, 150, 159–160, 200; board of deacons, 147, 156, 158–159, 161, 163–166, 168–170, 173, 175, 180, 186, 200, 202; Brooklyn branch, 162, 175, 186–187, 190; Chen, Sheng, 163; Chen, Shewo, 158–161, 165, 166; Chen, Shufan, 151, 154, 172, 206, 208; Chen, Yonghuang, 159, 161; Chen, Zhaoqing, 159, 184; class, 166, 169–170, 180; clerical leadership, 158–163; communion, 165–166, 200; contemporary growth, 173–175; conversion, 148, 190–193; Fuzhou dialect, 149, 150, 155–156, 158, 163, 170, 177; history, 150–166; Home of Grace, 162–163, 166,

About the Author

Kenneth J. Guest is Assistant Professor in the Department of Sociology and Anthropology at Baruch College, CUNY, and Senior Research Consultant at the International Center for Migration, Ethnicity, and Citizenship.